TWAYNE'S WORLD LEADERS SERIES

EDITOR OF THIS VOLUME

Hans L. Trefousse, Brooklyn College

The Emperor Julian

TWLS 53

Emperor Julian

THE EMPEROR JULIAN

By CONSTANCE HEAD

Western Carolina University

TWAYNE PUBLISHERS
A DIVISION OF G. K. HALL & CO., BOSTON

Library of Congress Cataloging in Publication Data

Head, Constance.
   The Emperor Julian.

   (Twayne's world leaders series)
   Bibliography: pp. 219–22
   Includes index.
   1. Julianus, Apostata, Emperor of Rome, 331–363.
DG317.H5   937'.08'0924 [B]   75–15724
ISBN 0–8057–7650–8

Contents

About the Author

Constance Head is Professor of History at Western Carolina University in Cullowhee, North Carolina, where she has taught since 1967 and where her areas of specialization include Roman and Byzantine studies. She received the Bachelor of Divinity, Master of Arts, and Doctor of Philosophy degrees from Duke University, Durham, North Carolina.

Professor Head's first book, *Justinian II of Byzantium*, was published by the University of Wisconsin Press in 1972. In addition, she is the author of a number of scholarly articles which have appeared in *Byzantion*, *Archivum Historiae Pontificiae*, and *The Catholic Historical Review*, as well as several popular history essays in *Mankind* and *History Today*. In 1972–73, she held a Younger Humanists Fellowship from the National Endowment for the Humanities, and it was during that period of study that her idea for a book on the Emperor Julian originated.

Preface

Although he reigned for less than two years (A.D. 361–363), the Roman Emperor Julian is one of the best-known figures of ancient history, a warm and very human person set in a rapidly changing environment he never really understood. Determined to alter the world for what he believed would be the better, he would meet disappointment, and then death in his early thirties.

Julian was a pagan, a worshiper of the "old gods" and a devotee of Greek Neoplatonism at a time when the triumph of the Christian faith was already assured. Zealous Christians through the ages since his time have responded to this genuinely devout young ruler by bestowing upon him the infamous epithet "Apostate," signifying one who through his rejection of the Christian faith is forever a "lost soul." Church historians decades after his time attempted to smear his memory with grim (and often completely unfounded) tales of how this last pagan emperor sought to combat the Christian faith.[1] Yet in spite of all this, thanks to the unusual wealth of source material from the pens of his contemporaries Ammianus Marcellinus and Libanius of Antioch, and most especially thanks to Julian's own voluminous writings, it is possible to glimpse him as he really was: a dedicated and mystical young man with an intense devotion to the truth as he saw it.

Moreover, while his strong attachment to ancient paganism and his attempts to restructure it to meet the needs of his time are important facets of his career, duly deserving emphasis, they do not by themselves comprise the whole story of Julian's life and reign. The young man who was the last pagan emperor of Rome was also a brilliant soldier and a statesman with high ideals for governmental reform in many areas besides that of religion. It is important to see Julian in this broader context and to realize that what he sought to accomplish during his brief reign was not so much a negative campaign against the

Church he had personally rejected as a positive return to a society built upon the highest ideals of classical Greece and Rome.

Julian died very young. What might have been, had he never ventured on his ill-fated invasion of Persia and lived instead to a normal old age, is a subject of perennial fascination. For this reason as well as for the intrinsic interest of his life story, Julian has received attention from numerous writers whose works represent widely varying approaches to their subject and estimates of his historic role. It is not the purpose of this volume to replace lengthier and more detailed works, but rather to introduce Julian to the general reader and, hopefully, to encourage the student to turn to the original sources themselves for further insights into the mind and environment of this extraordinary ruler. Our concluding chapter (which some may prefer to read first) presents a more detailed look at precisely what these sources are and their relative value. Throughout our study, while modern scholars' opinions will be noted from time to time, the reader will find principal emphasis placed on Julian as he appears in the works of his contemporaries and as he reveals himself in many autobiographical passages of his own.[2]

Julian spoke of his literary efforts as his "children," the only children he had to survive him; while his friend the rhetor Libanius of Antioch, in the Emperor's funeral oration, says of Julian's works: "He has left them as his offspring for all eternity, and time cannot remove them as it does the colours of his official portraits."[3] There is considerable truth in these words. The best sources for the study of Julian are his own writings. As long as these survive, the memory of this often surprising and always fascinating emperor will endure in the pages of history.

Acknowledgments

To everyone who has had a part in the growth of this project I am truly grateful. Special thanks are due to the Interlibrary Loan staff at Western Carolina University who located much hard-to-find material and to Ms. Heni Cason of the University Archives; to the Graduate School for a research grant that facilitated the project; and to Ms. Rebecca Hilliard, a loyal and efficient secretary who typed the manuscript—much of it twice.

And most of all, my gratitude is to my mother who never ceased to provide her unfailing encouragement.

Chronology

331	Julian (Flavius Claudius Julianus) born in Constantinople, son of the prince Julius Constantius and Basilina.
332	Julian's mother Basilina dies.
337	Emperor Constantine the Great, Julian's uncle, dies. Accession of Constantius II, Julian's cousin.
337/338?	Julian's father executed.
c. 337–342	Julian attends school in Nicomedia and Constantinople.
342–348	Julian and his older brother Gallus in exile in Macellum.
348–355	Julian's student travels.
350/351?	Probable date of Julian's initiation into the Mithra cult in Ephesus.
351	Gallus appointed Caesar of the East.
354	Gallus executed.
355	Julian in Italy for seven months; then (August–October) in Athens. Returns to Milan and (November 6) proclaimed Caesar of the West. Marries his cousin Helena. Leaves for Gaul (December 1).
355–361	JULIAN IN GAUL (Winter Quarters: 355/6, Vienne; 356/7, Sens; 357/8, 358/9, 359/60, Paris; 360/1, Vienne).
356/357?	Julian's only child, a boy, dies at birth.
357	(May) Helena goes to Rome. (August) Battle of Strasbourg. (Autumn) Julian's army crosses the Rhine for first time.
358	Second crossing of the Rhine: many prisoners recovered from King Hortarius. Julian lowers taxes and has difficulties with Prefect Florentius.
359	Third crossing of the Rhine. Salustius recalled to the East.

360   (February) Julian proclaimed Emperor by his troops
           in Paris; attempts negotiations with Constantius.
           (Summer) Fourth crossing of the Rhine; Julian's
           wife Helena dies. (November) Julian celebrates his
           quinquennalia in Vienne.

360/361?   Empress Eusebia dies.

361   (Early) Vadomar's raids; Constantius marries Faus-
           tina of Antioch. (Summer) Julian begins his east-
           ward march; composes his "Letter to the Senate and
           People of Athens." (October) Sirmium surrenders;
           Julian moves on to Naissus. (November 3) Con-
           stantius dies; Julian becomes undisputed Emperor.
           (December) Julian enters Constantinople. Chalce-
           don trials.

361–362   (December–May) JULIAN IN CONSTANTINO-
           PLE.

362   (May–July) Julian touring Asia Minor on the way
           to Antioch. (June) School Law issued.

362–363   (July–March) JULIAN IN ANTIOCH: (Summer)
           Grain Crisis. (October) Destruction of the Temple
           of Apollo at Daphne. (Winter) Julian composes
           "Against the Galileans" and "The Misopogon"; plans
           to rebuild Jewish Temple.

363   (March 5) Julian leaves Antioch. (April) Roman
           army crosses frontier into Persia; many victories.
           (Late May) Battle outside Ctesiphon. (Early June)
           Roman retreat begins. (June 26) Julian dies as the
           result of injury received in battle; succeeded by
           Jovian.

CHAPTER 1

Julian's Childhood

ON the twenty-second of May, 337, Constantine the Great, who had ruled the Roman Empire for more than a quarter of a century, died in Nicomedia. He was about sixty-three years old, and for the past thirty years had been much occupied in changing the face of history. Not many miles from where he died stood the beautiful new capital city of Constantinople, founded by him a few years earlier and designed to rival Rome as the center of the Western world. An even more dramatic change was his recognition of the Christian faith. The religion that had heretofore been sporadically persecuted by the Roman governing authorities and despised by many of the Empire's intellectuals, had become under Constantine the religion of the Emperor's favor. The Christian Church would never be the same, as, for good or ill, the fourth century and all subsequent ages would be irrevocably affected by the decisions of the Great Constantine.

The Emperor left five children, offspring of his Empress Fausta, the wife whom he had had murdered. His eldest son and favorite, the illegitimate Crispus, was dead, executed earlier through Fausta's intrigues. The Empire was thus to be divided among his three surviving sons, to whom he had given the interesting but confusing names of Constantine II, Constantius II, and Constans. His elder daughter was Constantina;[1] the younger was Helena, named for her grandmother. There was no imperial inheritance for the girls of the family, save through their inevitable fate as marriage pawns. On the other hand, there were other close male relatives, nephews whom Constantine thought it wise to conciliate. Two of these, Delmatius and Hannibalian (the latter of whom was married to the Emperor's daughter Constantina), were designated for high posts in the Empire: Delmatius was to be *Caesar*, and Hannibalian King of Pontus. Such were the terms of Constantine's will.

Through the long summer of 337, although none of his sons was present in Constantinople, the arrangements for the succession seemed to be working out smoothly enough. Constantius, the middle son, a short, bowlegged, dark-skinned youth of nineteen, was due to arrive in the new capital to claim his share as Emperor of the East. Weeks passed; decrees were still issued in the name of the dead Emperor Constantine. Constantius would come eventually from the Persian frontier where military duties had called him. Meanwhile the older and younger sons of the late Emperor, Constantine II and Constans, were ready to take over their respective provinces in the Western Empire.

Finally, in the late summer of 337, Constantius arrived in Constantinople. He was a somber young man, full of his own self-importance, devoutly religious in his own fashion, a Christian with pronounced inclinations toward the Arian sect and a passion for theological disputes. Beneath his ever placid exterior lay the memories of a frightful childhood, of his mother drowned by his father's orders. Constantine the Great, it was said, was a kind father and devoted to his sons, but this could not erase the reality of Fausta's death. Constantius, the new Emperor of the East, had grown up hard and ruthless in a milieu where the execution of one's own family was not an unreal nightmare, but an act sometimes justified as political necessity.

Among the surviving kin of the old Emperor Constantine were his half-brothers, three harmless, wealthy, politically inactive gentlemen of middle age, including Julius Constantius, a widower with four children who resided in Constantinople. One day late in 337 or early 338, quite without warning, Julius and his eldest son were slain by soldiers of the Emperor Constantius. There were other victims in the same massacre: the princes Delmatius and Hannibalian who had been supposed to share in the imperial power, their father (also named Delmatius), their uncle Hannibalian, and several cousins whose identity is uncertain.[2]

In sum, all of the close adult male kin of the late Emperor Constantine were dead—all except his own three sons, Constantine II, Constantius, and Constans. Now the brothers could rest assured that there would be no rivals to their throne. Constantine II and Constans were far away in the western provinces; it was Constantius who must have been the moving force behind the atrocity. In later years, truly enough, there were those who sought to gloss over the young man's responsibility for the death of so many of his relatives; the army, it was alleged, had taken matters into its own hands and acted without his direct orders.[3] But even if this is true, which is open to doubt, the all-powerful autocrat Constantius, present in the city and quickly informed of all matters of importance, could have acted to save his kin. It suited him better that they should die.

The unfortunate Julius, however, as we have seen, was the father of four children, and only the eldest son was killed with him. There was one girl, probably named Galla,[4] who at some point either previous to the massacre or soon thereafter, became the bride of none other than Constantius himself. This unhappy princess vanishes like a wisp of morning mist on the pages of Roman history; nothing is known of her subsequent fate, and before long we will find Constantius married to the woman who would be his lifelong partner in Empire and the sometime power behind his throne, Eusebia of Macedonia.

Then there were Julius' two little sons, Gallus[5] and Julian, aged twelve and six respectively. These, it was decided, were too young to execute: it would not be Christian to slay little children. Besides, Gallus was a puny lad, likely to die anyway.[6] According to one account, the boys were spared the fate of their relatives only at the last moment when sympathetic Christians, including one Marcus of Arethusa, whisked them off to sanctuary in one of Constantinople's many churches.[7] In any event, when the horror of the massacre had subsided, the brothers were still alive, orphans at the mercy of their cousin Constantius.

Of the two brothers—rather, half-brothers, since they had had different mothers[8]—it is Julian who is the subject of our study: Julian, who would grow up to be a philosophically inclined, mystical young man, a soldier of great repute, and eventually one of the most unusual and in many ways appealing Emperors ever to sit on the throne of the Caesars.

Julian was born late in 331, perhaps on the sixth of November.[9] At that time there was no hint of the coming tragedies of his childhood; rather, as the first child of the imperial family born

in the new capital city of Constantinople, the arrival of Flavius
Claudius Julianus must have been welcomed with great rejoicing.
Some notice needs to be taken of the strange system of late
Roman nomenclature, as completely different from that of early
Rome as it is unlike modern practice. In this instance, "Flavius"
was a family name in the Constantinian dynasty, practically the
equivalent of a modern surname. "Claudius" was also a family
name, in memory of their presumed (but probably fictitious)
kinship with the Emperor Claudius Gothicus; while "Julianus"
or "Julian" was the child's actual given name, which he would
be called by his family. A variant of his father's name, Julius,
it was also the name of his maternal grandfather, the provincial
governor of Egypt.[10]

Julian's mother was Basilina, a well-educated, immensely rich
and aristocratic young lady who lived only a few months after
the birth of her only child. As Julian wrote of her many years
later, she was "snatched away while she was still a young
girl . . . from so many misfortunes that were to come."[11] Of
course, he had no real memories of his mother; he would know
her only through the stories of Mardonius, an old eunuch who
had been Basilina's teacher when she was a child and who in
time fulfilled the same function for Julian himself. The boy
would always cherish fond memories of the mother he knew
only through his tutor's reminiscences, a mother who, like him,
loved to read and study the heritage of the classical past. There
is, in Munich, an ancient cameo bearing a profile portrait of a
young woman named "Basilia," whose resemblance to Julian
is striking enough to make it almost certain that the girl there
depicted is his mother.[12]

Already motherless, Julian, as we have seen, was six when
he lost his father as well. At the time of the massacre, the
boy apparently did not know the cause of his father's death.
A few years later he would discover it, for it was a secret that
could not be kept forever. On learning the truth, Julian recalled
long afterward, that he felt as if he had been plunged into
Hell.[13] It was a terrible reality that would stay with him all
his life, and that had a great deal to do with making him what
he was.

Rarely were there two brothers more different than Julian

and Gallus: Julian with his bright, inquiring mind; Gallus, both dull and violent. Yet it is clear from his writings that Julian sincerely loved his difficult half-brother with a desperate love born of the fact that Gallus was his only close kin.

It was Mardonius, the old tutor, who in many ways must have been the center of Julian's childhood. Although he was very strict, Mardonius was deeply devoted to little Julian, and Julian in his later years always spoke of him with affection and gratitude.[14] Probably the boy had already started school before the massacre. Mardonius, his pedagogue, walked to school with him and home again, discussed his lessons, taught him manners, and told him stories of the old gods who ruled the earth before the Christians came. If Mardonius was a Christian himself—and he probably was, at least nominally—it made little real difference.[15] The old eunuch was a Hellenist through and through, devoted to the classics of ancient Greece with a fervor he imparted in full to his young pupil.

Almost equally important from Mardonius' standpoint was the business of educating his charge in correct behavior. He insisted, for instance, that Julian walk with his eyes downcast, not staring about in every direction. It became a habit Julian could never break; years later, when criticized for his stooping posture scarcely becoming an Emperor, he replied that it was the ingrained practice of his boyhood days.[16] After the massacre, Mardonius, slave though he was, seems to have been assigned the principal responsibility for Julian's upbringing. The boy longed to go places: to the theater, to the chariot races in the Hippodrome, or to many another festivity which the thriving capital offered. Mardonius, who must have realized how risky it was to expose the little prince to the crowds, curtailed these impulses with his advice to the effect that it is better to read about something than to go there.[17] So Julian read—and seemed unable to get his fill of books.

As a little boy, it appears that Julian continued to attend a school with other children for several years after his father's death. Libanius, the orator of Antioch, years later reported that the child Julian never expected or received any special privileges in school because he was the Emperor's cousin.[18] Only Mardonius and one other attendant escorted him to school;

this was not at all unusual since practically every upper-class boy had a pedagogue who performed the same function.

Julian's manners, thanks to Mardonius, were exemplary. "He spoke to people before he was spoken to," which was apparently deemed somewhat remarkable in a prince. When the other children were told to stand up, Julian stood up with them. His clothes were like those of his schoolmates; if a stranger had looked into the classroom, he never could have guessed which boy was the descendent of emperors. "However," Libanius adds significantly, "he was not on a level with them [his class-mates] in every particular, for in his understanding and appre-ciation of his lessons, in his grasp and retention of them, and in his perseverence in his labours, he opened up a great gap between himself and the rest..."[19]

Where were Julian and Mardonius living during these years that Julian was growing up? There is considerable uncertainty on this point. Constantius had confiscated all the properties that Julian and Gallus should have inherited from their father, but apparently Julian had received substantial wealth from his mother's family, perhaps including a home in the capital city. Libanius speaks of the child Julian's schooling in Constantinople, yet for a while at least the young prince and his pedagogue stayed in Nicomedia, where Julian's official guardian (and dis-tant kinsman) Eusebius was the Arian Christian bishop. Later, in 339 or 340, Eusebius was transferred to the bishopric of Constantinople and the boy and his tutor may well have come back to the capital with him.[20]

On holidays, Julian was allowed to visit the home of his maternal grandmother near Nicomedia, a place he always re-membered as "most delightful," with a garden, many trees and a "charming bath."[21] Julian loved the outdoors; he especially enjoyed lying in the fragrant grass, reading or simply watching the sky. Although he admitted that the nearby beach itself had no appeal for him—he did not like to walk among "seaweed and brambles"—sometimes he would climb a certain hill to a com-fortable spot from which he could see the coast and watch the ships on their way to Constantinople from the far corners of the Empire and beyond. At night, the boy loved to study the stars; he learned to recognize the constellations and no doubt delighted in the ancient myths connected with many of them. "When the firmament was clear and cloudless, I abandoned all else without exception and gave myself up to the beauty of the heavens," he remembered long afterwards.[22]

And always there were his books, the beloved poems of Homer and Hesiod, and old Mardonius to discuss their hidden meanings with him in endless detail. It was as pleasant a life as an orphaned prince could wish for.

CHAPTER 2

Macellum

WHEN Julian was about eleven, in the year 342, everything suddenly changed.[1] Constantius, worried, perhaps, that the boy was too much in the limelight in the big city, banished him. In the mountains of Cappadocia, northeast of Caesarea, was a place called Macellum, a remote castle formerly used as an imperial hunting lodge. Gallus, who had been attending school in Tralles and had been separated from Julian for several years, would join him there.

For six years, the two brothers remained at Macellum. Julian's recorded memories depict the place as completely dismal, although the ecclesiastical historians insist that it was a palatial estate, surrounded by beautiful scenery, and that the young prince was guilty of vast ingratitude toward his cousin Constantius, who had provided him with such a lovely home. Julian's unhappy recollections of Macellum are probably the result of its isolation and his loneliness there. Mardonius, it is almost certain, was not permitted to accompany him and, in all likelihood, Julian never saw his old tutor again. As for any real companionship with his brother Gallus, the six-year difference in their ages and the fact that they had so little in common must have made them poor company for each other. There were a few slaves there, unquestionably spies of Constantius, with whom nevertheless the boys associated "as equals"; there were Christian tutors who supervised the princes' education; otherwise the place was quite desolate. "We ... were watched as though we were in some Persian garrison, since no stranger came to see us and not one of our old friends was allowed to visit us," Julian recalled long afterwards. "No companion of our own age ever came near us or was allowed to do so."[2] If there was anything wrong with Gallus' character, Julian remarked

some years afterward (knowing full well that Gallus had turned
out to be a complete disaster), it was because he had had to
live too long in "those mountains."[3]
   Fortunately, Julian could always find relief for his own bore-
dom in reading: "From childhood, I have been penetrated by
a passionate longing to acquire books."[4] While the castle of
Macellum probably had almost nothing in the way of a library,
young Julian was allowed to borrow books from an Arian
Christian bishop, George of Cappadocia, who lived nearby.
Although George's library included not only Christian theology
but a wealth of classical literature which Julian certainly preferred, it was during his years at Macellum that he gained his
thorough knowledge of the Christian scriptures. His teachers
(of whom he reports absolutely nothing) must have been
pleased that the boy memorized lengthy passages from the
Bible.[5] And yet, even as he studied, his discontent with the
Christian religion was beginning to take shape.
   One may wonder why young Julian did not find the stories
of the Bible at least as appealing and fascinating as the Greek
myths he admired, but it is actually not difficult to discover
several reasons why the sensitive, lonely boy felt repelled by
Christianity. First, the faith that counselled "Thou shalt not
kill" had produced Constantius, who had killed Julian's father
and so many others, and who, the boy firmly believed, had
intended to kill him and Gallus also. Among the teachers sent
to Macellum to instruct Julian in Christian principles, there
was none who dared face the tumult stirring in the child's heart.
Nor do we know if he even dared to express the uncertainties he
felt. Constantius, who had struck such cruel blows, could well
strike again. Indeed, the Emperor actually visited Macellum
once, and Julian had his first face-to-face encounter with the
terrible cousin who held his life in his hands. Young as he was,
Julian was learning to be extremely cautious; above all, he
wanted to stay alive.
   It is possible, too, that as Julian matured he found a further
reason to be repelled by Christianity in the theological arguments of Arians versus their Athanasian (or Orthodox) rivals.
The principal point of dispute between the two factions was the
nature of Christ: according to the Arians, there was once a

time when Christ *was not;* in other words, he was less than God the Father, of *similar*—but not *the same*—substance. The Athanasians, on the other hand, stressed the absolute likeness of substance of God the Father and God the Son. The late Emperor Constantine had wavered for years between the two views, thoroughly confused, but generally inclined toward the Athanasian viewpoint. Constantius, however, was an ardent Arian; under his rule the Arians flourished and persecuted their Athanasian opponents with a zeal that was anything but Christlike. Under Constantius' directives, Julian was receiving thorough grounding in Arian theology. While the subtle differences of this faction from the Athanasians apparently left the young pupil unimpressed, in later years Julian would make it amply clear that he found the inability of Christians to get along among themselves one of their most unlovely traits.[6]

Not to be overlooked as an additional factor contributing to Julian's distaste for Christianity was the literal-mindedness with which his Christian instructors interpreted the scriptures. All Bible stories were presented as completely and historically true. The classical Greek myths, however, which Julian continued to admire so enthusiastically, were interpreted by devout Hellenists as allegorical tales. While they might be taken literally by simple believers, true philosophers would understand them as revealing deeper truths, hidden mysteries about the nature of the gods. The contrast between Christianity and Hellenism on these matters must have been striking indeed to a young person with Julian's inquiring mind.

It also seems clear that Julian was unmoved by the Christian emphasis on baptism and its accompanying guarantee of forgiveness for sins. So far as we can tell, his life at Macellum was almost monastic in its disciplined asceticism. He grew up innocent of many of the temptations that often caused adolescent Christians in other environments to stray from "the straight and narrow path" and then to repent vigorously. The sternly moral atmosphere of Macellum probably had a great deal to do with Julian's lifelong adherence to moderation and moral decency; yet at the same time caused him to be repelled by the oft-repeated Christian message to be cleansed from the stains of sin. He had not sinned, at least not outrageously, and he had nothing of which to repent.[7]

These problems notwithstanding, in due time Julian came to receive Christian baptism:[8] a rather odd happening in itself, for even Constantius was not baptized.[9] Like Constantine the Great and many other Christians of the time, the Emperor preferred to wait until he was at death's door to receive the valuable sacrament that could be performed only once and that he believed would wash all his sins away. Perhaps young Julian was undergoing a bout with some illness so serious that death seemed likely and baptism advisable.

In any event, the rite was probably celebrated at Macellum, rather than earlier. In his writings Julian never mentions his baptism directly, but he seems to have worried a great deal in later life how he might most effectively "erase" the effects of the sacrament, which was supposed to leave an indelible though invisible mark on the soul. Probably no one considered giving the boy any choice in the matter; if, perhaps, he was questioned about his readiness for baptism, he must have felt it wise to pretend to sentiments he did not feel. Thus, very young and under far too much restraint to be held truly accountable for his action, Julian became a full member of the Church which he would later reject. And only if such rejection is construed as "apostasy," does he merit the infamous epithet that traditional Christian history has bestowed upon him.

Although Julian was repelled by Christianity, it is important to realize that even in his boyhood he was searching for a sense of permanent religious commitment. In his later years, he would have little to say concerning his life at Macellum, but the few recollections he did report show clearly how introspective he was throughout this crucial period of his adolescence. He had then—as he would always have—a deep, mystical longing to give his complete allegiance to some divine Power, to dedicate himself totally to an ideal and to feel that he was accepted and loved in return. Nowhere does he express these emotions more clearly than in his "hymn" of praise to Helios the Sun God, which he composed as Emperor some twelve or thirteen years after he left Macellum: "From my childhood an extraordinary longing for the rays of the god penetrated deep into my soul . . .

The heavenly light shone all around me, and . . . it roused and urged me on to its contemplation."[10] Again in a little "myth" that forms a part of his reply to the Cynic Heracleios, Julian speaks of being accepted by the gods, and especially by Helios-Mithra, while still a youth.[11] In return for his wholehearted consecration of himself to their service, the gods promise Julian their protection and watchful care. In the strange, isolated world of Macellum, these thoughts—forbidden by his Christian upbringing, yet unutterably sweet—must have thrilled Julian to the depths of his being. He must learn more of philosophy and the mysteries of the gods, and so he would someday, if ever Constantius would see fit to set him free.

Still, for the present, he knew he must conform outwardly to Christianity as was required of him. Thus as he grew older, but probably when he was still in his early teens, Julian became a lector at an Arian church near the castle.[12] This post, which was customarily entrusted to young boys, called for public reading of the scriptures and was often regarded as a first step toward ordination as a Christian priest. Many a young man, however, held a lectorship for a time and never went on to join the ranks of the clergy, so there is no reason necessarily to think that a clerical vocation was being planned for Julian. He probably had no more real choice in this matter than he had had in his baptism: it was expected of him and he must appear agreeable. Gallus, too, was a lector; and whatever else was to be said for the job, it at least meant an opportunity for the brothers to leave the dreary castle for a few hours in the limelight, performing before the public. Julian, who always loved attention, must have enjoyed this aspect of his lectorship, if no other.

It is also reported that when they lived at Macellum, Gallus and Julian at times held debates, with Julian taking the role of a pagan and Gallus the Christian seeking to convert him. When asked why he preferred the part of the unbeliever, Julian would reply cagily that it was the harder, more challenging role.[13]

In later days, Julian's Christian foes delighted in recounting an incident which (if it ever actually happened at all) seemed an even surer revelation of his future "apostasy." Gallus and his brother, it seems, determined to build a shrine near Macellum in memory of a local martyr, Saint Mamas, and workmen were employed for the construction. One half of the building was assigned to each brother; and while the part sponsored by Gallus rose speedily and without difficulty, Julian's half of the building soon collapsed into rubble—a sign that the saint wanted no part of Julian's offering.[14]

Although Julian states definitely that he and Gallus remained at Macellum for six years,[15] there is considerable uncertainty about the exact date (probably in 348) and the circumstances of their departure. Constantius had plans for Gallus, and the young man, now in his twenties, went to Ephesus, but soon thereafter was summoned to the Emperor's court in Italy.[16] Meanwhile for Julian, now in his late teens, a new world was opening up. The freedom so long denied him at Macellum was his at last and he could become what he wished to be, a student of philosophy.

Although the Emperor Constantius would have never dreamed it, the time was drawing near when his young cousin Julian, so studious, seemingly so Christian, so harmless, would become irrevocably committed to the ancient gods.

CHAPTER 3

Student Travels

THERE are a number of revealing hints of Julian's personal appearance as a young man in the years immediately following his departure from Macellum. Although the fashion of the times dictated that men be clean-shaven, Julian was determined to grow a beard.[1] After all, a beard was the sign of a philosopher, and he was resolved to fulfill the philosophic ideal. While there seems to be no hint in the early sources of the color of this controversial beard or of his hair, his brother Gallus was strikingly blond[2] and it is possible that Julian was too,[3] particularly since his skin was noticeably ruddy, so florid that he frequently seemed to be blushing. His eyes, though again there is no hint of their color, were reportedly beautiful and fiery, revealing his deep intelligence. Julian was not tall; and though he always ate sparingly, he was inclined to be somewhat stocky. Like most of the Constantinian family, he had a thick, muscular neck and chest. His nose was straight; his lower lip noticeably large.[4]

Julian readily admits that he was never particularly neat.[5] Clearly he cared nothing, either as a young student or later as Emperor, about presenting a princely appearance. His hands were often covered with ink stains, his fingernails too long, and his famous beard dishevelled. As a student, he dressed in the accepted costume: a tunic topped with a *pallium* or "student cloak."

The young man possessed great reserves of energy; he slept very little and commonly spent a large part of the night as well as the day at his studies. It was as if he was determined to accomplish as much as possible in the time allotted to him, for there was always a grim possibility that cousin Constantius might have another change of heart. Another Macellum, or something far worse, could be awaiting Julian at any time.

There is much uncertainty concerning the chronology of the years immediately following Julian's departure from the hated Cappadocian castle where he had spent his long exile. Eunapius, whose *Lives of the Sophists* is the best source for Julian's student travels,[6] gives practically no hint of the sequence of events, while Libanius, in his reference to Julian's education, complicates the matter still further by his curious omission of any reference to Macellum whatsoever.

In spite of these difficulties, it is most probable that upon leaving Macellum, Julian went straightway to Constantinople,[7] where he undertook a course of study under the grammarian Nicocles and the rhetor Hecebolius. Constantius, it seems, was glad to encourage Julian's scholarly habits, "rather than leave him to reflect on his own family and his claims to empire."[8]

But even though the prince now possessed considerably more freedom than he had earlier, he was still spied upon by agents appointed by Constantius "to keep watch that he might not waver from the Christian faith."[9] Outwardly, Julian continued to conform to Christian practices, and his teacher Hecebolius was a Christian and an outspoken opponent of the old gods.

One interesting hint of Julian's continued conformity to Christian appearance is a little poem he composed on the subject of an organ he saw at the Church of the Holy Apostles.[10] Julian would never be a successful poet, and the verse, aside from its value as a factual description of this early instrument, is interesting solely because it provides a clue that he was still attending Christian (Arian) services.

While the Emperor apparently had no suspicions of Julian's true religious inclinations, he was jealous of Julian's growing circle of friends in Constantinople and feared "some untoward consequences for himself"[11] if Julian were to become too popular and well known in the imperial capital. Accordingly, the young man was ordered to move to Nicomedia. At that time the great attraction offered by this city, some sixty miles from Constantinople across the Straits in Asia Minor, was the fact that the famous rhetor Libanius of Antioch was teaching there. Julian unquestionably hoped to attend Libanius' classes, but as it turned out, he was not permitted to do so. Libanius, years later, blamed Hecebolius for this prohibition, and attributed it to professional jealousy.[12] Hecebolius, it seems, accompanied Julian to Nicomedia and bound him by mighty oaths that he would study with no other teacher. It may be, however, that Constantius was the real moving spirit behind the ban on Libanius, for the noted professor from Antioch was an ardent follower of classical philosophy and of the old gods.

In any event, Julian circumvented the order as best he could by buying copies of Libanius' lectures, taken down verbatim by shorthand writers. The young prince had plenty of money and was willing to spend extravagantly for what he really wanted. The notes he acquired through this subterfuge he studied diligently, and as Libanius never tired of pointing out in later years, his rhetorical style had a deep influence on the future Emperor.[13] Although Julian never studied with him directly, Libanius proudly spoke of him as one of his best students.

It is very possible that in spite of his growing inclinations toward the old gods, Julian served as a lector in one of the churches in Nicomedia just as he had done at Macellum.[14] He was, it is clear, continually watched by Constantius' agents, and it was necessary for him to follow a politic course. Though it is clear that Julian had a comfortable income (probably from the properties left him by his grandmother), there is a great deal of information about Julian's student years that is simply unavailable. Where did the young man live? Perhaps while he studied in Nicomedia he made his home at the family villa he had visited so often in his childhood, but there is no real evidence. What sort of household did he have? How closely guarded was he? How long was he compelled to remain a student of Hecebolius when obviously he preferred studying with a teacher who followed the old Hellenic religion? Historical novelists may make intriguing suppositions on these matters, but these are guesswork at best. Julian himself in a letter written long afterward offers a few small but unexplainable hints that he traveled a great deal in his student days, visiting friends and using his influence on their behalf. On two occasions, he says, he made a journey to the province of Phrygia to assist "that admirable woman Arete," who had suffered great wrongs from "her neighbors," but we have no further information as to her identity. On the second of these journeys, Julian (who almost never complained of poor health) recalled that he was "physically very weak from the illness that had been brought on by former fatigues."[15]

After what was probably a rather long stay off and on in Nicomedia, Julian traveled on to Pergamon (Pergamum), where he hoped to study under the famous but aging scholar Aedesius, one of the greatest Neoplatonic philosophers of the day. From Eunapius' account it seems that old Aedesius was a bit overwhelmed by the enthusiastic Julian who "longed to drink down learning open mouthed and at a gulp."[16] The prince, "old for his boyish years," was thoroughly fascinated by Aedesius and filled with "amazement and admiration for the divine qualities of his soul."[17] Aedesius was pagan, and it seems altogether likely that Julian confided in him something of his own doubt about Christianity. Hoping to be accepted as one of his regular students, he showered the old teacher with lavish gifts, but Aedesius refused to accept them—or Julian himself. Perhaps because of his advanced years and perhaps, too, because he realized how potentially dangerous it would be to have the Christian Emperor's supposedly Christian cousin as a student, Aedesius urged Julian to seek out other instructors. He recommended particularly Chrysanthius of Sardis and Eusebius of Myndus, two of his disciples who still lived and taught in Pergamon, and regretted that Maximus, his prize pupil, had moved on to Ephesus.

Julian straightway contacted Chrysanthius and Eusebius; he went frequently to hear their lectures and soon realized that although both were Aedesius' disciples, they represented vastly different approaches to philosophy. Chrysanthius was a devotee of *theurgy*, including the whole field of wonder-working, divination, and occult lore designed to bring man into closer contact with the gods, while Eusebius followed the more traditional course of philosophical rhetoric. Julian admired them both, but was puzzled by the outspoken denunciation of theurgy and "magic" with which Eusebius ended every one of his lectures. The historian Eunapius tells how Julian finally "took Chrysanthius aside and said, 'If the truth is in you, dear Chrysanthius, tell me plainly what is the meaning of this epilogue that follows his exposition?' " Chrysanthius replied that Julian should ask Eusebius

himself and when he did so, the philosopher "spread the sails
of the eloquence that was his by nature" and launched into a
description of the wonder-working powers of Maximus, which
he clearly hoped Julian would find as repellent as he did himself.
Before he left for Ephesus, Maximus had invited a number of
"philosophers" to the temple of Hecate where he conducted
a rite in which he made the image of the goddess appear to
smile and the torches in her hands burst into flame. Eusebius
admitted that he was impressed by the display, but only
momentarily. "You must not marvel at any of these things
even as I marvel not," he warned Julian, "but rather believe
that the thing of the highest importance is the purification of
the soul which is attained by reason."[18]

The prince's reaction to this report was not what Eusebius
had anticipated. "You have shown me the man I was in search
of!" Julian exclaimed, and as soon as possible thereafter, he
moved on to Ephesus.[19]

The theurgist Maximus, who would ever afterward exercise
a profound hold upon Julian's imagination, is a controversial
character. Eunapius, who knew him personally, found him most
impressive and formidable with his bright flashing eyes and
immensely long beard. Even more overwhelming were his
powers of speech: "In discussion with him no one ventured
to contradict him, not even the most experienced and most
eloquent, but they yielded to him in silence and acquiesced in
what he said as though it came from the tripod of an oracle;
such was the charm that sat on his lips."[20]

While many modern historians depict him as a charlatan and
deplore his influence over Julian as most unfortunate, it is
important to understand that in their own time, theurgy as
practiced by Maximus and many of his contemporaries was
considered a perfectly valid means of communication with the
gods. There were relatively few like Eusebius of Myndus who
felt these methods to be opposed to philosophical principles.

From the start Julian was strongly attracted to the mystical
aspect of worship; and he was, like most men of his time,
inclined to attach great importance to omens. Without abandon-
ing the philosophy he genuinely respected and admired, he

became at the same time an ardent devotee of theurgy and would remain so throughout his life.

It was probably in Ephesus in about 351 that Julian was initiated into the Mithra cult under the guidance of Maximus. Years later, Julian looked back to the time of his decisive break with Christianity as occurring when he was nineteen years of age[21] and the evidence clearly suggests that it was his Mithraic initiation that took place at that time .The worshippers of Mithra practiced such secrecy in their rites that even today there is relatively little definite information on this "mystery cult" which was very widespread in the Roman world.

Mithra was the Persian god of light. His story, far older than the official Zoroastrian religion of Persia and incorporated into it, told of his birth from a rock on December 25th, while shepherds gathered around in adoration. Subsequently, according to the legend, the god Mithra slew a bull from whose blood sprang forth all plant and animal life. By conferring this blessing upon mankind, Mithra was looked upon as a savior and worshipped as the divine intercessor between humanity and the higher gods.[22] In the Greco-Roman world, Mithra was often identified with the sun-god Helios. Julian in his writings seems to consider them identical, though others described Mithra more precisely as the companion of Helios.[23]

Cult meetings of the Mithraists were regularly held in underground cells or caves, where the only light was artificial and where a statue or bas-relief of Mithra slaying the bull usually dominated the area. For all its occultism, Mithraism emphasized a high standard of moral behavior, and with its stress on courage and brotherhood, it has often been described as the most inspiring and ethical of the oriental mystery religions that were such active rivals of Christianity in the early Christian centuries. The similarities between the two faiths have captured the imagination of many: not only in the birth-story of Mithra, but in the Mithraic "holy communion" service—a mystic meal of bread and water—and in the emphasis upon the Second Coming of Mithra, there are startling likenesses about which historians of religion can say with certainty only that there was much mutual "borrowing" among the cults of those times. The Mithraists, of course, believed that the Christians copied *them.*

Because of the secrecy maintained by Mithraic initiates little is known definitely of the rites for progressing through the seven degrees of the cult. One of the ceremonial acts frequently mentioned in the early sources was the *taurobolium*, the Mithraic baptism with bull's blood. While the initiate stood in an enclosed pit below, a bull would be slaughtered and its blood would pour down upon him through openings in the ceiling of the pit. This gory act was viewed by the loyal Mithraist as a spiritual cleansing. Many commentators have assumed without any concrete proof that the *taurobolium* was the rite that nineteen-year-old Julian went through in Ephesus. This is unlikely since he was a new convert to the cult and the *taurobolium* apparently was granted only after the initiate had progressed through the lower degrees.

Another Mithraic rite, designed for one of the lower orders of membership, involved the presentation of a crown to the initiate who was required to reject it (and any further wearing of such headgear, for instance, at a banquet) with the statement, "Mithra is my only crown."[24] (This regulation would cause considerable difficulty for Julian as reigning Emperor, for although he seems to have preferred to wear a "fillet" or narrow tie around his head, he could not completely avoid the wearing of an imperial crown on ceremonial occasions.)[25] We know, too, that another Mithraic ceremony called for the initiate to submit to the branding of some mystical symbol upon his body, probably on his forehead or the back of his hand. Although Julian reportedly "admired" this practice,[26] he cannot have risked having such a mark branded upon himself, since it would have provided all too vivid evidence for Constantius' agents who continued to report on his actions.

Indeed, in view of the fact that practically all his activities were subject to the spying eyes of the Emperor's agents, Julian must have been remarkably discreet to have managed any contacts with Maximus whatsoever. It is possible that among those whom Constantius assigned to his bodyguard were some who sympathized with Julian's inclinations toward the worship of the old gods, though there is no proof for this supposition.

From the writings of the Christian bishop Gregory Nazianzen (who knew Julian and despised him) comes an anecdote that seems almost certainly a distorted reference to Julian's Mithraic initiation.[27] According to this story, Julian and his "guide" (who is not named but who must be Maximus) descended into a cave, where they were immediately assailed by "unearthly noises, unpleasant odors, and fiery apparitions." Julian, terrorized, makes the sign of the cross; the demons disappear; but they soon return, at which Julian again makes the wonder-working Christian sign to banish them. Maximus convinces him this is not the thing to do; those seeking initiation will overcome their fear of the demons in a different manner. Julian is won over to follow Maximus and proceeds to be initiated.

It is hard to know what to make of this nonsense, for certainly neither of the two participants, Julian or Maximus, would have ever given an eyewitness report to Gregory Nazianzen, and the imaginative bishop probably concocted most of the details out of rumors he had heard of the various cultic mysteries.

Throughout his student years and in spite of his growing attachment to the occult, Julian continued his regular course of philosophic and literary studies. As a native speaker of Greek and fully imbued with the current idea that that language was far superior to Latin in every way, he devoted most of his attention to Greek writings. But unlike many of his fellow students, and perhaps because of his awareness of his Roman heritage, he was also determined to master Latin. While he was never an expert Latinist, it seems certain that he was able eventually to read some of the classics of that language, including writings of Cicero, Vergil, Horace, Ovid, Livy, Pliny the Elder, Seneca, Suetonius, and Aurelius Victor.[28] Later as a military commander in Gaul he would have ample opportunity to improve his knowledge of the spoken language, for Latin was still the official tongue of the Roman army.[29]

Wherever Julian went throughout the years of his student travels, he attracted a large number of friends. Perhaps as a result of the long isolation at Macellum, he was an extremely talkative, enthusiastic person, who greatly enjoyed discussions. Among those who sought him out must have been some who felt it was wise to cultivate him merely because he was the Emperor's cousin and a generous spender, but there is still considerable truth in Libanius' report that Julian's circle of friends increased "not just by his eloquence but by his natural attractiveness. By his gift for deep affection he instilled the capacity for it into others."[30] Julian would always possess a deep sense of loyalty; the friends of his student days would still find themselves welcome in his circle as Emperor.

From all indications, Julian was contented with life as a student, though he admits that he sometimes dreamed of the emperorship and the possibility that the gods had chosen him to restore their worship.[31]

Meanwhile, something very near to imperial grandeur descended upon Julian's brother Gallus.

CHAPTER 4

Gallus

CONSTANTIUS in the year 351 elevated Gallus to the rank of Caesar, a sort of junior partner in Empire. To understand why the Emperor took this surprising step it is necessary to realize that from the start Constantius' reign had been plagued by civil wars. His own brothers, Constantine II and Constans, had early turned against each other; in the ensuing conflict Constantine II was killed in battle in 340. Ten years later, in 350, Constans was assassinated, an act which proved to be the start of a widespread revolt by Magnentius, a Roman general of barbarian birth, who declared himself Emperor in the West. As it turned out, Constantius would successfully crush Magnentius' attempt on the throne (as he had other would-be usurpers before him), but the Emperor was growing increasingly aware of the painful fact that he might never have a son of his own to succeed him. His first wife Galla, now long dead, had given him no children, nor had his beloved Empress Eusebia of Macedonia. Was his inability to sire an heir a curse for his destruction of so many of his own kinsmen when first he succeeded to the throne?[1] Devout in his own way, Constantius apparently believed this to be true, as did Eusebia. In order to make amends and to secure the help he so desperately needed in governing his large empire, he decided to appoint Gallus to the caesarship. Since the revolt of Magnentius demanded Constantius' personal presence in the West, his young cousin's territory would be the Eastern half of the Empire.

The title "Caesar," derived from the family name of the first imperial house, was originally an epithet of the emperor himself, but at least since the time of Diocletian (who reigned from 284 to 305) the concept of the caesarship was that of a rank *second* to the emperor: a sovereign-in-training who was granted extensive responsibilities and who could reasonably expect in time to inherit the throne. Not long after Gallus left Macellum, Constantius summoned him to his court in Milan, with the idea perhaps already in his mind for his young cousin's future.

Though Gallus had very little of his brother Julian's intelligence or common sense, and possessed a fiercely ungovernable temper, he could at time be as completely charming as he was strikingly handsome. The very reserved Constantius, surrounded by the protective walls of intricate protocol, probably had little real contact with Gallus. The young man *seemed* satisfactory: he was rewarded with a bride, the Emperor's widowed sister Constantina. A thin-faced, unattractive, middle-aged woman (at least if her mosaic portrait in Rome's Santa Costanza is any reliable witness),[2] she was some years older than Gallus. Temperamentally, however, they were well matched, for she was to prove just as harsh and unnecessarily cruel as he in their exercise of power. Ammianus Marcellinus, ordinarily a most objective historian, can think of nothing but evil to report of Constantina: she was one of the Furies in human form; she "constantly aroused the savagery of Gallus" with the result that "the pair in process of time gradually became more expert in doing harm."[3] The new Caesar and his wife were stationed in Antioch of Syria, one of the largest and most beautiful cities of the East, where they would reign for three disastrous years from 351 to 354.

There is somewhat of a trend among modern historians to rehabilitate Gallus, to see him merely as a high-spirited and perhaps misguided, but not altogether unsatisfactory, young man.[4] Nonetheless it is difficult to dismiss the uniformly dismal picture of his conduct presented by such reliable, and varied witnesses as Ammianus Marcellinus and Libanius, both native Antiochenes who knew firsthand his reign of terror. Frequently, Ammianus reports, individuals were sentenced to death on false evidence and for the flimsiest of reasons, while many others lost their properties and were driven into exile. Chronic rioting by the unhappy Antiochenes only seemed to intensify Gallus' ferocious temper; yet no matter how oppressively he governed, he seemed unable to establish order in his capital city.[5] Even Julian, who undoubtedly loved his brother and was forever loyal to his memory, never tried to claim that Gallus was a capable or just ruler; he emphasizes rather that Fate was unkind to him.[6]

Julian knew Gallus well enough to stay away from the new Caesar's headquarters in Antioch. "My brother pursued his course of action without my having a sight of him even in a dream," Julian recalled later. "I was not with him, nor did I visit him or travel to his neighborhood; and I used to write to him very seldom and on unimportant matters."[7] Gallus was probably more agreeable to granting Julian freedom to travel about than Constantius had been; very likely, Julian's move to Pergamon and then to Ephesus in his quest for knowledge of theurgy and the old gods occurred soon after Gallus was installed in Antioch.

Nevertheless Julian clearly realized that Gallus had no sympathies with Hellenism. He was instead an ardent Christian after his own fashion. Even while the young Caesar was rapidly becoming the scandal of the East with wild carousings and anonymous trips "on the town," while he was carelessly governing his provinces and terrorizing the Antiochenes by his habit of listening to professional "informers," he also professed to be worried about the state of his brother Julian's soul. Was it possible, as he had heard rumored, that Julian was not completely true to the Christian faith, Arian variety? Perhaps Gallus remembered their play-acting at Macellum and the enthusiasm with which the "Hellenist" Julian had tried to "convert" him. In any case, he sent a noted (and notoriously radical) Arian theologian, Aetius, to check up on Julian's activities.[8] (As if it was not enough for Julian to be watched by Constantius' agents, Gallus now had his spies in operation as well!) Seemingly, Julian was warned of Aetius' intentions for he gave him a thoroughly winning demonstration of his loyalty to Christianity and in particular to the cult of the martyrs which Gallus especially admired. Aetius in turn convinced Gallus that his scholarly younger brother was no cause for worry.[9]

Aside from this encounter, Julian and Gallus exchanged occasional short letters. That was all, until the fateful day early in 354 when the student received a summons to meet his brother the Caesar in Constantinople.[10] There Gallus would be sponsoring a series of games in the Hippodrome.

Behind this seemingly innocuous invitation lay a mass of unspoken trouble. For all his show of imperial grandeur, Gallus knew when he left Antioch for Constantinople that he was probably going to meet his death. Constantius, disturbed by ever-increasing reports of his cruelty and his inability to rule, had deprived him of most of his troops, then summoned him West for a "conference." Constantina had left Antioch before Gallus, planning to meet with her brother the Emperor and smooth things over for her husband, but on her journey, she had suddenly—and mysteriously—died.[11]

There is no way of knowing how much of this Julian knew: possibly none of it. When he received his brother's summons, Gallus was still officially Caesar. He had demanded a meeting and Julian would obey. Julian met Gallus in Constantinople. The games—which Julian cannot have enjoyed since he now considered such entertainment an unphilosophical waste of time—were duly held in the Hippodrome in full imperial style.[12] Gallus, aged twenty-eight, was putting on a grand show, though he knew full well that disgrace awaited him further along the road to the West. There is no indication of what the brothers may have talked about during this, their last meeting, nor is there any clear evidence of Julian's whereabouts after Gallus left the capital city. He may well have remained in Constantinople.

Meanwhile, Gallus traveled on to Petobio in the province of Noricum, where he was taken into custody by Count Barbatio, formerly the commander of Gallus' household troops, now his deadly enemy. Not long thereafter, stripped of his official regalia and dressed in ordinary soldier's clothing, Gallus was conveyed by carriage to nearby Pola. There he was held in a palace surrounded by armed forces. He was given no trial; but in the informal hearings before his sentence was pronounced, the captive Caesar railed loudly against his dead wife: every act of misgovernment in Antioch was Constantina's fault. What Gallus hoped to gain by these accusations is difficult to imagine. In any event, he was pronounced a traitor; his hands were bound and he was beheaded.[13]

A special messenger hastened to Constantius in Italy, bringing along Gallus' red shoes—a token of his former status. These were tossed as a trophy of victory at Constantius' feet, and the Emperor reportedly was as pleased as if he had triumphed over the King of Persia, his greatest external foe, while his courtiers congratulated him on his great victory.[14]

It was not difficult to imagine Julian's alarm and horror when he learned of Gallus' fate, not long thereafter. "My brother," he wrote later, "was ill-starred above all men who have ever yet lived . . . Surely he deserved to live, even if he seemed unfit to govern."[15] Gallus, Julian believed, was the victim of at least partially false accusations, and should have "been allowed to speak in his own defense." Though these remarks were written at a time when Julian himself no longer stood in fear of Constantius, his loyalty to his brother's memory dated back even to the time of Gallus' death.[16] Although it would have been politically wise for him to do so, he never wrote and was never heard to say anything derogatory toward the fallen Caesar.

Gallus was executed late in 354. Sometime in the winter of 354-55, Julian was taken into custody by Constantius' agents, who would escort him to Italy. In recent years the Emperor had spent much of his time in his palace in Milan; Julian, however, was to be housed temporarily at nearby Comum. It is not in the least surprising that he left on this somber journey believing that he, like Gallus and like their father before them, was going to meet his death at Constantius' order.[17]

CHAPTER 5

The Summons to the West

JULIAN had no choice but to obey the Emperor's summons. He was determined nonetheless that in the course of his journey he would at least stop on the way to visit one place he had always wanted to see, the site of ancient Troy on the Asia Minor coast.[1] Apparently the Emperor's guards who were under orders to conduct him to Italy had no objection to this excursion which, in any case, was not far out of the way. When Julian arrived at Troy, he was met by the local Christian bishop, Pegasius, who naturally believed the prince to be a Christian, but who was pleased all the same to conduct him on a tour of the old city's famous Homeric shrines. There was a small temple with a bronze statue of the Trojan hero Hector; opposite it in an open court was a statue of his great adversary Achilles. Julian was surprised (and immensely pleased) to discover the altars at these shrines were still warm, and that Hector's statue showed signs of much recent anointing. When he questioned the bishop about these obvious indications of survival of the old cult, Pegasius cautiously replied: "Is it not natural that they [the local inhabitants] should worship a brave man who was their own citizen just as we worship the martyrs?" He then conducted Julian to the temple of Athene where there were many choice statues of the gods and goddesses perfectly preserved. When Pegasius neither made the sign of the cross nor hissed at these pagan mementos, as Christians regularly did, Julian realized clearly that the bishop was, like himself, a secret devotee of the old gods.[2] Before he left Troy, he took time for a further visit with Pegasius to the tomb of Achilles. Probably neither the prince nor the bishop dared to speak at that time about the problems of religion that were so important to them both. But Julian did not forget Pegasius and years later as

40

Emperor, he would reward the erstwhile bishop with a pagan priesthood, recalling how under the guise of Christianity, Pegasius had helped to preserve the relics of Troy's ancient glories.[3]

After this pleasant interlude in Troy, Julian all too soon had to resume his fateful journey to Constantius' court. Later he would remember the seven months he spent in Italy as a terrible time, with Constantius "dragging me hither and thither...and keeping me under guard."[4] He was not actually imprisoned, but as Libanius reports, "he was surrounded by armed guards, grim of face and harsh of tongue, whose behavior was such that imprisonment seemed a mere trifle in comparison."[5] Any day might bring the death sentence for this twenty-three year old student of philosophy who by accident of birth was so dangerously close to the throne and whose brother had died a condemned traitor. Julian knew he had enemies at court: some of those who had hated Gallus now hated him by association. Evidence of the fact that Julian was dangerous, they alleged, was his daring to visit his brother in Constantinople. Moreover, it was charged, several years earlier, he had left Macellum without permission.[6]

Chief among Julian's enemies was Constantius' most trusted eunuch, the grand chamberlain Eusebius. ("Eusebius," incidentally, was one of the most popular names of the fourth century. Its meaning, "pious," was in this particular case singularly ill suited to its owner.) Eusebius was the epitome of craftiness, and so powerful in the counsels of Empire that a witticism of the time stated: If you want something done, see Constantius—he is supposed to have some influence with Eusebius.[7] Particularly ominous for Julian was the fact that Eusebius had been one of the prime movers in Gallus' execution.

The months passed by. Julian studied; this may be the period when he seriously set about perfecting his Latin. He was also determined to clear himself of the charges against him. In answering Gallus' summons to Constantinople, he was merely obeying the reigning Caesar, he pointed out; it was an argument that was difficult to challenge. He seems, too, to have possessed written evidence that he had permission for his departure from Macellum.[8] He had done nothing to cast even the faintest suspicions upon his loyalty to Constantius.

But, Julian also knew, at the court of Constantius evidence could be manufactured where it did not exist. There were agents everywhere: unscrupulous creatures like Paul "the Chain," so called for his habits of "linking" seemingly innocent happenings into a case of treason; and Mercurius, the "Count of Dreams," whose specialty was finding and interpreting treasonable signs— that could be offered as valid condemnatory evidence—in people's dreams.[9]

Fortunately, Julian found an unexpected friend in the Empress Eusebia. There is no evidence that they had ever met; in the strictly regulated etiquette of the court they probably had not as yet. But Eusebia, who was deeply devoted to Constantius and concerned over their own childlessness, urged her husband to deal kindly with the young man who was his last surviving male relative—the only one he had not killed.

After several months Constantius finally agreed to see Julian, and told him he had decided to let him go. Julian owned a house that he describes as his inheritance from his mother;[10] perhaps it was the same villa near Nicomedia that he speaks of elsewhere as his grandmother's home. He was to retire there, in seclusion, but *alive*. Then on his eastward journey, he was intercepted by a messenger. Constantius had changed his mind again: prompted by Eusebia's advice, he had decided that Julian was to go to Athens.[11] Nothing could have pleased him more.

Fourth-century Athens, though no longer the splendid city it had been in the great days of classical Greece, was still an important center of educational activity. To a dedicated Hellenist like Julian the bustling university town seemed the center of the intellectual world. Libanius in several of his orations praising Julian insists that the young prince had no further need of schooling; that in Athens he knew more than his teachers, who were astonished by his abilities.[12] Julian himself, however, seemed delighted to be a student again. Moreover, to live in Greece, he wrote, "had long been my dearest wish, and I desired it more than to possess treasures of gold and silver . . . For we who dwell in Thrace and Ionia are the sons of Hellas, and all of us who are not devoid of feeling long to greet our ancestors and to embrace the very soil of Hellas."[13]

Though many of the teachers and students who clustered in

Athens were Christian, the city's ties with the old religion were still strong. The Parthenon stood on the Acropolis in undamaged splendor, and there and at many other temples and shrines throughout the city, the worship of the old gods continued unhindered.[14]

At nearby Eleusis the mystery cult of Demeter and Persephone still attracted hundreds of initiates annually to the holy spot where Persephone supposedly reappeared from the underworld. The hierophant or high priest of this cult was greatly revered for his wisdom and his predictions of coming events. Eunapius (who was himself an initiate into the Eleusinian mysteries and as such was not permitted to speak or write the hierophant's name) reports of him how he prophesied the imminent end of his cult. He was, he declared, the last legitimate hierophant. There would be one more to hold the post after him, but he would not be ritually qualified, and then the Eleusinian mysteries would cease forever.[15]

Information of this sort always fascinated Julian, and although Eunapius is not clear as to whether he actually heard these prophecies, he was definitely eager to meet the hierophant. He probably hoped also to be initiated into the Eleusinian cult. The pagan "mystery" religions were not, like Christianity, mutually exclusive, and there was no reason why an initiate of the Mithra cult like Julian could not also be admitted into the mysteries of Eleusis.

There were, however, other serious obstacles in the way of the prince's inclinations toward seeking initiation. The ceremonies at Eleusis occupied several days and were, in part, public. Even if Julian could have eluded his bodyguards or persuaded them to permit him to take part, some observer would have reported his activity to agents of Constantius. He did manage to visit the hierophant, but this is probably as far as his connection with the Eleusinian cult went.[16]

The restrictions that surrounded Julian in Athens did not, however, keep the young man completely isolated from the world of ordinary student life. Here, as everywhere he had traveled, his outgoing personality and complete lack of royal pretentiousness attracted a great number of acquaintances. As Libanius recalled, "there could always be seen about him swarms of men, young and old, philosophers and rhetors . . . Everyone enjoyed the kindness of his disposition, but it was only the best among them who enjoyed his confidence."[17] One of these was almost certainly the famous teacher Priscus, who was a generation older than Julian and noted for his extreme aloofness and lack of warmth, yet who became Julian's firm, lifelong friend.[18]

On the other hand, among the young men who almost certainly did not win Julian's confidence in Athens were two future Christian bishops from Cappadocia: Basil of Caesarea and Gregory Nazianzen. Like Julian they were students of Prohaeresius, a Christian sophist. Julian got along with Basil well enough, but Gregory, it would seem, took an intense dislike to the student prince with his paganistic tendencies. In later years, Gregory was to claim that he had known Julian well, and suspected even then "what a monster" he would turn out to be. Gregory's description of the future Emperor is a spiteful caricature: he recalls Julian's nervous energy, his bursts of laughter, his breathless questions, his rather ungainly posture, all as bad signs of his later-to-be-revealed apostasy.[19]

Julian, happily oblivious to all this animosity, believed that to live in Athens forever would represent "the most perfect bliss."[20] As it turned out, his stay in the city was to be cut short; he was there only about two months (August to October) when he received a summons to return to the imperial court in Milan.

Even in that era when men often wept freely and openly, Julian was not one who cried easily, but to leave Athens, when he had only just arrived, was a blow he could scarcely endure. "What floods of tears I shed and what laments I uttered!"[21] he recalled afterwards. Stretching out his hands toward the Acropolis, he prayed to Athene. It would be better, he thought, to die at once, there in beautiful Athens, than to go back to the imperial court: or so he later recalled his emotions, looking back to this time of grave disappointment compounded with the terrible uncertainty of his impending fate.

CHAPTER 6

The New Caesar

UNWILLING as Julian was to return to Italy, there could be no escape from Constantius' order. The prince left Athens and arrived in Milan in October of 355. The gods sent him "guardian angels" for this dangerous journey, he declared;[1] more visible was the Empress Eusebia's very real concern for his well-being. While he was in Greece, Eusebia had continued to work on his behalf with Constantius. The Emperor, although still very ambivalent in his feelings toward his young cousin, appeared increasingly inclined to honor him as befitted his birth and to find a use for him in the business of rulership. The situation in Gaul had deteriorated badly in recent months: there would be a place for Julian there.

Julian had no way of knowing the Emperor's plans. He must have been somewhat consoled, however, to receive in the first few days after his arrival in Milan a series of letters from the Empress urging him not to worry and to write her whenever he wished. Later he would recall how he finally composed a reply, pleading with her that he might be allowed to go home— probably he meant back to Athens. "But," he added, "I suspected that it was not safe to send to the palace letters addressed to the Emperor's wife."[2] There was never the slightest hint of a romantic intrigue between Eusebia and Julian; they probably still had not met face to face. But Julian was a young, attractive man, much closer to Eusebia's own age than Constantius was, and at the imperial court there was always room for suspicions. Julian besought the gods as to whether he should send the letter; they warned him (perhaps in a dream) that if he did so he would surely die an ignominious death. The letter was not dispatched.[3]

Meanwhile, Constantius finalized his plans for Julian's future. The young student was being transformed—outwardly at least—

into a royal personage. Much to Julian's regret, his "philosopher's beard" had to be shaved off; he was dressed in military garb, though he knew that Constantius' courtiers secretly mocked him as "a highly ridiculous soldier."[4] Their hints that he try to walk like a courtier—"staring about me and strutting along"—went unheeded.[5] There were some things about Julian that simply could not be changed.

During the weeks after he first arrived in Milan, Julian was not housed in the imperial palace, nor did he wish to be; but finally he was ordered to move there. "I submitted and . . . consented to dwell under the same roof with those whom I knew to have ruined my whole family and who, I suspected, would before long plot against myself also."[6]

It is completely understandable why Julian suspected the worst of Constantius; however, at this point, at least, he seems to have judged the Emperor unfairly. On November 6, 355, in a magnificent public ceremony, Constantius officially proclaimed Julian his Caesar in the West, a position which would give him authority over Gaul, Spain, and Britain. The historian Ammianus Marcellinus gives a detailed account of this momentous occasion.[7] Firmly grasping Julian's right hand, Constantius addressed the crowd of soldiers surrounding the platform where they stood. The ever placid Emperor spoke "in a quiet tone"; he commented on the dangerous situation in Gaul where German barbarians were overrunning the frontiers, then announced that he had chose his cousin Julian to serve as Caesar there and asked the army's approval.

The soldiers cheered enthusiastically, as they had no doubt been instructed to do: there was surely no other cause to rejoice in the promotion of a twenty-four-year-old philosophy student with no military experience. Constantius then clothed Julian in a purple cloak, and addressed him as "my brother, dearest to me of all men," charging him to defend Roman interests in Gaul. At the end of the Emperor's short speech, the assembled troops struck their shields against their knees, the signal of their enthusiastic approval of the new Caesar. As he rode back to the palace in the same carriage with Constantius, it is reported that Julian muttered under his breath a line from Homer: "By purple death I'm seized and fate supreme."[8]

In the days that followed, Julian found that in spite of the honor bestowed upon him he was virtually a prisoner in the imperial palace, and later he would claim that he had been in fear for his life throughout the whole of November, 355. "I was continually thoughtful and gloomy," he recalled.[9] "My doors locked, warders to guard them, the hands of my servants searched lest one of them should convey to me the most trifling letter from my friends!"[10] Julian had been allowed to bring only four of his own servants to court with him, two young boys and two older men. Only one of these, who has been identified as the African eunuch Euhemerus,[11] knew of Julian's allegiance to the gods, and sometimes joined him in secret worship services. Julian's close friend, the physician Oribasius, was also present at court, but was only allowed to remain there, Julian believed, because the Emperor did not know of their friendship.[12]

Obviously, the enigmatic Constantius for some unspecified reason had decided to subject Julian to another period of testing, in spite of his already having been proclaimed Caesar. It seems likely that throughout these weeks, the eunuch Eusebius who hated Julian was still attempting to find some reason for the new Caesar's disgrace, while the Empress Eusebia continued to urge her husband to deal fairly with the young man. Constantius, so easily influenced by the advice of both his wife and his favorite eunuch, was temporarily at a loss to know what to do when their advice conflicted. As days passed, the will of the Empress prevailed, possibly because the continued bad news from Gaul (including the fall of Cologne to German tribesmen) made Julian's departure for that troubled province seem the most logical move.

One day, apparently fairly soon after his investiture as Caesar, Julian was granted an audience (likely his first) with his benefactor, the Empress Eusebia. His description of their meeting provides a revealing glimpse of the ceremonial formality of the early Byzantine court:

"Now when I first came into her presence it seemed to me as though I beheld a statue of Modesty set up in some temple. Then reverence filled my soul and my eyes were fixed on the ground for some considerable time, till she bade me take courage. Then she said: 'Certain favours you have already received from us and yet others shall you receive, if God will, if only you prove to be loyal and honest toward us.' This was almost as much as I heard. For she herself did not say more . . ."[13]

Very soon thereafter, Julian discovered that among the "favours" he would receive was a bride: Constantius' "maiden sister," Helena. She was at least thirty if not somewhat older;[14] Julian was himself twenty-four. Though there is nothing to indicate that they were actively unhappy, the bride and groom probably had little in common. Helena was no doubt a Christian and perhaps a devout one. Since she was Constantius' sister, Julian could scarcely be blamed if he regarded her as an agent of the Emperor (though he never expresses this suspicion). In fact, in all his voluminous extant writings he only mentions Helena three times.[15] His letters to her, written while he was on campaign in Gaul, unfortunately have not survived, though he claimed he would not mind if the whole world were to read them.[16]

With their departure for Gaul imminent, the Empress Eusebia showered gifts upon the newlyweds. "Perhaps you wish to hear also the list of her presents . . ." Julian notes, "but I have no time to gossip about such matters."[17] He was especially pleased, however, by the fine collection of books that the Empress gave him, enough to turn Gaul into "a temple of the Muses."[18] To these, Constantius added a contribution of his own: a booklet which he had written out with his own hand, listing approved menus for the Caesar's table![19]

Armed with this collection and furnished with a bodyguard of about three hundred men, Julian and Helena set out for Gaul on December 1, 355. Ahead lay a most uncertain future.

CHAPTER 7

The First Year in Gaul

DESPITE the near approach of winter, the passage over the Alps was unusually smooth, the weather spring-like and warm. Omen-conscious Julian must have considered this a good sign, though he had less reason to be pleased with his bodyguard, a troop of Christians who "only knew how to pray."[1] These forces comprised Julian's only military contingent; even though he was Caesar, and technically second in rank only to the Emperor himself, the actual command of the Roman armies in Gaul was in the hands of Ursicinus and Marcellus, generals appointed earlier by Constantius. Naturally Julian felt wary of these two; he was certain they had orders from Constantius "to watch me as vigilantly as they did the enemy."[2] While some have seen the Emperor's reluctance to give Julian any real power in Gaul as a sign of his continued hostility, his decision on this matter was actually very sensible: the young Caesar had absolutely no military experience, and to have expected him to assume immediate command would have been thoroughly unrealistic.

The Alps crossed, Julian and his entourage headed for the fortified town of Vienne in southern Gaul. Here, as he was making his ceremonial entry, an aged blind woman cried out as he passed by that he was chosen by the gods to restore their worship.[3] On the same momentous occasion, Libanius reports, a wreath of greenery, hanging up over the street as a decoration, came loose as Julian was riding by and landed on his head—a wonderful omen indeed.[4]

The Gaul which Julian entered under such happy auspices had been under Roman rule for four hundred years; the inhabitants, whether of Celtic stock or decendants of Roman colonists, were thoroughly romanized and Latin was spoken by practically all. Somewhat larger than present-day France, *Gallia* stretched at least in theory to the west bank of the Rhine; to the north, the territory included what is now Belgium and Luxembourg, as well as part of the Netherlands and the German Rhineland. Until the recent incursion by German tribesmen, "Allemani" from across the Rhine, the Gallic provinces had been accustomed to long decades of peace and prosperity, but the reign of Constantius had witnessed continued disruption of the area. As Libanius says, "The barbarian flood had inundated the wealth of Gaul, or rather had rendered up to the barbarians all that Gaul possessed."[5] German raiders appeared annually, looting, burning, slaying, and carrying off numerous prisoners of war, while Constantius (in spite of his talent for subduing rival claimants to his throne) had been completely unsuccessful in halting the German threat. It is little wonder that the Gallic provincials hoped that the arrival of Julian would signal the beginning of better times.

Julian spent the winter of 355-356 in Vienne.[6] Immediately he set out to familiarize himself with the administrative routine, a business in which he was greatly aided by the prefect Salustius, an appointee of Constantius who turned out to be a true friend to Julian and a worshipper of the old gods. Julian, of course, had to keep his own religious inclination concealed: he even attended Christian church services on occasion, though his closest associates realized fully where his real sympathies lay.

To the surprise of many, Julian was also determined to learn the military arts through firsthand experience. In the winter afternoons he would practice daily with sword and shield; and he soon learned to march in step to the tune of military pipes. Though sometimes when he was discouraged, he was heard to sigh, "O, Plato!"[7], the scholarly young man was developing a surprising gift for, as well as interest in, the art of soldiery.

In spite of his heavy duties, Julian never neglected his earlier interests in literature and philosophy, and usually devoted several hours of each night to reading, study, and writing.[8] He was never one to require much sleep, only about four or five hours per night. His reading now included large amounts of military history and tactics; in time, he would write his own commentaries on his campaigns in Gaul.[9] Although this source is no longer extant, it was probably used by Ammianus Marcellinus in his history, the best record now available for the Gallic period of Julian's career. Ammianus was himself in Gaul during part of Julian's term there; he was an officer of relatively low rank, under the command of the general Ursicinus.[10] He probably met Julian somewhere along the way, but he was by no means one of the Caesar's close confidants. That he admired Julian tremendously is obvious on practically every page of Ammianus' work; he is at the same time a careful and objective reporter, who does not hesitate occasionally to point out his hero's mistakes.

Libanius' "Oration 18" composed not long after Julian's death also contains detailed information on the Caesar's years in Gaul[11] and is probably based on information from his commentaries, though Libanius' high-flown rhetorical style and habits of compressing and rearranging material make it a more difficult source to use.

On New Year's Day of 356, Julian became consul for the first time with the Emperor Constantius as his colleague.[12] The consulship, an ancient heritage from the Rome of republican times, was by the fourth century A.D. simply a ceremonial office, but one that carried tremendous prestige. Each year (not yet officially numbered by the scheme based on the birth of Christ) was named for the pair of consuls who served during that year. The Emperor himself was not automatically a consul; he nominated himself to that post only occasionally. Constantius' choice of Julian to serve as his colleague seemed an indication that the Caesar was now solidly secure in the Emperor's favor. Perhaps Eusebia was to thank for the honor; it is possible, too, though it is only a conjecture, that Helena may have had something to do with it.

Throughout the winter of 355-356, Julian apparently recruited a considerable number of volunteer troops from among the Gallic citizenry to increase the scant bodyguard supplied him by the Emperor.[13] With the coming of warm weather, the inevitable German raids would recommence, and Julian intended to be prepared. By summer he had under his direct command both infantry and cavalry troops, although Ammianus does not specify their number.

The Emperor Constantius, it is clear, was not unaware of these activities, but apparently he still did not expect Julian to play an active military role. "About the summer solstice (of 356) he allowed me to join the army," Julian reports, "and to carry about with me his dress and image."[14] The imperial paraphernalia may have included a cloak with Constantius' picture embroidered on it, to be worn by Julian on all public occasions; it has also been suggested that a small bust of the Emperor adorned the Caesar's crown.[15] In any event, as Julian noted: Constantius "had both said and had written that he was not giving the Gauls a king but one who should convey to them his image."[16]

It was June when word reached Vienne that the enemy had laid siege to the ancient city of Autun. The old town's fortifications were reported to be in poor condition, crumbling with "the decay of centuries."[17] The small garrison stationed there, apparently consisting mainly of overaged, semi-retired veterans, was trapped inside but putting up a gallant defense. Apprised of this situation, Julian and his forces set out from Vienne to lift the siege. The plan proved successful beyond his hopes: at the approach of the Caesar's army, the Germans scattered in all directions. Julian had won his first victory.[18]

With Autun secure and the summer campaign season just beginning, Julian determined to lead his troops further into endangered territory. Consulting with his advisors about possible routes to Troyes, he selected the shortest, reputedly most dangerous route, through heavily forested territory. The choice proved justified. They safely reached Auxerre where Julian ordered a short rest; then they pushed on toward Troyes. There were a number of skirmishes with the Germans along the way; the Romans were uniformly successful in beating them off, and arrived outside the walled town of Troyes so unexpectedly that the local authorities were reluctant to let them in until thoroughly convinced that this Roman army was not really the enemy in disguise.[19]

After a short rest, the army proceeded from Troyes to Rheims, headquarters of the general Marcellus. There Julian intended to formulate campaign plans for the rest of the season. Since Ammianus specifically states that the resulting strategy was the outcome of "many various opinions,"[20] it appears that Ursicinus and Marcellus probably were little inclined as yet to give serious consideration to Julian's ideas.

In the ensuing campaign, on a very cloudy day as Julian's forces were passing through a thickly wooded area, the two legions that formed the Caesar's rearguard were ambushed by Germans lurking in the forest. What could have been disaster for the Romans was only narrowly averted, as the endangered forces sounded the alarm and were joined by reinforcements. From this experience, Ammianus reports, Julian learned to be particularly wary of ambushes, and to take special precautions lest one happen again.[21]

The remainder of the summer of 356 was marked by a string of successes for Roman arms. Brumath was recovered, and then the important fortress city of Cologne on the Rhine.[22] Julian remained in Cologne for some weeks thereafter, negotiating a truce with the Frankish (German) kings. After additional inspection tours, during which he arranged for the stationing of garrisons in various strategic fortresses along and near the Rhine, he withdrew with a much diminished force to winter quarters in Sens. "There I was exposed to utmost danger," he recalled later, ". . . while I was quartered apart with only a few soldiers."[23]

Custom demanded suspension of hostilities during the winter months; but it was a convention often disregarded by both sides. When the Germans learned that Julian was at Sens with only a nominal force, they advanced upon the town and set up siege. The Caesar realized the folly of attempting to go out to meet them, and much as he would have preferred this course of action, he ordered strengthening of the town wall, prepared for what might be a long siege, and hoped daily to receive reinforcements from Marcellus whose forces were stationed not far away. Julian could be seen "day and night," reports Ammianus, "with his soldiers among the bulwarks and battlements."[24] His willingness to share the hardships of his men was one of Julian's most winning characteristics. Not only in times of crisis but as a general practice, he was perfectly content with the same rations as the ordinary soldiers. He slept under a coarse woolen blanket and seemed completely unconcerned about material possessions. During the siege of Sens, when food apparently was very scarce, his courageous example must have provided inspiration to his hard-pressed troops and to the townspeople.

After about a month, the Germans, who were seldom particularly skilled in siegecraft, withdrew and Sens could again breathe freely. The reinforcements expected from Marcellus had never arrived.

Even Constantius was displeased on learning of Marcellus' appalling failure to send aid to the beleaguered town.[25] The general was summoned to the imperial court in Milan to answer charges. Since Ursicinus was transferred to the Eastern frontier at about the same time, Julian would find with the coming of warm weather in 357 that he had two new generals to work with, Severus and Barbatio.[26] While Severus, commander of the cavalry, would prove (for a while at least) a helpful ally, Barbatio, who was deeply implicated in the execution of Gallus, made up his mind at the outset that he had no use for Gallus' brother either, and was destined to give Julian more trouble than the enemy.

Meanwhile, Marcellus was busily spreading rumors against Julian at the imperial court, charging him especially with being overly ambitious. Julian considered the situation so grave that he dispatched a trusted eunuch, his grand chamberlain Eutherius, to Milan to present his side of the case. Ammianus Marcellinus, who ordinarily has little use for eunuchs, praises Eutherius to the skies: he was a person of outstanding integrity and genuine kindness, and a devoted friend of Julian.[27] His calm presentation of the Caesar's cause before the Emperor won the day: Marcellus was banished and Julian thoroughly vindicated.[28]

It is probable that Julian's cause was considerably helped by a document he had composed during the winter just past and which Eutherius in all likelihood brought with him to Milan.[29] This was Julian's first "Panegyric in Honor of the Emperor Constantius," a highly complimentary (but in light of further knowledge of Julian's thought) completely insincere work lauding the Emperor on every page. Julian could not have enjoyed writing this piece, in which he was obliged to say a great deal that he did not mean, but it was a part of the business of staying alive. Panegyrics were very fashionable and Constantius would surely expect his scholarly cousin to produce one sooner or later. From all indications, too, the Emperor was pleased by the results.

Nor can modern students of Julian's thought afford to dismiss this First "Panegyric on Constantius" as nothing more than a hypocritical exercise in rhetoric. Though Constantius probably did not have the wit to read between the lines, the piece is full of irony: the virtues Julian professes to find in Constantius are qualities that he hoped to find in an ideal ruler, "doing good to all men and imitating the divine nature on earth."[30] Particularly striking is this statement addressed by Julian to the autocratic Constantius: "You ever behave toward the people and the magistrates like a citizen who obeys the laws, not like a king who is above the laws."[31] This was an ideal of old republican Rome, not of the proto-Byzantine Empire of the fourth century, and there is no hint that the gentle suggestion made the least impact on Constantius' heavy-handed methods of government. Julian, however, was not merely voicing a pious sentiment. Personally, he was a firm believer in a strictly limited monarchy, and as a ruler himself, he would strive diligently to uphold this ideal.[32]

Julian seems, too, to have made a real effort in the First Panegyric to be honest when possible, and to laud with particular enthusiasm the few genuine virtues that Constantius appeared to possess. The Emperor's well-known fidelity to his Empress Eusebia called forth Julian's enthusiastic praises,[33] as did Constantius' affection for and sense of duty toward his father, Constantine the Great.[34]

Fortunately for Julian, since the rhetorical customs of panegyric writing were derived from classical sources, he did not find it necessary to touch upon the matter of Christianity at all, aside from one veiled remark that the "last hours" of Constantine the Great were "peculiarly blest"[35] (no doubt a reference to the late Emperor's deathbed baptism). Otherwise there is nothing (either hypocritically Christian or daringly pagan) to suggest Julian's own religious sentiments at the time, and Constantius apparently still remained oblivious to his cousin's Hellenic tendencies.

In fact by the start of 357, Julian, who had been named consul for the second time, apparently stood in higher favor with Constantius than he ever had before. Ammianus, however, casts a ghoulish hint of doubt upon this otherwise rosy picture. Sometime in 356 or early 357, Julian's wife Helena gave birth to a baby boy. The midwife cut the umbilical cord too short and the infant died. Ammianus, who ordinarily avoids unfounded gossip, seems convinced that this was a deliberate murder: the midwife was bribed by Julian's enemies "that this most valiant man might have no heir."[36] Later in 357, Helena went to Rome to attend her brother Constantius' triumphal celebration there. While on this visit, Ammianus charges, the Empress Eusebia gave Helena a "rare potion," which she apparently presented under the guise of a fertility drug. Helena on her return to Gaul took the potion regularly, and though she became pregnant at least once more, the drug caused her to suffer a miscarriage. Eusebia, the historian indicates, being childless herself, could not bear for Helena and Julian to have children.[37]

It is very difficult to know what to make of these allegations, but since everything else we know of Eusebia suggests that she was an honest and loyal friend to Julian, it is doubtful that she was behind these machinations. It has been theorized that she may indeed have given Helena a "wonder drug" of some sort, but with the best of intentions, for Eusebia seems to have tried many exotic medications herself in the hope of having a child.[38] Julian, at least, gave no credence to such rumors if he ever heard them. Sometime after Helena's return from Rome,[39] he composed a "Panegyric in Honor of the Empress Eusebia" in which he has nothing but the warmest praise for her unfailing kindness to him. It is a much more obviously sincere piece than the "Panegyric of Constantius" and as such seems a strong clue that the usually reliable Ammianus was grievously misinformed on the matter of Julian and Helena's offspring.

CHAPTER 8

Gaul: 357

THE new infantry commander, Barbatio, arrived at the southern Rhine with an army of 25,000 men in the spring of 357.[1] Roman strategists planned to trap the Germans in a pincers movement in which Julian's and Barbatio's troops would join forces, but a surprise raid by the Laeti tribe upset their careful plans. The Laeti attacked the walled town of Lyons; unable to storm the fortifications, they ravaged the outlying areas and took considerable plunder. Julian, anticipating their next move would be withdrawal with their spoils, sent a squadron of cavalry to patrol each of the three roads leading away from Lyons, and as the Laeti attempted their withdrawal they were ambushed by the Romans. Many of the enemy were slain and their plunder recovered. The only disappointment to mar the victory was the fact that a number of the Laeti escaped unhindered "past the rampart of Barbatio." It was the first of many indications that the infantry commander was deeply involved in intrigues to damage Julian's military reputation, even at the cost of secretly assisting the enemy.[2]

In the following weeks, Julian concentrated his efforts on the recovery of several islands in the Rhine now inhabited by Germans. In order to launch his planned attack he needed boats, and Barbatio, Julian knew, had some craft that he intended to use for the construction of pontoon bridges. When the Caesar sent a request for seven of these boats, Barbatio's response was to set fire to his entire fleet, and then to report that he was unable to send aid. It is no surprise that the ordinary soldiers began to wonder if Barbatio were simply a "fool" or acting on secret orders from Constantius.[3]

Julian's attack on the islands of the Rhine succeeded anyway. From enemy prisoners of war, he learned of a spot where the river was fairly shallow at that time of year, as far out as the nearest island. To this point he dispatched some auxiliaries, who managed to reach their destination by wading, then floating on their shields. According to the fierce but widely accepted practice of the time, the Romans slaughtered everyone they found on the island; the boats they found there provided transportation to other islands up and down the river. Many Germans were slain, while many more fled back to the relative safety of the east bank of the Rhine. In a whirlwind campaign, Julian's men had wiped out a number of dangerous nests from which the enemy customarily launched their raids into Gaul. During the same season they also recovered the ruined fortress of Tres Tabernae on the west bank of the Rhine and rebuilt it.[4]

Meanwhile other soldiers were assigned the task of harvesting for their own use crops planted by the Germans who had now at least partially evacuated the area.[5] Julian was always deeply concerned that his troops should have sufficient rations. Occasionally supplies were sent across the Alps from Italy; in the summer of 357 a large amount of sorely-needed food reached Barbatio's camp via this route. Barbatio set aside as much as he thought his men could use, but the rest, which was supposed to be forwarded to Julian, he ordered put to the torch instead.[6] One can well imagine Julian's dismay and anger on learning of this second instance of the general's senseless firebug habits.

Not long afterwards, while attempting to cross the Rhine, Barbatio's forces were taken by complete surprise by a "horde of savages." Roman losses were very heavy; Barbatio hastily retreated to his camp at Augst; the Germans followed in hot pursuit, helping themselves to the Roman baggage and pack animals and taking numerous prisoners.[7]

It was midsummer, but Barbatio ordered his surviving troops into "winter quarters" and betook himself back to Milan to complain about Julian. Of all of the officers with whom Julian had to contend during his years in Gaul, Barbatio was no doubt the greatest trial. Perhaps it is kindest to assume that he was mentally disturbed. Despite the rumors that he was Constantius' henchman, the Emperor, on learning what had happened, quickly had him transferred, and several years later he was executed for an alleged plot against Constantius' throne.[8]

As the summer of 357 wore on, the Germans east of the Rhine, encouraged by their easy defeat of Barbatio, began to mass their forces under seven tribal kings for an all-out campaign against Julian. A Roman deserter supplied the interesting, but apparently mistaken, information that there were only about 13,000 men under the Caesar's command. The Germans, with vastly superior numbers, were so heartened by this news that they sent messengers to Julian demanding Roman withdrawal from what they called "their" territories in Gaul. Julian refused terms and held the envoys captive. Battle was inevitable.[9]

Julian clearly realized it would be to the Roman advantage if the Germans had to fight with their backs to the river, and having discovered that thousands of them had crossed to the Gallic side of the Rhine and were massed near Strasbourg, he departed with his forces from Tres Tavernae. A distance of about twenty-one Roman miles separated the two armies.[10]

It was a hot August day and when the men halted around noon for a short rest, Julian spoke to them briefly, suggesting (but by no means ordering) that they pitch camp there for the night and proceed against the enemy the next morning lest they be too exhausted to fight.

No one liked this seemingly sensible advice. As Ammianus Marcellinus reports: "The soldiers did not allow him to finish what he was saying, but gnashed and ground their teeth and showed their eagerness for battle by striking their spears and shields together."[11] Even Florentius, the praetorian prefect who accompanied the army and who was one of Constantius' trusted agents, favored fighting that day: if they should wait till the morrow, the Germans might disperse and the Romans lose their advantage. Or, worse still, more Germans might arrive from across the Rhine, where reportedly thousands were mustering. It is possible that Julian intended all along that his speech would produce the reverse psychology of inciting the men to fight without delay. In any case, the march was resumed.

As the Romans drew nearer to the German camp they were sighted by three mounted enemy scouts who hastened back with news of their approach. Julian had lost the advantage of surprise. The Germans readied their battle lines, planted an ambuscade in a swampy spot well concealed behind a "curtain of reeds" and awaited the Roman attack.

Ammianus Marcellinus' lengthy account of the ensuing battle presents vivid glimpses of the Germanic foe. The typical German was much larger than the average Roman; as they rushed into battle "they gnashed their teeth hideously and raged beyond their usual manner, their flowing hair made a terrible sight, and a kind of madness shone from their eyes."[12] Most were armed with javelins and swords, though they lacked the sophisticated armor of the Romans. Chnodomar, chief among the seven German kings, was resplendent in his helmet with a flame-colored plume.

From the outset, the Roman left flank under the command of Severus pushed back the German right. The planned ambush in the marshy spot failed completely, since the Romans caught sight of the enemy there and avoided the trap. Meanwhile, the cavalry on the Roman right was hard pressed by mixed forces of German cavalry and infantry. Ammianus explains that the German infantrymen were particularly effective in this sort of fighting: they concentrated on wounding the Roman horses, thus facilitating the slaughter of unhorsed cavalrymen.[13] Hard pressed by waves of German attackers, the Roman cavalry, even some of the standard-bearers, broke ranks and attempted retreat, only to run into a solid wall of Roman infantry reserves, their shields locked together in "tortoise" formation, who held them back at least for the moment.

Julian rode over hastily, his purple dragon banner blowing conspicuously in the breeze. In a brief speech, he warned his panicked forces that if they intended to desert they would have to kill him first. He reminded them that there would be no refuge for them anywhere should they flee, and encouraged them with news that things were going well for the Romans on the opposite side of the field. The scattered cavalry regrouped; Julian's speech, says Libanius, was so rousing that even some of the baggage guards rushed into the fray.[14] The infantry reserves were called in and moved forward, giving their battle cry that "rises from a low murmur and gradually grows louder, like waves dashing against the cliffs."[15] The air was thick with javelins and darts; in a few moments, there was heavy hand-to-hand combat between the Germans and this fresh wave of Romans.

Finally, the Germans, seeing so many of their number fallen on the field, began to retreat. Romans followed in rapid pursuit; the ranks of German dead increased tremendously as the survivors neared the Rhine, often tripping over the bodies of fallen comrades. Those who reached the river had no alternative but to try to swim for safety. Julian ordered the Romans to stay out of the river; they stood on the bank peppering the fleeing enemy with darts. So many wounded Germans were pulled under by the rapid current and drowned that the Rhine ran red with blood.[16]

It was estimated later that about six thousand Germans were slain on the battlefield that day while perhaps two thousand more perished in the Rhine. Roman losses were exactly two hundred and forty-seven including four officers.[17]

For the cavalry troopers who had tried to flee in the midst of battle, Julian later decreed the punishment of being paraded before the rest of the army dressed as women. It was a humiliating experience for them, but legally they could have been sentenced to death for attempted desertion, so they had cause to be grateful for the Caesar's mercy. The historian Zosimus, the sole ancient source for this anecdote, adds that they fought with extraordinary bravery in subsequent battles.[18]

The same evening a troop of Romans returned to camp with a prize captive, King Chnodomar himself, whom they had caught beside the riverbank trying to escape. Chnodomar was a very large, fat man; having been thrown from his horse, he was easy prey for his captors. With him surrendered three of his close friends and about two hundred bodyguards who thought it dishonorable to seek freedom once their king was a prisoner. When Chnodomar was brought before Julian, the once-proud barbarian pleaded abjectly for his life. Julian treated him kindly and sent him to Constantius who kept him in honorable confinement in Rome until he died some years later.[19]

While the detailed report of the battle of Strasbourg by Ammianus Marcellinus, a professional soldier, is vastly superior to any other source, Libanius the rhetor finds a more congenial theme in the celebration after the victory was won: "What festival in Greece could have been compared with that evening, when the combatants were drinking together, recounting to one

another how many they had killed in the battle, laughing, singing, bragging, while anyone kept away from the feast by his
wounds found ample consolation in his very wounds? Why,
even in their dreams they fought and beat the enemy over
again, and all night long they enjoyed the pleasure of their
labours of the day, for at last, at long last, they had set up a
trophy over the barbarians and were the more delighted at
its very unexpectedness."[20] The exhausted but victorious Romans
clearly realized that the day had vastly altered the situation
in Gaul. With the Germans crushed and King Chnodomar a
prisoner, the Gallic side of the Rhine, at least in the area between
Strasbourg and Cologne, was more secure than it had been
in years.

It was widely known, too, that Julian had exposed himself
to constant danger throughout the entire battle, darting from
place to place to keep a watchful eye on every development
and urge his men on to greater valor. For the victory that was
won that day, the twenty-six-year-old philosopher prince deserves
a great deal of personal credit. It was to be his largest single
success in Gaul.

In view of the suspicious and jealous nature of the Emperor
Constantius, his reaction to the news from Strasbourg, though
disappointing, must have been exactly what Julian expected.
Constantius took full credit for the victory himself and celebrated a triumph in which the prisoner King Chnodomar was
displayed to cheering crowds in Italy. "So it came about that,
though I had done all the fighting . . . it was not I but he who
triumphed," Julian recalled with understandable bitterness a
few years later.[21]

"The Rhine flowed on peacefully after the battle of Strasbourg," remarks Ammianus at the start of Book XVII of his
history.[22] It would not remain peaceful for long, however, for
although it was late in the season (August), Julian soon announced his next plan: to bridge the Rhine at Mainz (Mayence)
and meet the Germans on their home ground. The army did
not care much for Julian's plan, but "by his eloquence and the
charm of his language he won them over and converted them
to his will. For their affection, warmer after their experiences
with him, prompted them to follow willingly one who was a

fellow-soldier in every task, a leader brilliant in his prestige, and accustomed to prescribe more drudgery for himself than for a common soldier."[23] Libanius indicates that just before crossing the Rhine, Julian inspired his forces with the idea that so far they had fought only a defensive campaign; now as "men of mettle" they would be carrying out a genuine reprisal against their enemies. Moreover, Julian predicted, the Germans were so weakened after their defeat at Strasbourg that the invasion would be a "pleasure jaunt."[24]

The Rhine was duly crossed by a pontoon bridge and for several weeks thereafter Julian's men wrought havoc in German territory, while the surprised and sadly unprepared Germans hid their women and children in the forests and sought to hinder the Roman advance by ambushes and barricades of felled trees. Nothing seemed able to stop the victorious Romans, though as September wore on, the cold weather was a cause for much complaint. When they happened upon a crumbled and abandoned fortress built by the Emperor Trajan, Julian ordered the place refortified. To this outpost the Germans sent envoys suing for peace. Julian agreed to a ten-month truce; a Roman garrison would remain at Trajan's fortress and the Germans would supply it with grain. These terms agreed upon, the Caesar planned to withdraw the main body of his troops back across the Rhine to winter quarters in Gaul.[25]

As it turned out, the return march was interrupted as they approached the Meuse (Mosa) River, when Julian learned that two small abandoned island fortresses in the Meuse had been seized by a band of about six hundred Frankish Germans. Julian's forces encamped on the riverbank with the objective of starving out the enemy. As the siege continued throughout December and well into January, 358, Julian ordered some of his men to row up and down the river nightly to break up the ice that continued to form, lest the enemy be able to slip away over the ice in the dark of the night. After a siege of fifty-four days, the Franks, who had run out of food, surrendered. It would not have surprised anyone (least of all the defeated Franks whose custom was "to conquer or die") had Julian ordered them all put to death. He decided, however, to send them in chains as a "gift" to Constantius, which meant that they would eventually become auxiliaries in the service of Rome in some other distant corner of the world.[26]

At last, with much of the winter already passed, Julian and his weary forces were able to withdraw into winter quarters. This time, he selected as his headquarters the thriving little town of Lutetia Parisiorum—or as some people already called it, Paris.

CHAPTER 9

On the Banks of the Seine

JULIAN liked Paris: in his "Misopogon" written several years later, he recalls "my beloved Lutetia" in some detail.[1] In those days, the city encompassed scarcely more than its original small island in the River Seine, completely walled for defense. Wooden bridges connected the island with both banks of the river, whose water, Julian says, was clear to the eye and pleasant to drink. The site was an ideal location for winter quarters, for although Julian was never one to complain about extremes of hot and cold, he appreciated the fact that because the ocean was not far away, winters in Paris were usually rather mild. Some of the natives even managed to raise fig trees, he noted, and kept them alive in the winter by carefully covering them with "a sort of garment of wheat straw."

Julian would spend three winters in Paris. He and Helena lived in a large house of at least two floors; the inside walls were plastered, which made him reluctant to have the house heated for fear of noxious fumes. In this connection Julian recalls one of his rare bouts with illness and incidentally provides an intimate glimpse of the Caesar at home.[2] One winter, when the weather was colder than usual and the Seine was full of ice that looked like Phrygian marble, he finally told his servants to place a coal-burning stove in his bedroom. As he feared, the heat drew out steam from the walls; it also made him very sleepy. When he awoke suddenly, he was violently ill, choked with the fumes that filled the room. His attendants carried him outdoors for fresh air; he lost his supper, but by the next day was feeling much better. Had he not awakened in time, he knew, the tumultuous career of Caesar of Gaul would have ended forever. It was as close a brush with death as any he had had on the battlefield.

In only one other source, a letter of Julian to his friend Priscus of Athens, do we find any detailed mention of his suffering from ill health, this time "a very severe and sharp attack of sickness" that apparently kept him bedridden for some days, too ill to bathe or to read his mail.³ Ordinarily, however, Julian's health was excellent and his energy seemed boundless. As in his student days, he slept only a few hours per night, firmly believing that "No one who is asleep is good for anything."⁴ He could always wake up without difficulty and customarily devoted the rest of the night to study, writing, and prayers to the gods, while the daylight hours were spent on government business.⁵

Throughout his winters in Paris, Julian devoted much of his time to administrative and judicial problems. It is difficult to date precisely all of his activities, but from his earliest days in Gaul, he was determined to participate personally in the governmental process whenever possible. He genuinely enjoyed being present at court trials and soon won a reputation for quick thinking and conscientious fairness. In this connection Ammianus reports a lively anecdote. Numerius, the ex-governor of Gallia Narbonensis, was accused of embezzlement and summoned to trial. The only evidence against him was hearsay which he staunchly denied. When it seemed likely that he would escape conviction, the angry prosecutor, Delphidius, exclaimed to Julian: "Can anyone, most mighty Caesar, ever be found guilty, if it be enough to deny the charge?" To this Julian replied: "Can anyone be proved innocent if it be enough to have accused him?" Numerius was found innocent, and the story was widely repeated as a choice example of the young Caesar's wisdom and humanity.⁶

Many people, it seems, selected the time just before Julian was about to leave on military campaign to present their appeals to him. In such instances, he had to refer them to the provincial governors, but he would customarily inquire when he returned to winter quarters about the sentences that had been pronounced in his absence. Often, he appears to have lightened the punishments. "The laws may censure my clemency," he once remarked (according to Ammianus Marcellinus), "but it is right for an emperor of very merciful disposition to rise above all other laws."[7] He was especially reluctant to impose the death penalty and preferred to sentence serious offenders to exile.

Julian was also much concerned with reforms in government spending, which he hoped would bring about a reduction of taxes. In this goal he was much encouraged by his trusted praetorian prefect, the "excellent Salustius," who was himself a native of Gaul with deep concern for his people. On the other hand, Julian's reform plans were much discouraged by Florentius, also a praetorian prefect, a professional bureaucrat and appointee of Constantius, who could not begin to understand Julian's real determination to lighten the burden of taxes upon the Gallic provincials. The collection of taxes was Florentius' specific job and he expected Julian to let him do it without interference. There were at that time both a land tax and a head tax. Revenues from these, Florentius reported (probably early in 358), were insufficient and with Julian's assent (which he assumed Julian would give automatically) a special levy would be collected. The Caesar answered calmly that "he would rather lose his life than allow it to be done."[8] By making a thorough study of the tax records, Julian then accumulated figures to show that the revenues already collected were ample for the government's needs. Florentius' proposal was defeated.

It was probably the following winter (Ammianus Marcellinus simply says "long afterwards")[9] when Florentius again sent the Caesar a request for higher taxes. This time Julian was not so calm; he tossed Florentius' report on the ground and loudly remarked, knowing that his comment would be repeated to the prefect, that the "shameful and wholly abominable reports" would have to be revised, "for they pass the bounds of decency." In a letter to his friend Oribasius the physician, Julian reflects further on his behavior on this occasion: "Ought I to have looked on while the wretched people were being betrayed to thieves or to have aided them as far as I could? To me, at least, it seems a disgraceful thing that . . . I should desert my post which is for the defence of such wretched people; whereas it is my duty to fight against thieves of this sort . . . and if any harm to myself should result, it is no small consolation to have proceeded with a good conscience."[10] "And so," writes Ammianus Marcellinus, "it came to pass then and thereafter that through the resolutions of one courageous spirit no one tried to extort from the Gauls anything beyond the normal tax."[11]

From another report by Ammianus it appears that not only did Julian resist efforts to raise taxes, but he was actually able over the course of several years to lower them considerably. When he first came to Gaul the land and head tax amounted to 25 gold pieces per person; by the end of his term five and a half years later, this had been reduced to 7 gold pieces.[12] It is little wonder that Julian, in spite of his troubles with Constantius' officials, was winning the enthusiastic devotion of most of his subjects.

The Emperor punished Julian's outburst against Florentius by removing Salustius from Gaul early in 359. (Significantly, however, Constantius did *not* require that Julian agree to Florentius' demands.) The loss of Salustius was a great blow to the young Caesar. He had been helpful to Julian from the first days in Gaul, and was clearly a man of great integrity and understanding. Although Salustius was considerably older, he and Julian had become very close friends; a pagan himself, Salustius was one of the few who knew of Julian's commitment to the old gods.

The Caesar made a real effort to accept Salustius' recall with the philosophic calm he valued so highly, but he was unquestionably angered and hurt by the unfairness of the entire matter. To console himself—and to bring the incident to the attention of others—he composed a short discourse "Upon the Departure of the Excellent Salustius."[13] In this very attractive little work, Julian recalls their great friendship, their mutual interest in philosophy and literature, and their remarkable likeness of purpose in matters of governmental reform. In a world where few were trustworthy, Julian *trusted* Salustius, and though some who hoped to detract from the Caesar's reputation, alleged that his good ideas were all really Salustius', Julian remained unperturbed by these comments. "In fact," he wrote, "to whichever of us credit may seem to belong, it belongs equally to the other, and malicious persons will gain nothing from their gossip."[14]

Most of all, Julian missed the opportunity for conversation with Salustius, "for I have no one now to whom I can talk with anything like the same confidence."[15] He would, he declared, just have to talk to himself, and trust in God. He believed firmly that someday he and Salustius would meet again; meanwhile they were still friends in spite of the great distance between them. Salustius was to be sent to the province of Thrace (most likely, to Constantinople) and Julian urged him to remember that this was his (Julian's) native land, a place that he loved very much.[16]

This discourse concludes with a prayer for his friend's well-being that may be fairly ranked among the finest pages of pagan literature:

May God in His goodness be your guide wherever you may have to journey.... May He receive you graciously and lead you safely by land; and if you must go by sea, may He smooth the waves! And may you be loved and honored by all you meet, welcome when you arrive, regretted when you leave them! Though you retain your affection for me, may you never lack the society of a good comrade and faithful friend! And may God make the Emperor gracious to you, and grant you all else according to your desire, and make ready for you a safe and speedy journey home to us![17]

In spite of the hopes expressed here, Salustius was not permitted to return to Gaul while Constantius was alive. Later, however, Julian as Emperor bestowed upon Salustius the governorship of Gaul and he returned to rule there on his friend's behalf.[18] He would also be honored with the consulship in 363.

Julian's discourse "Upon the Departure of Salustius" is but one example of his prolific literary output during his years in Gaul. Notice has already been given to his "Panegyric on Eusebia" and first "Panegyric on Constantius." Before he left Gaul, he produced another panegyric on "The Heroic Deeds of the Emperor Constantius." As is to be expected, this piece like its predecessor is full of necessary but insincere flattery. They differ considerably, however, in style. In the "Heroic Deeds," Julian uses the device frequently employed by panegyrists of comparing his subject with the Homeric heroes. Constantius, he says, is braver than Hector and Achilles, more eloquent than Odysseus, wiser than Nestor. Though a large part of the composition is laced with references of this sort

of Hellenic literature, Julian remains carefully evasive on the
subject of religion. His few references to "the gods" could well
be interpreted as deliberate archaizing, in complete conformity
with current rhetorical style. The Homeric classics were "safe,"
studied and admired by Christians and pagans alike.

More important, composing the "Heroic Deeds" gave Julian
another opportunity to reflect on the virtues of the ideal ruler:
devoutness, family loyalty, justice, generosity, courage, moderation and self-restraint.[19] For pages at a time, Julian reflects
on these qualities without making any direct application to
Constantius, a rather daring way of withholding the praise he
could not give sincerely, and subtly pointing out some of the
qualities that his imperial cousin in reality sadly lacked. As in
the First Panegyric, there is a very interesting section on
Julian's belief that the Emperor is subject to the laws of the land:

He [the ideal ruler] cares for justice and the right, and neither parents
nor kinsfolk nor friends can persuade him to do them a favor and
betray the cause of justice. For he looks upon his fatherland as the
common hearth and mother of all, older and more reverend than
his parents, and more precious than brothers or friends or comrades. . . . For law is the child of justice, the sacred and truly divine
adjunct of the most mighty god, and never will the man who is
wise make light of it or set it at naught.[20]

There is some uncertainty whether Julian ever dispatched
the "Heroic Deeds" to Constantius.[21] It is possible that he
completed it only shortly before their break and thus never
sent it. In any case, he considered it important enough to be
preserved among his literary works.

There remain, too, a few of Julian's letters from Gaul,
significant for their insights into his thought at the time. For
instance, it is interesting to notice how Julian frequently addresses his various correspondents as "dearest brother." Such
effusiveness is typical both of the times and of Julian's own
character, but may also indicate that those so addressed were,
like him, initiates of the Mithra cult and thus brothers in a
mystical sense.

In spite of his many victories on the battlefield, Julian declares in a letter to two old school friends in Athens that there

is nothing more delightful "than to pursue philosophy at one's leisure without interruptions"[22]—a privilege he obviously no longer enjoyed. In fact, he complained, it was a wonder he could still speak Greek, "such a barbarian have I become because of the places I have lived in."[23] Though he had become fluent in Latin, he apparently had little real enthusiasm for Latin literature: a fact that is not surprising when it is recalled that the Greek educators of that era considered Latin culture so far inferior to their own.

One of Julian's favorite correspondents was the philosopher Priscus of Athens, whom he repeatedly asked to come and visit him in Gaul. Priscus was to be thanked for arousing Julian's increased interest in Aristotle; they also corresponded on the subject of Iamblichus, a Neoplatonic philosopher whose writings Julian vastly admired, though he did not possess a reliable copy of his works and urged Priscus to send him one.[24] We do not know the outcome of this request, but it does seem clear that Priscus finally visited Gaul, at least for a short time. Upon his departure Julian presented him with a poem (no longer extant) that he had composed in his honor.[25]

Nor was Priscus the only friend from Julian's student days to visit Gaul. Libanius indicates that "swarms of orators," former acquaintances of Julian, journeyed to Paris.[26] Among the most distinguished of these visitors, adds Eunapius, was the hierophant of the Eleusinian mysteries.[27]

For all these guests, the chief entertainment awaiting them at Julian's court in Paris was philosophic conversation. There were none of the floor shows, acrobatic acts and dancing, that many other aristocratic Romans considered essential elements of a successful dinner party; such things, thought Julian, were unphilosophic and a shameful waste of time. Disregarding the elaborate dishes recommended in Constantius' menu book, his dinner table was supplied only with simple foods.[28] Beer, the Gallic national beverage, may have been served to those who liked it, though according to a little light verse he wrote on the subject, Julian was not favorably impressed by the taste of beer himself,[29] preferring watered-down wine or plain water.

Unquestionably there were many letters written by Julian in Gaul that have not survived; for instance, those he wrote to

his wife whenever he was away on campaign. Nor have his
military commentaries been preserved. And though, thanks to
Ammianus and other sources, one can scarcely complain of a
dearth of material on Julian's years in Gaul, the loss is still
unfortunate, for had more of Julian's own works from this
period survived, we would have a much fuller picture of
this crucial period in his career both as a warrior and a man
of letters.

CHAPTER 10

Further Victories: 358 and 359

AMONG the many matters demanding Julian's attention every winter was that of requisitioning sufficient food for the next season's campaigning. Early in 358 Julian determined to ease this ever-present problem by importing grain from Britain.[1] It was a project hedged by numerous difficulties. Although *Britannia* was divided into several Roman provinces and theoretically part of Julian's territory, there was little communication with Gaul because of the Germanic tribes who still controlled the lower (Northern) Rhine from Cologne to the sea.

While Julian ordered the construction of a fleet of six hundred ships (two hundred of which were old ones refurbished for new service), the problem was how to get them past the barbarians at the mouth of the Rhine and thus on their way to Britain. Florentius, who was always ready to spend government money, favored paying the Germans two thousand silver pounds for the right of passage, a policy which met with Constantius' full approval. Julian, however, regarded the idea of tribute as disgraceful—thus, his prime military objective for 358 was to restore Rome's hold on the Rhine all the way to the North Sea.[2]

While it is not necessary to pursue all the details of Julian's military campaigns in the summers of 358 and 359, it is worthwhile to notice that these two seasons were marked by a series of further victories that meant steadily increasing security for Gaul and the happy fulfillment of Julian's plans for the British grain fleet.[3] Julian undertook offensives across the Rhine; numerous Germans who surrendered were sent to Constantius to serve as auxiliaries in the East where the Persian menace was growing.[4]

The spring of 358 started out badly for Julian, inasmuch as rations were very low. Undoubtedly more food would be available as the season wore on, but the Caesar was determined to

73

start out early with what was available—hard, dry biscuits. Moreover, no funds had yet arrived from Constantius to pay the troops; this lack, combined with hunger, produced mutinous murmurings among the soldiers. Forgotten was their previous devotion to Julian, forgotten his courageous leadership on earlier occasions. Nor did it help that he had no more to eat than did his men. All of a sudden he was being reviled as a "little Greek," "an Asiatic," a deceiver and a fool.[5] After a rapid and successful attack on the tribes of Salii and the Chamavii, followed by a pause to rebuild three fortresses on the Meuse, food was running shorter than ever.

Julian coped with this discontent, Ammianus says, by "various sorts of fair words."[6] He was unquestionably a very able speaker (apparently unhindered by the fact that his addresses to his men had to be in Latin rather than his native Greek), and somehow he was able to win back the devotion and respect of his troops. It is likely that he emphasized the fact that food and rich plunder awaited them when they crossed the Rhine into enemy territory.

Scarcely had the river been crossed when one of the German kings, Suomarius, appeared on the scene with an army, but seeking peace rather than battle. Julian agreed, provided that Suomarius' tribe should supply the Romans with food. This arrangement made, the Romans proceeded further into the interior of Germany to combat the tribe of King Hortarius who was holding numerous Gallic and Roman prisoners. It proved a difficult campaign. The German forests were ideal for setting up almost impenetrable barricades of felled trees, and only after many discouraging detours did Julian's forces reach their goal. The Romans burned and devastated the countryside, slaying any Germans who refused to surrender promptly. Apparently Hortarius was ill-prepared for this Roman onslaught when it actually arrived. He hastily asked for terms and Julian agreed, provided that all prisoners be returned.[7]

Ammianus reports that in spite of his promises Hortarius tried to hedge on the matter of prisoner return; only after much difficulty did Julian persuade him to restore all the captives. In this connection there is a more detailed anecdote in the work of the fifth-century historian Zosimus (though it may date

back to Julian's first crossing of the Rhine in the previous year).[8]
Whenever it occurred, the Caesar provided himself with a
careful list of known prisoners, gathering data on them from
fugitives who had already escaped their German captors. Then
when the King sent in those he had chosen to release, Julian's
secretaries checked their names against this list and realized
plainly that many were still missing. Julian inquired about
these by name and stormily threatened that unless they were
repatriated at once, war would be resumed. The prisoners
were released.

Julian returned to Paris for the winter of 358–359. The following spring saw the resumption of activity along the Rhine
as seven abandoned towns recovered from the Germans were
rebuilt. These ranged from Castra Herculis (apparently near
the mouth of the Rhine) to Vingo (Bingen) somewhat south
of Cologne. At each of these locations granaries were built for
storage of the grain now coming in regularly from Britain.
Hortarius' Germans, by the terms of their treaty the previous
year, provided timber for the reconstruction work, while auxiliaries in the service of Rome furnished the manual labor.
Ammianus was particularly impressed that Julian somehow convinced these builders to work willingly, when under most
circumstances soldiers scorned such non-military assignments and
could scarcely be forced to undertake them.[9]

Meanwhile Julian had sent Hariobaudes, a German-speaking
spy, across the Rhine, ostensibly as an envoy to Hortarius, but
actually to accumulate information on other tribes still un-
subdued.[10] When he returned, Julian with Florentius and Lupicinus (a new cavalry commander who had replaced Severus)
made final plans for what would be the Caesar's third crossing
of the Rhine. Ammianus Marcellinus describes the campaign
in detail. Particularly noteworthy is Julian's strict insistence that
the lands of German kings now counted as allies (such as
Hortarius and Suomarius) remain unharmed. For the unsub-
missive German tribes there was the usual Roman treatment
of widespread slaughter and burning of property. Ultimately
several kings agreed to surrender and, as always, Julian arranged
for the return of many prisoners.[11]

By the end of 359, the Gallic provinces were safer and prob-

ably more prosperous than they had been in many years. Julian
himself summed up the military accomplishments of his first
four years in Gaul in a revealing passage: "Three times, while
I was still Caesar, I crossed the Rhine; 20,000 persons who were
held as captives on the further side of the Rhine I demanded
and received back: in two battles and one siege I took captive
ten thousand prisoners, and those not of unserviceable age, but
men in the prime of life; I sent to Constantius four levies of
excellent infantry, three more of infantry not so good, and two
very distinguished squadrons of cavalry."[12] He might have added,
too, that many more Germans had voluntarily come over to
the Roman side and now remained in Gaul as auxiliaries, with
the Caesar's promise that they would never be sent across the
Alps. Far from proving a danger to the Roman Empire, these
men tended to be intensely loyal to Julian. His report continued,
"I have now [in 361] with the help of the gods recovered all
the towns, and by that time [359] I had already recovered
almost forty."[13]

Julian knew well, however, that his almost miraculous restora-
tion of Gaul was not appreciated by Constantius and those
who surrounded him. The Emperor's unwillingness to give Julian
due credit for his work was already evident in 356 after the
battle of Strasbourg, when Constantius produced the "official"
report of the battle depicting himself as present and personally
responsible for the tactics that won the day.[14] Julian had taken
this and similar slights with his usual philosophic calm: after
all, everyone knew that Constantius had a habit of claiming
other's victories as his own.

A more serious problem was the sycophants who surrounded
the Emperor and tried to convince him that the young Caesar's
successes were minor achievements. Contemptuously, they referred to Julian as "Victorinus," the "little conqueror."[15] They
delighted in rude descriptions of his appearance: he was "hairy"
like a goat (a hint that perhaps he had let his beard grow
back);[16] he was "an ape in purple." He chattered too much;
he was a "Greekish pedant." Their insults even reached to
the point of downright lies: Julian, they alleged, was "lazy" and
"timid"![17] Constantius, it seems, swallowed all this with real
delight.

In many ways, Constantius was not a bad emperor, as Roman emperors go. Devoted to duty, conscientious, a man whose private life was impeccable, he was widely respected by his subjects. Even his gift for immobility was much admired; at public appearances he seemed more like a statue than a living man, but far from being condemned as unfeeling, he was praised for his wonderful dignity.[18]

So much for Constantius' good points. On the other hand, among his many failings was his absolute inability to comprehend that Julian had turned out to be not only valuable, but loyal. While one may blame Constantius for failing to appreciate Julian, it is not difficult to understand why he thought as he did. Julian had no real reason, so far as Constantius could see, to remain loyal. Many a successful general had turned into a usurper and Julian had far more reason to seize such an opportunity than most men had. After all, there was that inescapable reality: Constantius was responsible for the death of practically all of his kin. In the highly laudatory panegyrics that Julian turned out, he might *seem* to have forgotten these tragedies completely, but both Constantius and Julian knew that the past that lay between them could never really be forgotten; Julian had been too greatly hurt. Unfortunately all Constantius could think of to do was to hurt him more. Sooner or later, serious difficulties were sure to arise.

CHAPTER 11

The Challenge to Constantius

WHEN did Julian cease to be loyal? This is one of the most perplexing questions in Julianic studies, though it is one that has attracted scholarly attention only in relatively recent times.[1]

Basically there are two theories on the origin of the *coup d'état* that took place in Paris early in 360 when Julian was acclaimed Emperor by his troops. One is based on his own testimony in his "Letter to the Athenians," written a little more than a year after the events it describes. Julian's account has been accepted by numerous historians from Ammianus Marcellinus and Libanius down to the present day, with due allowance for the fact that he naturally wanted to impress his readers favorably. Contrariwise, there is the ingenious suggestion that Julian's version of the events in his "Letter to the Athenians" is nothing more than a tissue of lies. Actually, say proponents of the latter theory, Julian and his friend Oribasius carefully pre-planned the seemingly spontaneous revolt against Constantius and Julian's assumption of the imperial title.[2] To accept this view is to see Julian as sadly lacking in integrity, though the overall body of his writings testifies that he was usually an honest, forthright man, little inclined to unsavory intrigues. If his claiming the throne was indeed so thoroughly pre-planned, one has to believe, too, that Julian was willing to undertake a desperate gamble— one that would almost certainly lead to his defeat and death. Thus his innate common sense and military ability, as well as his integrity, argue against such an interpretation.

How then does there come to be any question concerning the spontaneity of the *coup* of 360? The idea that Julian secretly planned his acclamation as emperor with the help of the physician Oribasius is based largely on statements apparently made by Oribasius many years later as a very old man. Sometime in the early fifth century, the aged physician boasted to the historian Eunapius that he, Oribasius, had made Julian emperor.[3] Eunapius consequently speaks of the physician as Julian's "accomplice," and from this evidence stems the idea that the soldiers who rioted for "Julian Augustus" on that fateful winter night in 360 were acting upon instructions.

Though the whole truth can never be recovered, perhaps the most reasonable interpretation lies between the extremes of seeing Julian either as completely innocent of any desire for the throne or actively scheming to get it. His account of the events in the "Letter to the Athenians" is entirely too important to dismiss, yet it is also important to notice carefully which events he neglects to mention at all. Thus Eunapius' version of the role of Oribasius is understandable, not so much as a contradiction of Julian's report, but as a preliminary episode, one which Julian discreetly thought best to omit in his famous "Letter to the Athenians" but for which there is some evidence elsewhere in Julian's writings.[4]

Oribasius of Pergamon came to Gaul with Julian in 355 as his personal physician. They had been friends since their student days in Pergamon and shared similar opinions on the worship of the old gods. As one of the few men who knew of Julian's secret paganism and interest in the occult, Oribasius was naturally one of his closest confidants. Sometime late in 358, Julian (who was then in winter quarters in Paris) wrote a letter to Oribasius in Vienne.[5] In it, we find the first hint that Julian is thinking hopefully of the time when Constantius will be no more. Apparently Oribasius had written him about a dream of his, portending the Emperor's death. (To discuss such matters was a capital offense, but the physician clearly knew he could trust Julian.) In his reply Julian reports that he too has had a highly significant dream: of two trees planted side by side, one large, the other small and young. The tall tree was struck to the ground and, says Julian, he was concerned that the small tree would also be destroyed. Then as the vision continued, a stranger (perhaps the god Hermes?) appeared to him telling him to take courage, for "the smaller tree will be uninjured and will be established more securely than before." "So much then for my dreams," Julian concludes, "God knows what they portend."[6]

Oribasius would not need any imagination at all to grasp Julian's message. Obviously his friend believed that the divine powers wanted them to know that while Constantius might not long survive, Julian would outlast him and go on to greater things. To a man of Julian's turn of mind this omen would be a very real encouragement.

Nor was the interpreting of dreams Julian's only effort to probe into the secrets of his and Constantius' future. Eunapius reports that about this time Julian invited the Hierophant of Eleusis to visit him in Gaul.[7] The Hierophant (whose name, one will recall, is not recorded for it was too sacred to mention) arrived in due time at Julian's court. His reputation as a prophet was widely known, and Julian did not neglect to consult him on questions concerning Constantius. "With his aid," Eunapius says, they "performed certain rites known to them alone"; and by this means Julian "mustered up courage to abolish the tyranny of Constantius." Oribasius and the African Euhemerus were "accomplices" in these ceremonies, a piece of information that Eunapius must have learned from Oribasius himself.

Though there is no direct hint that they discussed it, one secret of Constantius' future that Julian must have wondered about was whether the Emperor would ever have a son. He had probably heard reports that the beautiful Empress Eusebia, though still young, was seriously ill of a disease of the womb.[8] Constantius, ardently devoted to her, would certainly remain faithful to her while she lived, but should she die, he would almost as certainly remarry. He was only in his early forties; there could yet be an heir whose claim as Constantius' successor would be better than Julian's.

Apparently, however, the researches that Julian and the Hierophant (and the "accomplices") conducted into the future revealed no such threats to Julian's career, but rather suggested (just as the prophetic dreams had done) that Constantius himself would not live much longer. The sources say next to nothing about these matters, but clearly Julian and Oribasius were encouraged.[9] This encouragement in itself renders questionable the theory that Julian took direct action to secure the throne for himself. If Constantius were soon to die, and if Julian, the gods' chosen one, was sure to be his heir, the best thing to do at this point might be to leave matters in the gods' hands, and make the most of the opportunities that developed.

Meanwhile, more than a thousand miles away on the Persian frontier, the perennial hostility between Rome and her ancient foe had erupted again. Constantius (who often before had come to terms with King Sapor of Persia after a display of Roman strength) planned to mobilize an immense army. Gaul was pacified now, so why should Julian retain such a large number of troops there? Such at least was the Emperor's stated reasoning. It is not unlikely that as Julian and his defenders professed, Constantius was also intensely jealous of the Caesar of Gaul and fearful of the consequences should he retain command of such a large force.[10] Therefore Constantius sent a tribune, Decentius, to Paris with orders for the immediate transfer to the east of Julian's four auxiliary legions: the Aeruli, the Batavi, the Celts, and the Petulantes. From each remaining division of Julian's forces, Lupicinus the cavalry commander was to select three hundred men. Constantius did not know that Julian had dispatched Lupicinus to Britain to fight the Picts and the Scots,[11] a circumstance that gave the Caesar some opportunity to stall for time. Those who believe that Julian was already carefully scheming to seize the crown, see in his sending of Lupicinus to Britain a crafty move to rid himself of this important officer who was firmly loyal to Constantius.[12] Be that as it may, at this point Julian openly stated that the Emperor's order for troop transfers to the East would have to be obeyed, though at least he would protest heartily on behalf of the men he had enlisted with the specific assurance that they would not be transferred away from Gaul and the Rhine frontier.[13]

Decentius ignored Julian almost completely, and having selected "the strongest and most active of the light-armed troops" who were not stationed directly in Paris, he began making plans for their march to the East. For some odd reason, although Julian warned him against it, the tribune decided to lead them directly to Paris. Perhaps he wanted to witness the Caesar's helpless discomfiture as the orders were carried out.

Meanwhile, Julian had written the prefect Florentius in Vienne to come to Paris at once for consultation. Florentius, fearing trouble, disobeyed. Lupicinus was ordered back from Britain, but it would take a long time for the message to reach him.[14]

Julian, seemingly very displeased but apparently still determined to carry out the Emperor's orders, listened to protests from those who had been assured they would never have to leave their native land, and from their families who would, it seemed, have to be left behind.[15] At this point a very rousing anonymous letter or pamphlet was found on the ground in the camp of the Petulantes. Julian says that the document was "full of invectives against Constantius" and of laments that he (Julian) was being subjected to such disgrace.[16] Emphasis, too, was placed on the Emperor's betrayal of Julian's guarantee of their remaining in Gaul: "We verily are driven to the ends of the earth like condemned criminals," quotes Ammianus from the highly-charged pamphlet; "and our dear ones, whom we freed from their former captivity after mortal battles will again be slaves to the Alamanni."[17] Those who see Julian as the engineer of his power seizure have imagined that he was himself the author of this invective, but without the slightest grain of evidence. Oribasius presumably could have written it, but there is no proof that the physician was even in Paris. It seems much more likely to have originated among the discontented soldiery themselves.

While Julian was completely sympathetic to his men's complaints, at the moment the best he could offer was the use of official transport wagons so that they might take their wives and children with them to the East.[18] The crisis simmered.

When Decentius neared Paris with the forces he had already collected, Julian went out to the "suburbs" to meet them. Ammianus describes him "praising those whom he personally knew and reminding each one of his valiant deeds, [as] with mild words he encouraged them to go with cheerful step to Augustus [Constantius] where . . . they would get worthy rewards for their toil."[19] That afternoon he held a dinner for the officers at his residence in Paris. This event apparently took place peaceably enough, but then, about sunset, the palace was surrounded by troops shouting for Julian to appear and acclaiming him as Augustus. Julian, according to his own account, was "feeling by no means confident." He went upstairs to a room near Helena's and there prayed to Zeus through an opening in the wall, asking for a "sign." Julian does not say how the prayer was answered, only that the god "showed me a sign and bade me yield and not oppose myself to the will of the army."[20] Ammianus has more detail: Julian, he says, fell asleep and as he slept a vision of the "Genius Publicus," the guardian spirit of Rome, appeared to warn him that this was his very last chance to increase his rank.[21] Later on, Libanius in several orations would stress the idea that Julian's promotion 'to the Emperorship was an instance of the gods acting through the soldiers in fulfillment of a divine plan.[22]

For some hours, however, Julian still did not go outdoors, and through the long February night, the troops continued their shouts of "Julian Augustus!" Finally, before daylight, he emerged from his house to confront his troops and make one final effort to calm them. He would, he promised, resist the Emperor's orders to send them east, but he did not want the crown for himself. At this point, in spite of Julian's protests, one can feel relatively confident that he was completely ready to become Emperor; that his seeming reluctance was a judicious move to give him a lever for bargaining with Constantius afterwards. In any case, the soldiers would have nothing to do with his objections. It was a highly dangerous situation: whatever previous planning he may have done, Julian's very life was in peril had the troops turned against him at this moment. "I could not singlehanded control so many," he recalled.[23] "Caesar was compelled to consent," says Ammianus Marcellinus.[24]

Following an ancient barbarian custom, some of the soldiers lifted Julian bodily upon an infantryman's shield and displayed him to the whole assembly. There were shouts demanding he be crowned, and when he explained that he possessed no "diadem," someone suggested that he should borrow one, or a necklace, from his wife. No, said Julian, it would be inauspicious to wear a woman's jewel. Another soldier proffered an ornament from a horse's trapping, which he likewise rejected. Then a standard-bearer of the Petulantes, Maurus by name, took off his metal neck chain and placed it upon Julian's head. The deed was done.[25]

Something of Julian's conflicting emotions at this crucial moment can be seen in his "Letter to the Athenians," written more than a year later. Though he was clearly pleased that he was favored by the gods, he was also, he says, "terribly ashamed and ready to sink into the earth at the thought of not seeming to obey Constantius faithfully to the last."[26] Ammianus also suggests that Julian was genuinely frightened concerning his fate had he continued to resist. He was a very brave man, but naturally he cannot have relished the thought of what his men would do to him if they turned against him. Hoping to disperse the crowds, he promised every man a pound of silver and five pieces of gold. After this he also gave specific orders that no harm was to befall Decentius or any of the other henchmen of Constantius who were in Paris at the moment, orders that were obeyed most reluctantly.[27]

The threat of crisis subsided; Julian Augustus was left to face the reality of what his soldiers—and he—had done. As an avid student of Rome's past, twenty-eight-year-old Julian knew well the alternatives that now confronted him: either he would make good his claim to the title he had accepted, or he would perish in the attempt.

CHAPTER 12

Calm Before the Storm

AFTER Julian's acceptance of the title of Augustus early in 360, dramatic action might be expected to follow rapidly as he sought to uphold his claim. The inevitable explosion was delayed for several reasons, however, and the summer of 360 finds Julian's forces still battling barbarians along the Rhine rather than engaged in civil war for the crown.

There are several hints that Constantius' followers in Paris, headed by the tribune Decentius, at first sought to solve the Julian crisis by attempted assassination.[1] The details are most unclear and may have been simply wild rumors. Surrounded as he was by thousands of loyal troops, Julian was, for the present, in no serious danger. As soon as possible Decentius returned to the East with his dismal report of Julian's activities. Constantius, who had trouble enough with King Sapor, was placed in a great quandary: whether to concentrate his forces on Persia, or upon Julian in Gaul?

Meanwhile Julian prepared two letters of his own to Constantius. Ammianus Marcellinus quotes what purports to be the text of one of these in which Julian declares that the title of Augustus was forced upon him by the soldiers, but that since the deed was done, he asks that Constantius ratify it officially.[2] While he must have realized how unlikely it was that Constantius would agree, Julian's request was not beyond the stretch of imagination, for there were many cases of co-Augusti in Roman history, and Constantius himself had earlier shared his title with his two brothers. Julian's letter continues with promises of his loyalty, but he also declares outright that he will not force his men to leave Gaul to fight in the East, emphasizing that Gaul must not be left defenseless. He will,

85

however, he says, send Constantius some volunteers from the
tribe of the Laeti, as well as a number of fine Spanish chariot
horses. As additional terms, Julian agrees to accept whomever
Constantius might choose as praetorian prefects, but otherwise,
he insists, he will select his own officials. The letter which Julian
signed as "Caesar" rather than "Augustus," is courteous but firm.

Along with it, however, he dispatched another letter which
Ammianus only describes as "written in a more reproachful and
bitter tone,"[3] though he also adds that he did know its exact
contents. If Julian genuinely hoped for a peaceful settlement,
sending this highly charged epistle would seem to be an extremely foolish action. Probably he realized that there was no
real chance for reconciliation with Constantius, and pondering
over the injustices he had suffered from him, impulsively dashed
off this injudicious composition.

Julian entrusted delivery of the letters to Pentadius and the
much esteemed eunuch Eutherius, who, after a difficult journey, reached the Emperor in Caesarea of Cappadocia. As he
read the letters, Constantius lost his usually immobile placidity
and "burst out in an immoderate blaze of anger."[4] The envoys
felt fortunate to escape with their lives. Julian reports also that
the various legions under his command dispatched letters on
his behalf to Constantius.[5] One can be sure these produced an
equally irate reaction from the Emperor.

As the months of 360 slipped by, however, Constantius still
had his hands full with the Persian crisis and continued to post-
pone any direct military action against Julian. Instead he dispatched his quaestor, Leonas, to Gaul with a letter stating that
he did not accept the changes that had been effected and that
Julian must content himself with the role of a Caesar. In place
of Florentius (who had quit the province for parts unknown),
Constantius appointed as prefect Nebridius, a eunuch who already served in a lesser post on the Caesar's staff, but who, the
Emperor believed, was devoted to his own interests. As Julian
had already agreed to accept whomever Constantius might choose
as prefect, he had no choice but to confirm this appointment.[6]

Then Julian assembled his troops in Paris for a public reading
of Constantius' letter. It must still have been early spring,
before the campaign season had begun. Leonas was present as

Julian read the letter aloud; there was a very vocal reaction from the soldiers.[7] Shouts of "Julian Augustus!" showed clearly how little the words of Constantius counted with the Gallic troops. Leonas, duly impressed, made his long journey back to the East with another dismal report for the Emperor.

About this time, Julian was faced with another problem: the imminent return of Lupicinus from Britain. The whole matter of Lupicinus' expedition into Britain is a curious one. Julian had sent him there with orders either to fight the perennially troublesome Picts and Scots or—a most un-Julianic alternative—to negotiate peace with them by means of subsidy payments. As noted previously, those who believe that the Caesar planned his *coup* in advance have conjectured, though without documentation, that the British expedition was from the beginning only a device to keep Lupicinus (a known partisan of Constantius) out of the way while Julian claimed the throne.[8]

Leaving aside such speculations as unprovable, it is nonetheless clear that by the spring of 360 Julian was not at all eager for Lupicinus in Britain to learn of the recent events in Gaul, for fear that he too might start a revolution. Consequently, Julian ordered that no one be allowed to cross from Boulogne to Britain until Lupicinus and his forces had crossed the Channel in the other direction.[9] The plan worked, and the general was greatly surprised on returning to Gaul to learn what had happened in his absence. He was further surprised to learn that he had been relieved of his command; Julian had already appointed his replacement, one Gomoarius.[10]

The time had come to set out for the summer campaign and although the banks of the Rhine were relatively quiet, Julian decided to conduct a surprise attack on the tribe of Atthuarian Franks, who still crossed the river on occasional raids into Gaul.[11] Julian's purpose was not merely further to strengthen the Rhine frontier; he also wanted to keep his troops occupied. The Rhine was duly crossed near Kellen (Tricensima) and the Atthuarii taken by complete surprise. After suffering many casualties, the barbarians shortly agreed to surrender. The remainder of the summer was spent in inspection tours and strengthening of fortifications all along the Rhine. At the end of the three-month campaign season Julian stopped briefly at Besontio (Besançon), a fortress town set high on a rocky cliff, which he described as almost inacessible even to the birds.[12]

For winter quarters that year, Julian selected not Paris but Vienne. Obviously he was seriously thinking of taking the offensive and moving east. It is just possible that there is a connection between Helena's death, which occurred late in 360, and Julian's hardening attitude toward Constantius, once her restraining influence was removed. This remains conjectural, however, since there is no information on Helena's attitude toward her husband *vis à vis* her brother. Nor is there any reliable data as to the exact date or the cause of her death. Her body was sent from Vienne to Rome where she was buried in a marble sarcophagus beside her sister, Gallus' wife, Constantina.[13] Julian would never remarry: as Libanius says significantly, he remained "in mourning for his wife."[14]

About the same time that Helena died, or perhaps a few months earlier, the disturbing news arrived from Constantius' court of the recent death of the Empress Eusebia. Without her to plead on his behalf, Julian's chances for any reconciliation with Constantius were fainter than ever. Moreover, scarcely was Eusebia dead than Constantius took another wife, Faustina of Antioch.[15] It was altogether possible that the new Empress would present her husband with an heir.

In view of these discouraging developments, it is no surprise to find Julian in the winter of 360–61 deeply immersed in the occult arts with the purpose of reading the future. Always conscious of omens and at least as superstitious as most men of his time, Julian had nonetheless a habit of trying to see good signs in those which seemed at first glance distinctly bad. For instance, Ammianus tells of an incident when Julian (still in Paris) was taking part in a military exercise, and accidentally broke his shield as he gave it a vigorous shake. As the broken pieces clattered to the ground, Julian triumphantly held up the handle and remarked: "Let no man be afraid; I hold firmly what I was holding!"[16]

Ammianus, incidentally, sets great store by happenings of this sort. Though he criticizes Julian for being too "superstitious," he personally believed there was considerable value in several different forms of divination: by the flight pattern of birds, by the examination of entrails of sacrificial animals, by prophetic text, and needless to say, by dreams.[17]

One night during his winter in Vienne, Julian had one of his typically vivid and impressive dreams. When "he lay almost awake," as Ammianus says, a "gleaming form" appeared to him and repeated several times a four-line verse (in Greek) promising the imminent death of Constantius. This so encouraged Julian that he appeared very "calm and tranquil" thereafter.[18] Meanwhile he was also attempting to convince his theurgist friend, Maximus of Ephesus, to come to Gaul. Apparently Maximus thought the journey entirely too dangerous, though Julian continued to hope for his arrival.[19]

In November, 360, to celebrate the fifth anniversary of his Caesarship, and no doubt to increase the good will of his troops, Julian held a series of "quinquennial games" in Vienne. Here he wore "a magnificent diadem" decked with jewels rather than his usual "cheap crown."[20] It might seem that, having broken with Constantius, the time had come for Julian now to take a clear stand on religious matters. Although one report has it that "he said directly within earshot of all that he would rather entrust himself and his life to the gods than to the words of Constantius,"[21] it seems in fact that he delayed revealing his paganism to the general public. At least once (probably only once) during the winter in Vienne he attended services at a Christian church; the date was Epiphany, January 6, 361. Ammianus says he did this "in order to win the favor of all men and have opposition from none."[22] Although a pagan himself, the historian was singularly detached on matters of religion, and it does not seem to have bothered him that his hero Julian resorted to this bit of subterfuge.

The army under Julian's command undoubtedly represented a wide variety of religious views. While few of his soldiers (or anyone else for that matter) would be able to work up great enthusiasm for Julian's highly intellectual Neoplatonism, many of them were, like him, initiates of the Mithra cult. The Celtic and German elements among his troops must have included pagans of many sorts. On the other hand, Christianity was well represented among the Roman forces by this time. After a half century under Christian emperors, the inherent contradiction between the military life and the pacificism of many earlier Christians had practically disappeared. During his five years in Gaul Julian had never made an issue out of religious preference: most of his troops probably assumed him to be a Christian, though he was obviously not a fanatical one. Probably in early 361 he was still uncertain as to the exact course his religious policy would take if ever he secured the crown. Certainly he wanted toleration, and he could well have hoped to keep the Christians as friends even after his own paganism became general knowledge.

While Julian was wintering in Vienne, Constantius in faraway Antioch-of-Syria was laying plans how best to cope with his rival. Orders were dispatched to imperial troops in Italy to be prepared for war should Julian's forces venture to cross the frontier. Meanwhile at several points along the border Constantius' men began stockpiling rations. Obviously the places they selected were too close to Julian's territory, for the Gallic army soon seized these provisions for themselves, a haul which Julian estimated at some six million bushels of wheat.[23]

Since support for Constantius was obviously weak among the Roman forces remaining in the West and since the Emperor himself and most of his army were still occupied with the Persian crisis, he next decided to enlist the aid of some of the Germanic kings who were allies of Rome. Among those contacted, the only one who agreed to go against Julian was Vadomar, who in return for a "subsidy" broke the truce, sent raiding parties across the Rhine into Gaul, and generally tried to keep Julian so busy defending the frontier that he would have no opportunity to move east. The barbarian king, moreover, was a crafty individual: while his men marauded along the left bank of the Rhine, on the border of Raetia, he personally continued to pose as Julian's loyal ally. An important encounter took place when some of Julian's forces under Count Libino crossed the Rhine and were ambushed by Vadomar's men. Vastly outnumbered, the Romans were severely trounced: though the casualties were fairly few, this was simply because the Romans panicked when Libino was slain and most managed to escape.[24]

Knowledge of the double game Vadomar was playing came to light when a letter from him to Constantius was intercepted by Julian's soldiers. To deal with such treachery, Julian concocted a little intrigue of his own, and managed to have King Vadomar arrested while he attended a banquet, still pretending to be a loyal ally. Confronted with the evidence of his misdoings, Vadomar fully expected to be executed. Julian, however, was surprisingly merciful: he sent the barbarian king into exile in Spain, but otherwise did him no harm.[25] In the days that followed Vadomar's arrest, we find Julian's forces again crossing to the German side of the Rhine for a surprise attack with the purpose of crushing any further ambitions against Gaul on the part of Vadomar's subjects. The barbarians, caught by surprise in the dark of the night, promptly begged for peace. Julian could be relatively confident that the Rhine frontier would remain calm for the rest of the summer. Now, if ever, the time had come to begin his march toward the East.

CHAPTER 13

From Gaul to Naissus

IT is a curious fact, and one that reveals a great deal about Julian's charismatic qualities, that the men who in early 360 were so reluctant to leave Gaul under any circumstances, were by mid-361 ready to follow him wherever his destiny might lead. When he announced his plans for taking the offensive against Constantius, Julian requested from his troops an oath of loyalty. Each man held his sword at his own throat (to symbolize the sanctity of the promise) and swore to "endure all hazards" for Julian, even to die for him if need be.[1] Not only ordinary soldiers, but the high-ranking officials took the oath. The only one who refused was the prefect, Nebridius the eunuch, who remained defiantly loyal to Constantius. Julian's troops were enraged and would have torn the poor creature to pieces had not Julian covered him with his military cloak—as Libanius puts it, enveloping him in a "cloud" of mercy.[2] Libanius obviously thought Julian was too soft-hearted here; but the would-be Augustus clearly understood and appreciated Nebridius' viewpoint even though he was not pleased by it. The prefect was allowed to depart without penalty for his home in Italy.[3]

Julian's conscientious efforts to conduct as bloodless a campaign as possible are seen in his admonition to his forces that on their eastward march they must do no harm to private citizens. The territories through which they would pass were Roman lands; their inhabitants were potentially Julian's own subjects, and in most instances probably not so fanatically devoted to Constantius that they would not welcome an apparent change for the better.

Modern historians have frequently commented upon the extreme hazards of Julian's enterprise. As Libanius remarks, his army was "remarkable not so much in numbers as in morale,"[4] while Constantius, with the huge force he had assembled for the Persian war, possessed an overwhelming numerical advantage. Julian himself believed that had Constantius struck earlier, while Julian was still in Gaul, he would "have had to face complete ruin."[5] Yet in spite of the logical unlikelihood of success, and perhaps because of his mystic assurances of victory, Julian refused Constantius' last overture: a guarantee conveyed by a Christian bishop, Epictetus, that the Emperor would spare his life if Julian would surrender all claims to the throne.[6] This proposal Julian dismissed as not consonant with his sense of honor. Besides, who could believe anything Constantius said, he whose words were "written in ashes?"[7]

At the outset of the march eastward, Julian, concerned by the relatively small number of his forces, decided it would be best to divide them into two groups: he felt that by spreading them out in this manner they would present the illusion of a much larger army.[8] One force was assigned to the command of two generals with the interesting pagan names of Jovinus and Jovius. They were to take a route through northern Italy, while Julian and his new cavalry commander, Nevitta (a barbarian by birth), led the remainder of the army through Raetia toward the Danube.

This strategy succeeded admirably. Once the Danube was reached, Julian's men took to the river, appropriating for their use a large number of boats which they happened upon "by a fortunate chance."[9] The voyage down the Danube was a curious combination of stealth and triumph. The invaders, sticking close to the center of the river, managed to slip by a number of fortresses unnoticed, while elsewhere rumors (no doubt originating from Julian's own staff) were being circulated about his huge army and the numerous victories already won. Some towns, on hearing of his approach, sent out representatives with gifts to surrender to the conqueror.[10] Julian's old antagonist, Florentius, and Taurus, his fellow-consul for the year, on hearing these reports fled eastward in a public post-wagon.[11]

Meanwhile in western Illyricum, at the capital city and important fortress of Sirmium, Count Lucillianus (father-in-law of the future Emperor Jovian) prepared for war. Apparently Julian's intelligence reports were far more accurate than the Count's. When Julian's forces were some nineteen miles away

from Sirmium, he dispatched a small troop overland on a very
dark night to take Lucillianus by surprise.[12] Security measures
around Sirmium were grossly inadequate: Julian's men entered
the lodging where the Count was asleep and took him prisoner
before he was able to make even a show of resistance. Hurriedly
he was placed "upon the first horse that could be found" and
brought before the imperial claimant.

Lucillianus, knowing well the ways of emperors, fully expected death, but when Julian showed himself willing to spare
his life, the Count plucked up the courage to admonish him:
"Incautiously and rashly, my Emperor, have you entrusted your-
self to another's territory." "Reserve those wise words for Constantius . . . ," Julian replied.[13] Lucillianus was no longer the
prefect of Sirmium but at least he was alive. And Sirmium, without shedding a drop of blood, was in the hands of the Emperor
Julian. It was around the middle of October, 361.

The day after Lucillianus' capture, Julian entered Sirmium
in triumph; great crowds turned out to welcome him "with many
lights, flowers, and good wishes."[14] The next day, in order to
please the soldiers and the people, and in spite of his personal
dislike for this sort of entertainment, he ordered a celebration
with chariot races. An air of festivity permeated the city; Julian
was happy himself, if we are to believe Ammianus Marcellinus,
vastly pleased with his easy and successful campaign thus far.

The important province of Illyricum (roughly equivalent to
modern Yugoslavia) was now almost completely in his grasp.
Italy was reported to be largely pro-Julian, though in the city
of Rome itself (which he had never visited) there were many
Senators outspokenly loyal to Constantius, the Emperor they
knew and who represented the idea of legitimate succession.
Julian inspired more enthusiasm in Greece where Neoplatonism
and the worship of the old gods were still thriving and where,
in philosophic circles, his views of these subjects were widely
known.[15] At this time, in the autumn of 361, with an eye on the
publicity they would undoubtedly attract far beyond their
designated destinations, Julian dispatched letters to the local
senates of Rome, Athens, Corinth, and Sparta.[16] Of these mani-
festos, which were probably very similar in content, only the
letter to the Athenians has survived.[17] Largely autobiographical,

it is Julian's justification for his claim to the throne: an important, naturally biased, yet often moving statement of a young man with everything to lose, who nonetheless faces his future with the optimistic assurance that the gods are on his side.

It is not clear at precisely what moment Julian saw fit to reveal to the general public his allegiance to the old gods and his total rejection of Christianity. Sometime during his eastward march he began the practice of offering public sacrifices. By the time he was in Illyricum, he was allowing himself to be outspokenly pagan. "I worship the gods openly" he wrote from Naissus to his great friend Maximus, "and the whole mass of the troops who are returning with me worship the gods."[18] Word of his activities spread rapidly. In Greece, especially after the news of Julian's successful penetration of Illyricum, there was a great upsurge in public worship of the gods. More surprisingly, there was no hint of widespread desertions of Julian's cause by Christians—not yet.

It was still October when Julian left Sirmium for Naissus (modern Nish in Yugoslavia), the birthplace of the Emperor Constantine. Winter was coming on; wars were rarely fought in bad weather in those days, yet he had received disturbing reports of Constantius' troops massing for a showdown somewhere beyond the Haemus and Rhodope Mountains,[19] perhaps in Thrace, the neighboring province that included Constantinople, the capital city. Unless a miracle occurred, Julian could expect great trouble on the other side of the mountains. While he made the most careful military preparations for the next stages of his campaign, Julian continued to believe in miracles.

In early November the news coming into Julian's headquarters at Naissus grew progressively worse. First, there were the two legions formerly under command of Lucillianus: not trusting their loyalty, Julian had dispatched them from Sirmium with orders for duty in Gaul. When the legions reached Italy they revolted; they had seized the town of Aquileia and were holding out for Constantius.[20]

And where was Constantius? As so often throughout his long reign, the Emperor had spent most of the summer along the Persian frontier trying to avoid war with King Sapor, who was equally busy trying to avoid him.[21] Romans and Persians alike

seemingly had come to believe that an annual show of force
was an inescapable necessity, though neither really wanted to
fight. Sapor, as soon as he could decently do so, announced that
the omens forbade him fighting that year and withdrew. Constantius, with most of his vast army (some troops, of course,
would remain in the eastern garrisons), could now concentrate
on Julian and, late as the season was, he fully intended to do so.

Constantius had never lost a civil war: the pretenders who
sought his throne had inevitably suffered defeat. Julian—that
ungrateful young man who had never really appreciated all
his cousin had done for him—would be no different. Constantius
had no need even to think of forgiving Julian as his only
surviving kinsman, for that problem would soon be resolved.
The Emperor's young wife Faustina was pregnant, and he
would soon have an heir of his own body.

Forty-four years old, Flavius Constantius, Emperor of Rome,
had everything to live for. But that autumn, as he traveled back
toward Constantinople from the eastern frontier, he was a soul
in torment: ever on the watch for ill omens, deep in melan-
choly by day and beset by horrifying nightmares when he slept.
His guardian spirit, his good *daimon,* had left him, he remarked,[22] a strangely pagan sentiment from the fanatical Arian
Emperor, but perhaps he was a bit confused on the distinction
between *daimones* and guardian angels. From Antioch to Tarsus,
from Tarsus to Mopsucrenae, he traveled rapidly, as if aware
that he was racing with time. At Tarsus he reported a slight
fever, but he had always been a strong man and he would
keep moving. At Mopsucrenae, near the border of Cilicia, where
he stopped to rest, his body was burning "like a furnace." He
requested baptism; like his father before him, he always intended
to wait till his last moments to receive the sacred rite: there
were so many sins to wash away. An Arian bishop was duly
summoned and the sacrament performed.[23]

There was still the matter of the succession to decide. He
would never live to see his and Faustina's child, and who could
say for sure that it would be a son? Even if it were, the Romans
would never accept an infant emperor. The Persians, he had
heard tell, had acclaimed Sapor as king while he was still in his
mother's womb, but that sort of thing was un-Roman. It would

never do: the Empire needed a grown man—a brave, intelligent, able leader to guide the state in peace and war, one who would command both the respect and the love of his subjects. Who else but Julian?

Ammianus Marcellinus confidently assures us that Constantius on his deathbed spoke the name of his cousin, designating him as heir.[24] In addition, there was supposed to have been a written will. Nevertheless, Gregory Nazianzen just as confidently declares that Constantius died deploring the fact that he had not killed Julian as a child.[25] Most likely Ammianus has more of the truth. Whatever his faults, Constantius was basically a man of peace: he had no desire to leave a legacy of civil war to the Empire he had ruled so long. Constantius died on the third of November. Immediately, two counts in his service set out from Mopsucrenae to carry the word to Julian in Naissus.

It was not until some weeks later that Faustina's baby was born. She was named Flavia Maxima Faustina Constantia Postuma, and out of this imposing collection, the girl would in time choose to be called "Constantia" for the father she had never seen.[26] Eventually, she would become an Empress, wife of the Emperor Gratian of the West, but in the winter of 361–62 any such possibility was far in the future. For the present, the Emperor was Julian, and Julian was on his way from Naissus to Constantinople to receive his crown.

CHAPTER 14

Julian in Constantinople

I AM alive by the grace of the gods," wrote the new Emperor from his headquarters in Naissus to his uncle Count Julian, his mother's brother and his only surviving close kinsman. Constantius was dead; the welcome news had thrown young Julian's court into a flurry of sudden activity. Well into the night, his secretaries were all so busy that the Emperor undertook to write his uncle with his own hand. "[I] have been freed from necessity of either suffering or inflicting irreparable ill," he reflected. "But Helios, whom of all the gods I besought most earnestly to assist me, and sovereign Zeus also, bear me witness that never for a moment did I wish to slay Constantius. . ."[1] What had happened was clearly the will of the gods; the fulfillment of their promises and omens to grant him victory. According to Libanius, Julian actually burst into tears when he learned of Constantius' death,[2] but if so they could have only been tears of blessed relief, with perhaps a mingling of regret that he and Constantius had gotten along so badly. Julian was never one to cry easily, or for long. Ammianus Marcellinus is probably more nearly right in saying that the new Emperor was "hugely elated" by his predecessor's death.[3] As for the late Emperor, "he was what he was . . . may the earth lie lightly upon him," commented Julian in another letter probably written in early December.[4] There was a great deal to be said for imperial solidarity, now that Constantius was dead.

On the eleventh of December, the new Emperor entered Constantinople. It had been about seven years since Julian had seen his native city; but he loved Constantinople, he said, better than any earlier emperor could have, for there he was born and there he had lived as a young child.[5] It was a large and thriving city, old Byzantium rebuilt on a lavish scale, still possessing an

98

air of "newness" about it that formed a great contrast to most
of the cities of Julian's world. The Emperor Constantine had
aspired to make his capital beautiful, and nature assisted this
goal with the striking view of the sea that surrounded the city
on three sides. Statues, transported on Constantine's orders
from all over the Roman world, adorned the public squares
and the Mesé (Middle Street) running the length of the city.
While Julian, no doubt, appreciated the many advantages his
new capital offered, he could not have been pleased that his
birthplace was planned as a specifically Christian center. The
great churches of the Holy Apostles and Sancta Sophia were
but two of the largest of many Christian places· of worship in
the city, while there was only one notable "Hellenic" shrine, the
small Temple of Fortune. But this was a situation that could
in time be altered. For the moment, Julian would simply have
to tolerate living in Constantius' Great Palace, directly beside
the Church of Sancta Sophia.[6]

The inhabitants of the capital who turned out in droves to
witness Julian's grand entry must have felt mixed emotions at
the sight of their native son. Though Ammianus asserts that all
welcomed him as if he had come down from heaven,[7] few
could have helped but notice the striking contrast between the
new ruler and his cousin Constantius. Julian was thirty years
old; youthful in appearance and conspicuously small of stature.
His beard, which for a while he had kept shaved, was beginning
to grow back. As it turned out, he would never shave again;[8]
this at a time when no fashionable gentleman would consider
wearing a beard. Philosopher that he was, Julian cared absolutely nothing for fine clothes. He wore the imperial costume
because it was expected of him, but as Libanius points out,
"he did not look himself up and down" with undue pride, nor
was he particular about the exact shade of imperial dye used
for his clothing: "he did not measure the happiness of his
reign by the depth of his purple."[9]

Ceremony demanded that he usually wear a golden crown. He
would have preferred not to do so, but convincing himself
that it was the will of the gods, he conformed to custom. Yet
even when Julian decked himself in the rich robes, diadem, and
red shoes of imperial majesty, he would never look the part of

an Emperor. He was, in his individualistic way, an attractive young man, but that famous self-control that was so much admired in Constantius was missing. Excitable, nervous Julian was never able to remain motionless for long. He lacked dignity, some said, though this is scarcely just, for he certainly possessed a deep and serious commitment to the office which the gods had given him. What he lacked, rather, was the imperial mystique: he could never learn to act the part of a statue, or a god on earth. He was simply a very human young man who happened to hold the highest office in the world of his day. There would be no more *proskynesis*, he declared, that elaborate ceremony of bowing to the ground and kissing the imperial shoes required of everyone who entered the Emperor's presence since the days of Diocletian. As Libanius recalled, Julian "did not think it heightened his majesty for them [suppliants at the court] to be frightened and silent, to fold their hands, to prostrate themselves to the ground and to study his shoe toe in preference to his face."[10]

What was the Roman Empire coming to! Those who doubted the new Emperor's suitability for his post may have been consoled somewhat by his admirable display of propriety at the funeral of his predecessor. The body of Constantius had been transported from Mopsucrenae under the care of a young army officer named Jovian (soon, though none would have dreamed it at the time, to be Emperor himself).[11] For most of the solemn procession, Jovian had ridden in a carriage with Constantius' casket. Then came the last stage of the journey by ship across the Bosphoros; finally, around mid-December the Emperor's remains reached Constantinople. Julian in spite of an abnormally strong aversion to funeral rites, hastened to the harbor to take part in the necessary ceremonies. Bareheaded and without any imperial ornaments except the indispensable purple cloak, he took his place among chosen men who lifted Constantius' coffin and conveyed it through the city streets to the Church of the Holy Apostles, the late Emperor's chosen resting place.[12] The Arian funeral rites conducted that day were the last Christian service Julian would ever attend. Had he known that, in time, his body would lie in the same church, not far from Constantius', one imagines he would have lost the philosophic calm that he so admirably displayed throughout what must have been an unusually difficult day.

If in most ways, he seemed completely unlike his recent predecessors, Julian resembled Constantine and Constantius in his interest in sponsoring lavish public building and improvements in the capital city. His major project was construction of a harbor on the south side of the city and near it a crescent-shaped stoa, which seems to have been a large and impressive structure. Inside the stoa was a library in which Zosimus says (with some obvious exaggeration) the Emperor "deposited all the books he had."[13]

For a person of Julian's simple tastes, Constantius' lavish household arrangements at the Great Palace proved a source of surprise—and considerable dismay. The great number (several thousand, according to Libanius) of cooks and barbers in Constantius' employ, he considered particularly unnecessary.[14] After all, Julian's tastes in food and drink were of the simplest, and as for his beard and rather longish hair, an occasional trim would be all he required—quite a different order than Constantius' carefully oiled, meticulously styled curls and smooth-shaven face. One day soon after his arrival he called for one of the court barbers, who appeared dressed in magnificent garb. On seeing him, Julian remarked: "I sent for a barber, not a fiscal agent," and he was not at all pleased to learn that this relatively minor functionary received a large salary, with numerous perquisites plus an allowance of twenty loaves of bread per day and fodder for his animals.[15] Julian had no inclination to imitate the life style of his predecessor. Rather, he felt, most of Constantius' servants were, like the barber, ridiculously overpaid; many were completely useless. The only solution was to fire most of them, a reform which he undertook without delay.

Among those who found themselves jobless were a number of eunuchs. Constantius, like many eastern monarchs of ancient times, had considered them particularly useful servants, while Julian (though he certainly appreciated the worth of certain individual eunuchs like the loyal Eutherius) tended to consider them unreliable as a class and much inclined to intrigue.[16] The vast reduction of the palace staff evoked considerable comment. Few, it seems, appreciated the idea that Julian was saving his

taxpayers' money and returning to a way of life more consonant
with the simple virtues of ancient Rome. More often heard
was the complaint that in diminishing his household the new
Emperor was detracting from his own grandeur: a serious mistake, for it was his imperial duty to maintain himself in suit-
able splendor.[17] Julian, ever sensitive to criticism, listened but
appeared unmoved.

More appreciated, at least by the average citizenry, was
Julian's firing of a considerable number of court hangers-on of
a higher level: "secretaries" and informers whose dishonesty
and insatiable greed for wealth had made them notorious in
the last reign. Libanius is most expansive in reflecting on the
wrongdoing of these unsavory characters who perverted justice to their own ends and mercilessly extorted funds from anyone whose property they coveted, not only in Constantinople
but throughout the Roman world.[18] Each of these secretaries
and informers had a large staff of servants of his own; and like
their masters, the servants too were noted for haughty and cruel
behavior "that made street, fortress and city tremble before
them."[19] Constantius had either been unaware of, or indifferent
to the enormity of their abuses. Now Julian, full of righteous
anger, removed from office almost all of the "secretaries"; the
few he retained would be expected to change their ways and
to serve henceforth in an actual secretarial capacity. The entire
class of "informers" was abolished completely. The men whose
business was collecting gossip, many of whom had made their
fortune through blackmail and false rumors, found themselves
suddenly jobless. Considering Julian's reforming zeal, they were
lucky still to be alive; but then, the new Emperor, as it soon
became clear, was extremely reluctant to pronounce the death
penalty.[20] For the unscrupulous agents of the late Emperor's
court it was punishment enough to find their lucrative careers
had come to an end.

Julian's determined and thoroughgoing reform of the court
bureaucracy was among the earliest acts of his reign. Whatever
else he might decide to do, his insistence on a more honest
and more efficient staff was a sign that augured well for the
future character of his reign.

More controversial, but from one point of view equally salu-

tary, was another of Julian's governmental reforms: his decision
to increase the number of men serving on the municipal councils
or senates of many of the empire's cities.[21] By the fourth century
no one wanted to be one of the *curiales*, as holders of this post
were called. It was an expensive, sometimes ruinous, job since
curiales were expected to expend their private fortunes in government service. Curial posts were hereditary; but many men
born to the upper class who would have had to serve in office,
managed to claim an exemption. For instance, some (like Libanius) became teachers; others (like Ammianus Marcellinus)
joined the army: both of these professions cancelled a man's
curial obligations, as did certain positions in the imperial government. Under Constantine and Constantius, Christian priests
were likewise excused; a situation that led to the recruitment
of some unlikely characters to the ranks of the clergy.[22] Julian
had no intention of cancelling the valid exemptions of profes-
sors, soldiers, and bureaucrats; in fact, he added physicians to
the list of those who could legally avoid curial duty.[23] He was,
however, determined that persons who had escaped duty only
by some special favor of his predecessor (including Christian
clerics and many others, Christian and pagan alike, who had
purchased exemptions from Constantius) would no longer be
excused.[24] Curial service, Julian realized clearly, was a heavy
burden, but if each city had more *curiales*, the burden at least
would be more widely distributed, and consequently not nearly
so difficult for any one individual. The reform could not be
carried out overnight: Julian was working on it when, in the
summer of 362, he moved from Constantinople to Antioch, a
city where he would meet particular opposition over this matter
as he did in many of the reforms he attempted.

On the other hand, a reform of Julian's that was almost universally applauded (even by the ill-natured Gregory Nazianzen)
was that of the postal system.[25] Under Constantius innumerable
free passes were issued by the Emperor and his subordinates
for persons to travel in state-owned postal wagons. This situation led to grave abuses. The beasts owned by the postal service (usually mules or horses, and some donkeys) were terribly
overworked, often beaten, and sometimes died from exhaustion
or insufficient food. It was the municipalities, not the central

government, that had to provide replacements: another heavy burden for the *curiales*. Julian's answer to this problem was a drastic reduction of the number of free passes for state transportation. In some areas, the comings and goings of the postal wagons declined so sharply that the animals' grooms had to make a special effort to provide them with sufficient exercise. Julian in his orders on postal reform made a special point of humane treatment of these animals. A further reform provided that when a beast died or was no longer able for service, the postal officials themselves had to supply the replacement: a notable improvement from the standpoint of the cities.

In spite of his strict curtailment of free travel privileges, Julian's letters reveal that he was not altogether opposed to granting an occasional pass for such a journey, particularly during his first months as emperor when he sought to gather around him a group of likeminded philosophers and other old acquaintances.[26] This influx of Julian's friends began along with the exodus of Constantius' servants and officials. Free at last to see and visit with exactly whom he pleased, the Emperor sent out invitations to many of his old acquaintances urging them to come to Constantinople and including the inducement of free transportation in the postal wagons. Of all his old friends, Julian was especially eager to see Maximus of Ephesus, the theurgist whose wonder-working had so fascinated him as a student, and with whom he had continuued to correspond. Maximus had resisted Julian's pleas to come to Gaul and later to Naissus: the omens forbade these journeys, he declared, but he would keep on consulting the gods hoping the omens would change.[27] Finally early in 362, the long-bearded philosopher of Ephesus and his wife, who was herself a learned student of theurgy, appeared in Constantinople.

The day that Maximus arrived, Julian was partaking in a meeting of the local Senate: one of the young Emperor's peculiar traits, it was observed, was his genuine enjoyment of public speaking. (Constantius would have never attended a Senate meeting, much less spoken there; his wishes were conveyed in writing and duly read by an appropriate official.)[28] Not so Julian, whose interest in such matters was based on a sincere belief that here, too, he was returning to the old Roman way, the ideals of the ancient Republic before it was corrupted by imperial absolutism and Christianity.

On this particular occasion, however, the arrival of Maximus preempted even Julian's interest in Senate business. He had asked to be informed immediately whenever his friend should appear in the city. Upon receiving the good news, he broke off his speech without regret, and ran to greet Maximus in the vestibule of the Senate house. Joyfully he escorted his old teacher into the meeting hall, embraced him before the whole assembly of city fathers, and introduced him in terms of warmest approval.[29]

Maximus, his wife, and their attendants presumably moved straightway into the Great Palace. The reign of the philosophers had begun.

Nor was Maximus the only "philosopher" to find favor at the new Emperor's court. If the theurgist of Ephesus was Julian's special confidant, there was room for others, among them his longtime correspondent Priscus of Athens.[30] On the other hand, no amount of coaxing on Julian's part could attract his former teacher, Chrysanthius of Sardis, to Constantinople. The Emperor even wrote directly to Chrysanthius' wife Melite, urging that she try to influence him to come to court. Chrysanthius replied that the gods absolutely forbade him to come, and Julian, who could scarcely reject that excuse, relented and awarded him an appointment as high priest of Lydia.[31]

Among the most serious problems facing the new Emperor during his winter in Constantinople was what to do with certain high-ranking officials of Constantius who had been notoriously inimical to Julian before his accession to the throne. To deal with this matter, he appointed a team of investigators headed by Salustius Secundus, a newly appointed praetorian prefect, and Arbetio, a former consul.[32] The special court was to meet at Chalcedon, across the Straits from Constantinople. Unwisely, once he had selected the six judges, he gave them completely free rein in whatever they should decide to do. Ammianus Marcellinus, ever reluctant to find fault with his hero, is impelled to admit that some of the Chalcedon proceedings were unjust and the penalties too harsh. Certain recent historians, however, have been more inclined to defend Julian.[33] He was not, they point out, directly to blame for the Chalcedon sentences; his mistake, rather, was the delegation of too much authority to others, trusting, it would seem, entirely too much in the ability of Salustius to incline the younger and more hotheaded judges in the direction of mercy.

Among the six judges only two were civilians, Salustius and Mamertinus, a noted orator and one of the consuls newly designated for 362.[34] The other four were army men: Arbetio, Agilo, Jovinus, and the other new consul, Nevitta, the barbarian-born general. It has been theorized that Julian was under some pressure from the officers who had supported his campaign to allow reprisals against those whom they considered their deadliest enemies.[35] In any event, all the victims of the Chalcedon trials were civilians.

In comparison to the severity of purges by earlier emperors the number of those condemned at Chalcedon is small, and most of them suffered nothing worse than banishment. There were, however, four executions; of three of the victims, even Ammianus admits that they scarcely deserved any better.[36] The former grand chamberlain, Eusebius the eunuch, seems to have been killed by being pushed off a high place; the notorious informer, Paul the Chain, and Apodemius, a secret agent who had been deeply involved in the execution of Gallus and other atrocities, were burned to death. The fourth victim of capital punishment was Count Ursulus, a treasury official who had been a valuable friend of Julian when he was in Gaul. Because of certain ill-advised and widely publicized remarks, Ursulus was extremely unpopular with the soldiery; this seemingly was the cause of his condemnation. Later Julian declared that he was unaware of the sentence until after it had been carried out. Apparently he was genuinely sorry; and though it was too late to intervene on Ursulus' behalf, he promptly restored most of the executed man's properties to the daughter who was his heir.[37] One additional death sentence decreed at Chalcedon could not be implemented: Julian's old antagonist, Florentius, a consul for 361, had disappeared without trace and was condemned *in absentia*. Later Julian, who despised informers more than he feared his missing adversary, refused to listen to a report of Florentius' whereabouts.[38] Thus the ex-consul survived Julian's reign by remaining in hiding.

The Chalcedon trials took place in December. On the first of January, 362, when the new consuls, Mamertinus the orator and Nevitta the general, had returned to Constantinople, they were formally installed in office.[39] By the fourth century, the consulship had become largely an ornamental office, hallowed by the traditions of nearly a thousand years but lacking in real authority. It is significant that Julian did not claim the consulship for himself in the first year of his reign. Why he selected Nevitta and Mamertinus for the post is not altogether clear. Probably he admired Mamertinus' rhetoric.[40] As for Nevitta, one may imagine that here as well as in the Chalcedon trials Julian was under some constraint from the army.[41] Not long before, Julian had stated that among the many misdoings of his uncle Constantine was that Emperor's appointment of barbarian-born individuals to the consulship;[42] in choosing Nevitta he now had committed the same offense. While there is no reason to believe that Nevitta was ever disloyal to Julian, it is altogether possible that the Emperor realized that the very existence of this powerful barbarian general contained a threat to imperial security if Nevitta were not awarded special favors.

Ever intent on the revival of old traditions, Julian walked to the consular inauguration, as emperors had done in earlier centuries of Roman history. Constantius, however, would have ridden in his chariot, and many inhabitants of the capital, knowing no other emperor with whom to compare the unpredictable young man who now held the title, considered Julian's decision to go on foot "as affected and cheap."[43] The people of Constantinople, Julian was discovering rapidly, were a difficult audience to please.

As part of the New Year festivities, the Consul Mamertinus sponsored games in the Hippodrome. It was the custom on such occasions to proclaim manumission of a number of slaves. These were duly led before the Emperor and the consuls, and Julian, this time forgetting the procedure that custom demanded, hastily pronounced the manumission formula, a privilege that should have belonged to Mamertinus. When someone in the Emperor's entourage informed him of his mistake, Julian good-naturedly admitted he was guilty of a procedural error and fined himself ten pounds of gold as a penalty.[44]

From such trivial incidents upon which Ammianus lingers with loving attention, as well as from his many notable efforts at government reform, a vivid picture of the new Emperor emerges: serious, devoted to duty, impulsive and always full of surprises. His commitment to hard work left him few free moments. "I have no time, heaven knows," he wrote (probably in April, 362) to his Uncle Julian who had reproached him for not answering his letters. "I do not even offer up many prayers, though naturally I need now more than ever to pray very often and very long. But I am hemmed in and choked by public business."[45] Just as in Gaul, he frequently took part personally in judging legal disputes, and with a disdain for court etiquette that never ceased to cause astonishment, he was often heard to address some nervous litigant as "My friend."[46] Among the citizenry of the capital (who obviously were not at all afraid of him), mannerisms such as this were always a lively subject of discussion.

And most of all, there was the matter of religion. Here, as elsewhere, it was almost impossible to anticipate what the emperor was going to do. Indeed, beyond the certainty of his commitment to the old gods, Julian himself in the early months of his reign, would have probably found it difficult to predict the eventual course of his religious policies.

CHAPTER 15

The Revival of Hellenism

JULIAN'S allegiance to the old gods of Hellenism was a complex matter, one that he was himself able to approach from several different and seemingly contradictory perspectives. Perhaps, at the outset, it is most essential to understand what he did *not* believe at all. As much as he loved the poems of Homer and the other ancient myths, he never accepted these as infallible sources of factual information on the habits of the gods. The ignorant common people might believe that the gods literally lived on Mount Olympus, quarrelled bitterly among themselves, and displayed every sort of human passion on a superhuman scale. But the truly educated pagans, the "philosophers" such as Julian himself, interpreted the old stories of the gods as allegories veiling higher truths, understandable only by those who studied to discover them and who were initiated into the various mysteries.[1] "It is the incongruous element in myths that guides us to the truth," Julian believed. "The more paradoxical and prodigious the riddle is the more it seems to warn us not to believe simply the bare words but rather to study diligently the hidden truth, and not to relax our efforts until under the guidance of the gods those hidden things become plain."[2]

Nowhere in Julian's writing is this method of allegorizing more fully applied than in his attempt to explain the spiritual meaning of the gruesome myth of Cybele, the Great Mother goddess, and Attis, her erring lover. Attis, says Julian, represents Mind which has "overstepped and transgressed due measure," but which after punishment "is led upwards again to the Mother of the Gods."[3] Thus interpreted, what seems on the surface an ugly and degrading story reveals a deeply hidden spiritual truth.

While Julian was very much a polytheist, it is also important

109

to realize that he considered all the gods and goddesses to be manifestations or emanations of The One, and thus at times he speaks of "God" in distinctly monotheistic terms. According to the teaching of Neoplatonism which Julian enthusiastically (if unsystematically) accepted, The One was completely incomprehensible to human beings, and could be known only through the lesser gods, who were assigned to various functions in the universe.[4]

Julian takes particular care to point out that the gods are the bestowers of all the good gifts that mankind enjoys.[5] Included among their blessings is the hope for a better existence in the world to come. Julian did not stress the idea of heaven, but he looked forward to the time "after the immortal soul has been separated from the body and the lifeless body has turned to earth" as a period of reunion with the gods.[6]

When it comes to distinguishing between these various gods, Julian at times is very explicit: Hermes, for instance is usually associated with learning and study; Asklepios with healing; Ares with war.[7] Asklepios, the healer god, was a special favorite of Julian's as he was with many of the pious pagans of the time. "When I have been sick, Asklepios has often cured me," he reports.[8] More than once, his descriptions of this god, who became man in the distant past and who traveled on earth "to Pergamon, to Ionia, to Tarentum"[9] and numerous other places, seem similar in terminology to Christian descriptions of Christ. Asklepios, says Julian, was begotten by Helios-Mithra (or Zeus) "to be savior of the whole world," and "even before the beginning of the world," Asklepios was pre-existent at the side of Helios.[10]

Different nationalities, Julian also believed, had their special creator deities, a theory that explained the differences in national character. For instance, while the Athenians paid particular reverence to Athene, the Egyptians favored Serapis. The Jews, too, he felt, worshipped a national god, and with all the good will in the world he could not understand why their god could not be added to the international family of deities.[11]

If sometimes Julian was careful to distinguish the functions of the various gods, at other times he describes them so that they seem manifestations of each other. Helios, his own patron-deity, is considered identical with Mithra; Helios is "King," a partner of Father Zeus, at times seemingly greater than Zeus himself.[12] The Syrian mother goddess Cybele is, surprisingly, so closely identified with Athene as to seem the same goddess under a different name.[13] Julian never seems to have been concerned over this disconcerting lack of precision in naming and describing the gods. To him this was simply not important: they were myriad in number, yet they all came from The One. The efforts of some modern scholars to comb his writings for a systematized hierarchy of the heavens would no doubt surprise him immensely.

While Julian genuinely relished Neoplatonic study of the nature of the gods, he was not himself an original thinker in this area, and his attempts at theological writing borrow heavily from the works of earlier philosophers, including Iamblichus, Porphyry and Plotinus. Julian particularly recognized his debt to "inspired Iamblichus." "Read the writings of Iamblichus," he urged, "and you will find there the most consummate wisdom which man can achieve ... I know well that no one can utter anything more perfect than he."[14]

In view of this lack of originality, it is fair to say that had Julian never been emperor, he might be remembered only as a very minor Neoplatonist in the era of Hellenism's decline. Far more important, therefore, than his theologizing are his practical attempts as sovereign of the Roman world to restore the worship of the gods to what it had been at its very best in earlier centuries. As emperor, he was also chief priest of the gods (a role that automatically accompanied emperorship but which Constantine and Constantius had ignored) and his consecration to this post was for him a matter of utmost sacredness. "I am indeed by no means worthy of so high an office," he reflected, "though I desire and moreover constantly pray to the gods that I may be worthy."[15] Whatever he did—whether planning for his forthcoming campaign against Persia, administering justice or conversing pleasantly with his friends—one senses that his mission as restorer of ancient Hellenic worship was never far from his consciousness. Not all of his warmheartedness and capacity for friendship could erase his conviction that the gods, in making him chief priest, had set him apart from other men; it was a responsibility to be accepted in humility, and gratitude. It was also a role that would demand a great deal of hard work, service that Julian rendered gladly. While there were still many practicing pagans in Julian's world, the Emperor found, too, that many old customs and practices had fallen into disuse. Now, he believed, these ancient rites must be revived, purified of corrupt and orgiastic overtones, and practiced in their original splendor. Temples that had fallen into decay were reopened and repaired at state expense. Public sacrifices, both of incense and the far more elaborate offering of sacrificial beasts, were encouraged.[16] While the gods do not actually need these things, Julian pointed out, the reverence that such acts induces in the worshiper is good in itself and will induce the gods to manifest good will to the worshiper in return.[17]

Julian personally appears to have derived great spiritual benefit from such acts of formal worship. His days regularly began with prayer; he would customarily arise very early in the morning, probably before daybreak, and his first official act of the day was his devotions to the gods, complete with the burning of incense before their statues in his private chapel. Both in Constantinople and later in Antioch, he would spend some time later in the morning conducting semi-public sacrifices of oxen and other beasts in the palace gardens. The meat roasted on these occasions would be served to participants as a sacred meal. It was never hard to attract a crowd, but although Julian professed himself encouraged by these throngs of worshipers, he sensed, too, that many of those who attended came only for the sake of eating the free food and witnessing the spectacle of the Emperor performing the role of high priest. His own troops who had come with him from Gaul were usually enthusiastic participants at such rites, though their conduct, Julian realized clearly, fell far short of the reverence he sought to cultivate.[18] In Antioch, where Julian's public worship services continued to attract characters of the worst sort, he responded to criticism by saying that none should be excluded. Certainly, the undesirables needed a religious rebirth more than anyone else, and to keep them away by force would be self-defeating.

Julian hoped to see temples throughout his Empire holding regular worship services along much the same lines as those he sponsored personally. The men and women consecrated to the various priesthoods of the old gods, Julian discovered, were disappointingly few in number, and he campaigned actively to recruit additional members. Many of his friends like Chrysanthius and his wife Melite were enrolled in high ranking positions in the various cults. Julian was fully aware of the importance of women in the old religion;[19] quite unlike their Christian rivals, many branches of "Hellenism" encouraged women to enter the service of the gods as priestesses.

The moral qualifications for the priesthood of the old gods were of great interest to Julian. Great though the need was for increased numbers, he did not encourage the insincere to seek enrollment. Under most circumstances, the Hellenic priesthoods did not require a vow of celibacy, but Julian did feel that priests should serve as moral examples to the rest of the community by avoiding scandal and practicing moderation in all things.[20] In return it was a duty of all pious Hellenes to respect and revere the priests who were the gods' representatives, as much or more than they respected the authorities of the imperial government.

But what if a priest should prove unworthy of his sacred office? This was a problem that most likely occurred often, and it is one to which Julian returns several times in his various writings. One who is merely suspected of misdoing, he says, still deserves the respect due to his office, but if after thorough investigation the charges are proven true, the unworthy priest must be dismissed.[21]

It is in the description of the way of life to be practiced by his followers—both the priesthood and the laity—that we find the most creative aspects of Julian's religious thought. It was his strong conviction that in order to be a true worshiper of the gods one must conform to certain ethical and moral standards. These ideals, while present in much of his writing, are given their most organized presentation in a long fragment entitled "A Letter to a Priest," written sometime in 362, probably when he was in Antioch. "Let everyone make the basis of his conduct moral virtues," Julian admonishes his readers, "and actions like these, namely reverence toward the gods, benevolence toward men, [and] personal chastity."[22] Of course, Julian was not the first pagan thinker to recommend such noble standards of conduct, but to find an emperor, a proven soldier of great capability and a talented legislator, also concerned with the implanting of higher standards of morality and generosity among his people, was unusual to say the least. Indeed the depth of his concern and his determination to model his own life upon his ideals are very nearly Christian in their fervor.

Many less dedicated pagans, as Julian would discover, reacted to his sincerity with open surprise, or worse still, with ridicule and contempt. Particularly was this true in areas of private morality, since, contrary to many of his contemporaries, Julian believed firmly that a true Hellene must live chastely, avoiding sexual excesses of any sort. For himself, he chose a life of complete austerity, a practice that he clearly did not expect many of his followers to adopt, but one that occasioned much comment.

From the time of Helena's death, Julian had bound himself by a vow of absolute celibacy.[23] By all accounts, he was completely faithful to this vow, though when he first became Emperor, most people expected him to remarry, and he frequently felt impelled to state publicly that he did not intend to do so. This fact notwithstanding, no one would have been surprised had he taken a mistress, or for that matter, a male lover, since homosexual relationships were not considered particularly scandalous in the world of his day. As it turned out, however, Julian did none of these things. Palace servants frequently remarked on the fact that, surprising as it might seem, the young Emperor "always slept alone."[24] As Libanius reflected, Julian was so pure that there was nothing sacrilegious in his bedroom in the palace in Constantinople being next to the room containing his shrine of the gods.[25] Even more convincing evidence of this aspect of Julian's personality is the fact that none of his Christian opponents, who seized every opportunity to slander him, ever charged him with sexual immorality of any kind. In this area, at least, his life exemplified the highest ideals of Christianity far more than it conformed to the liberal standards typical of Hellenism and one surmises that his attitudes can only have had their origin in the strict Christian atmosphere of his childhood.

Closely associated with Julian's attitude toward sex is his strong distaste for what he considered obscenity and sacrilege in literature and on the stage. Most plays, he felt, particularly the comedies, were unspeakably lewd. As Emperor, he says, he contemplated closing the theaters but his understanding of human nature forbade this move which he knew could have only resulted in his widespread unpopularity. Rather, he demonstrated his disapproval of the theater by staying away personally and urging the priests of the gods to do the same.[26] As for works of literature on what he deemed unworthy subjects, he counselled those who entered the priesthood of the Hellenic gods to avoid these altogether. Many ordinary people would continue to read such trash, he knew, but those who were consecrated to the service of the gods (as was he) must devote their time to better things.[27]

Just as the true servants of the gods must avoid salacious literature and entertainment, so also, Julian advised, must they in everyday life "hold fast to deeds of piety . . . neither saying nor listening to anything base."[28] Priests, especially, he warned to avoid licentious and obscene conversations, an ideal to which he apparently adhered firmly in his own daily living.

According to Julian, another important practice of moderation in living was the avoiding of excesses in eating and drinking. As has been noted, Julian was himself never a hearty eater. At a time when gigantic banquets were fashionable, and it was not at all uncommon for a person to eat so much that he had to induce vomiting in order to continue eating still more, Julian prided himself on the fact that never in his life had he resorted to this unpleasant habit.[29] Nor was he an excessive drinker: his usual beverage was one cup of wine per meal, and that heavily diluted with water; nor did he object to drinking plain water.[30] Some remarked facetiously that he talked so much at every meal that he had little time to eat or drink; while there probably is a measure of truth in this remark, his abstemious habits also sprang from his ingrained conviction that over-indulgence was morally wrong. His whole life, he reflected, was a "war" against fat,[31] and though he would never be uncommonly thin, those who shared his table amply testify that he was satisfied with remarkably little.

It is also worth observing that the many strange restrictions imposed upon him by his membership in the Mithra and Cybele cults limited Julian's diet still further. A loyal Mithraist, he explained, would not eat anything that grew "below the ground."[32] He seems to have entertained doubts, too, on the suitability of fish, which after all swam below the water. In this connection, too, might be noted the religious amulets which he wore at all times. They were, he said, "bound" to him[33] and though we have no precise description, they were probably Mithraic cameos (like many that have been found by archaeologists) carved with mystic symbols of the cult and hung on a cord around his neck.

Except for ceremonial appearances, Julian's clothes were deliberately simple, for here, too, the Emperor hoped to display a "moderation" pleasing to the gods. His lack of concern for his imperial wardrobe was notorious, and is reflected in a curious ancedote reported by Ammianus. It happened that Julian was informed of a certain ambitious man who was said to own a cloak of imperial purple. Under Constantius, such an act would have been considered a crime, but Julian merely listened placidly, then ordered a pair of red shoes (a sign of emperorship) sent to the man with the purple cloak, since they would be needed to complete his costume.[34] In spite of his obvious lack of interest in dress, and the fact that he was never outstandingly neat, Julian encouraged priests to look and dress their best for sacred occasions.[35] Certainly there is no valid ground for believing that he encouraged physical dirtiness in the name of piety as many of his Christian contemporaries did.

The competition that Christianity offered to Julian's revived Hellenism was very much in the Emperor's mind as he sought to outline the way of life pleasing to the gods, and it leads us to the most interesting and unusual facet of his entire program. Following the right rituals and practicing chastity and moderation were simply not enough in Julian's opinion. There was also the matter of positive action, reverence for the gods manifested through one's treatment of his fellow man. Here the qualities of life that are most essential to cultivate are generosity and benevolence. These, he insists with great urgency, must be instilled both as private and public virtues. Let the worshipers of the gods offer organized charity; let them provide for the destitute, the traveller, the aged and the ill.[36] Generosity came easily to Julian: long before he became Emperor he had always been liberal with whatever funds he had.[37] The gods, he believed confidently on the basis of his own experiences, rewarded a willing giver with additional blessings. Now, as ruler, he envisioned engrafting the practice of charity upon Hellenism reborn: in the new understanding of the old gods that he longed to establish everywhere, even prisoners, he suggested, would be entitled to help in the form of food and clothing. "The helpless and poor" should be able to turn to the priests for financial aid.[38]

As these suggestions prove, though Julian was at times unquestionably a dreamer, he also possessed a firm grasp of reality: of the disappointing lack of idealism among most individuals and the need for practicality in making his ideas palatable to them. The organized benevolence he hoped to offer in the name of revived Hellenism would not only please the gods, but would have the very earthly result of attracting new members to the worship of the old gods.

Would his plans ever have succeeded? Had he reigned twenty years instead of twenty months, would the western world be "Hellenic" today? Almost certainly not. While his early death makes it extremely difficult to evaluate the positive implementation of his ideals, even while he lived Julian seems to have realized he was fighting a hard battle. He usually remained optimistic, for irrepressible optimism was a part of his nature; yet at times, especially in Antioch, he gave way to periods of grave disappointment and disillusionment. The cause was twofold: His own people, the non-Christian Romans, were not sufficiently with him; many of them found Julian's sincerity more ludicrous than inspirational. He was a man born several hundred years too late; there was no place for him in the fourth-century world.

Conversely, the role he might have fulfilled as a Christian, he rejected. All the noble impulses in Julian's character seem, to the detached observer, natural ties to Christianity in the society of his time. If he had not been high priest of the pagans, he might well have become a Christian saint. Julian himself realized that in urging the adoption of organized benevolence by Hellenism he was taking a leaf from the Christian book: the Galileans (as he always called them) had made more converts by their charity than by their doctrines.[39] Yet in the same passage of his "Letter to a Priest" where he makes this observation, he gives one of the most forthright statements of his unbridgeable hatred for the Galilean faith. Christians with their acts of charity, he reflected bitterly, were like slave dealers who abducted little children with the inducement of a few cookies, then carried them off on slave ships so "that which for the moment seemed sweet, proves to be bitter for all the rest of their lives."[40] Rarely does one find an expression in Julian's existing writings that so clearly reflects his own very deep repulsion by Christianity. In effect, he is saying that to be baptized (as he had been himself, much to his regret) is as degrading and as deplorable as being enslaved. It is little wonder that the Christian copyist who preserved this portion of Julian's "Letter to a Priest" broke off at that point, unable to tolerate further expressions along these lines. People then and people now have pondered: how could Julian be so near to embodying the moral and ethical ideals of Christianity, and yet so very far from possessing any empathy for its doctrines? If he could not in sincerity be Christian himself, was there not room in his vast eclectic scheme for coexistence of the Galileans along with the many other cults of his time?

As Emperor, Julian faced these problems courageously and with the determination that characterized all his efforts to purify his Empire of what he genuinely believed to be sources of corruption. That he failed indicates a great deal about the innate strength of Christianity. On the other hand the attempts he made to come to terms with his Galilean adversaries through limited tolerance, reasoned argument, and occasional harshness tempered by surprising mercy, reveal a great deal about the character of the Emperor Julian.

CHAPTER 16

Trouble in Antioch

BEFORE turning to Julian's relations with the Galileans, it is important to notice that whatever his difficulties with this sect, they comprised only one aspect of the multi-faceted business of emperorship. Coming to terms with the Christians, from his perspective, was not even the major part of his religious program, where the emphasis was on a positive revival of the old religion with all its new ethical, moral, and ceremonial trimmings. There were, in addition, numerous other matters demanding Julian's attention, from planning for a huge invasion of Persia to coping with the problems of curial service. The Galileans, for all the outspoken hostility of some of their membership, seemed but a tiny cloud on Julian's horizon, when in the spring of 362, he decided to leave Constantinople for Antioch.

Julian had spent only about five months in his capital city. Emperors in those times frequently lived for months, or even years, in residences other than the Great Palace of Constantinople. Wherever the Emperor went, there was the center of government. Since his long-range plans called for war against Persia, Julian decided to relocate his court at a point further east.[1]

Antioch-on-the-Orontes in Syria was one of the Empire's largest cities, a cosmopolitan center where Greeks, Syrians, and many other nationalities lived side-by-side. For the most part, whatever their ethnic origins, the Antiochenes were intensely loyal to their city, believing it to surpass in beauty, culture, and prosperity all others in the Roman world.[2] They were, on the whole, a luxury-loving people; for those who chose a dissipated way of life, Antioch offered numerous distractions. As far as religion was concerned, the population was largely Christian;[3] many of them perhaps not as satisfactory in their practice of the

119

Christian life as their more devout spiritual leaders wished, but Christian nonetheless.

Julian could scarcely have picked a more unlikely spot for his headquarters. Why he selected Antioch is, in fact, something of a mystery.[4] Its geographic location had much to recommend it, but this was all, except for the fact that Antioch was the home of a man Julian had never met but whom he had admired vastly ever since his student days: Libanius the rhetor. Julian no doubt looked forward to making the acquaintance of Libanius, and as it turned out, the warm friendship that developed between the young Emperor and the aging professor was one of the few pleasant memories that Julian would have of Antioch. On the other hand, the Syrian city would offer him numerous problems: a first-class crisis resulting from the scarcity of grain, an uncooperative local Senate determined to resist reform, some surprisingly ardent Christians, and a citizenry who, as a whole, simply could not understand their serious-minded Emperor.

The journey from Constantinople to Antioch was a leisurely one. At every important stop along the route, there was the inevitable business of a welcoming ceremony for the Emperor, with sacrifices to the gods and speeches by the provincial dignitaries. Julian seems genuinely to have enjoyed all this: a good speech, he declared, was a far more welcome gift than any number of material treasures.[5] Custom demanded that each municipality he visited should present the Emperor with a golden crown. Julian, who cared very little for crowns but a great deal for custom, strictly limited the amount of gold that might be used in these items, a real relief to the municipal governments.[6]

It was early May of 362 when Julian and his retinue left Constantinople. Having crossed the Bosphoros, the imperial party stopped at Nicomedia, where despite Julian's reluctance to cry, he shed a few "silent tears" for this city of his childhood, now largely in ruins because of a recent earthquake.[7] He awarded generous sums for rebuilding, then traveled on to Ancyra and from there to Pessinus, the location of the most famous shrine of Cybele, the Great Mother goddess.[8]

Julian remained at Pessinus for several days, and it was likely

there that he composed his long (about 30 pages in modern type)
prose "Hymn to the Mother of the Gods." This treatise, while
it is one of the most interesting of Julian's theological writings,
shows in its lack of organization clear signs of the haste in which
he wrote. "Nay, I had not even planned to [write it] until I
asked for these writing tablets,"[9] he admits, but once begun he
must have worked in a frenzy of activity since he completed
the entire work in one night. As has been noted, Julian believed
that the myths of the gods contained hidden meanings, and the
purpose of this "hymn" is largely to show that the myth of Cybele's love for Attis, the infidelity of Attis, his subsequent castration,
and eventual rebirth are allegories of the sinful nature of mind
and the Great Mother's restorative powers. It is worth noticing
how Julian interpreted the entire Cybele myth on a spiritual
plane; there is no place in his scheme of things for the gross and
orgiastic practices sometimes connected with the legend and
worship of the Great Mother. The treatise includes, too, an
interesting historical digression on the introduction of the
Cybele cult in the city of Rome, and a detailed description of
dietary laws prescribed for Cybele (and Mithra's) devotees.[10]
Perhaps most significant of all, however, is Julian's closing
prayer to the goddess; here, laying aside all the complexities
of Neoplatonism, he voices his hopes for his people and himself
as he strove to carry forward the great reform he had undertaken:

Grant to the Roman people in general that they may cleanse themselves of the stain of impiety; grant them a blessed lot, and help
them to guide their Empire for many thousands of years! And for
myself, grant me as fruit of my worship of thee that I may have
true knowledge in the doctrines about the gods. . . . And in all that
I undertake, in the affairs of the state and the army, grant me virtue
and good fortune, and that the close of my life may be painless
and glorious, in the good hope that it is to you, the gods, that
I journey![11]

From Pessinus, Julian and his retinue returned to Ancyra. All
throughout his journey across Asia Minor, Julian was continually
being approached by individuals with cases to appeal to him
personally. Many of these, he found, were men who wanted

exemptions from his new policy of strictly enforced curial duties. Toward such petitioners, Julian was inclined to be severe: there was to be very few exceptions to his rule that those born to the curial class must serve, though Ammianus Marcellinus reports that there were some instances where a judicious bribe bought exemption. In spite of this, Ammianus on the whole found Julian a conscientious judge, one who refused to listen to malicious informers and who strove to render justice impartially.[12] The Emperor, it seems, was so concerned that he might lose his temper and act with a haste he would later regret, that he asked his close confidants to restrain him if ever he seemed inclined to be overly harsh.

As it turned out, in his efforts to avoid excessive cruelty, Julian came to have a reputation for abundant mercy, displayed at the most unexpected times. One famous incident of this sort took place a few months later when he was at Antioch. He was on his way to sacrifice to Zeus on Mount Cassius when he encountered a man lying flat on the ground before him. Inquiry revealed that the abject suppliant was Theodotus of Hierapolis, ex-governor of that town, who, at the time when civil war seemed imminent, had asked Constantius to send Julian's head to Hierapolis for public display. Now Theodotus was living in daily fear for his life and thought best to approach Julian directly and meet his fate. Ammianus records the essence of the Emperor's reply: "I heard of this speech of yours long ago from the mouths of many; but go to your home carefree, relieved of all fear by the mercy of your prince who ... strives to diminish the number of his enemies and increase that of his friends."[13]

Julian's journey across Asia Minor continued on through the provinces of Cappadocia and Cilicia. He seems to have been especially pleased by the welcoming speech of the noted orator Celsus, who was governor of Cilicia and a former fellow student of Julian in Athens. Celsus met the imperial party at the Cilician Gates, at the boundary between his province and Cappadocia, and from there rode in the imperial carriage with Julian to the provincial capital of Tarsus.[14]

Aside from this one mention of the Emperor's "carriage," we have almost no details of the actual mechanics of Julian's trip to Antioch. Nor is it clear how large was the party traveling with the Emperor: there must have been a considerable number, despite his vast cutback of Constantius' household staff. Among the most honored members of his retinue were the philosophers, Priscus and Maximus, and the physician Oribasius. There were also the inevitable bureaucrats, secretaries, attendants and servants of all descriptions.

On July 18, 362, the Emperor and his party entered Antioch.[15] Oddly, for all his interest in festival-days of the various gods, Julian had failed to notice that this was the day of mourning for the death of Adonis, a sort of Syrian counterpart of Attis. The lamentations of the Antiochenes bewailing the death of the god formed an ominous background for the Emperor's entry into the city.

In the days that followed, Julian's superstitious fears seemed well founded. Antioch, supposedly the city of abundance, was suffering the effect of a severe grain shortage. A recent drought had made the last harvest a very poor one, while the presence of vast numbers of soldiers, mustering in the city for the forthcoming Persian campaign, increased the demand for food.[16] It was the sort of problem that occurred frequently in the ancient world, and for which there seemed to be no really satisfactory solution. Modern historians have been quick to point out Julian's mistakes in dealing with the crisis and to suggest that he should have tried a rigidly enforced system of rationing.[17] The steps he did take, well intentioned though they were, would prove ineffective and contribute greatly to his unpopularity in Antioch. In fact, had it not been for the grain crisis, Julian and the Antiochenes would have probably gotten along well enough; this problem, far more than any trouble with the Galileans, seems to be the root of Julian's troubles in Antioch.

As a first step, the Emperor promised to remit the city's arrears of tribute, an easing of the tax burden that he hoped would prove a boon to the local economy.[18] Next, pursuing his firm belief that an increased number of men in curial service would help distribute the tax burden more fairly, he requested the Antioch Senate to increase its size to two hundred. Since Julian believed in local autonomy, the senators themselves were entrusted with the selection of their new colleagues. To his dismay, he would soon discover that the new appointees included some of Antioch's shadiest characters, notoriously lacking in business ethics, and likely to practice the same principles in their service of the city.[19]

The grain crisis, moreover, showed no signs of abating. Dealers who had grain hoarded it; prices were rising at fantastic rates. The citizenry jeered at their Emperor when he made public appearances; it was plainly his duty to do something.

Julian's first action was to ask the grain dealers for a voluntary lowering of prices,[20] a move which seems to indicate a strangely unrealistic faith in human nature. As an effort to do his part in easing the crisis, at about this same time he reduced the number of his household staff still further, sending away from Antioch those *domesticii* not absolutely necessary for the maintenance of his court.[21]

If Julian hoped that voluntary efforts would solve the crisis, he was doomed to disappointment. By October, prices were still vastly inflated and famine conditions growing more severe. Realizing he could not count on any effective support from the Antioch Senate (whose membership included many of the profiteers who were making a fortune out of the crisis), Julian issued an edict setting a maximum price for grain.[22] It was a fair figure, low enough to promise relief, especially since he also began importing grain from Egypt, wheat that was his personal property as Roman Emperor. This he would place on the market at the low price specified in his edict.[23] In addition to this generous provision, Julian also reduced local taxes by twenty percent and provided that certain municipal lands be transferred to small landowners.[24]

Contrary to the Emperor's fond hopes, the grain crisis did not disappear. The municipal lands, it seems, came into the hands, not of the needy, but of undeserving profiteers so that Julian had to revoke the grants. Even worse, the maximum price edict was a complete failure, so much so that Libanius, looking back on it in later years (and ever reluctant to find any fault with Julian), declared it must have been inspired by an evil *daimon*.[25]

Then at the height of his frustration with the local government authorities, Julian ordered the arrest of some of the leading senators. This, it seems, was a move designed merely to humiliate and frighten the victims, for they suffered no actual harm and were released after only a few hours.[26]

It is easy to criticize Julian for failure as an economist: whatever his varied talents in philosophy, soldiery and administration, he seemingly lacked even an elementary grasp of the laws of supply and demand. His edict placed no limit on the amount of grain that might be bought at the authorized price. The immediate result was the buying up of huge quantities by wealthy speculators, who then transported it out into the country and resold it to ordinary citizens at a much inflated price.[27] The modern critic of Julian is quick to suggest that he should have imposed a strict limit on the amount of grain each individual could purchase, yet this remedy fails to account for the numerous slaves, freedmen, clients and other assorted henchmen whom the speculators no doubt would have rounded up to make purchases for them, had there been a per capita limit. While Julian may have lacked economic sense, he was always willing to listen to advice; apparently no one at the time considered a per capita rationing system a viable possibility. As in almost all time of shortages, ancient and modern, profiteers managed to find ways to enrich themselves at the expense of ordinary people.

It was Julian's misfortune that these ordinary people failed to understand the efforts he had made on their behalf. Angered by the emptiness of their pantries and their purses, the Antiochenes focused their disgust on the peculiar young man whom they felt had brought these troubles upon them. It was typical of the lighthearted city that most of their hostility was released in the form of mockery; no one seemed to fear jibing at the Emperor publicly. He was, after all, notorious for allowing freedom of speech. Julian, extremely sensitive to criticism, listened; one wonders how the worst of it reached him unless he deliberately sought it out. He saw himself scorned, and was deeply hurt and depressed.

One facet of Julian that lent itself particularly to the levity of the Antiochenes was his appearance. His beard (long, and getting longer) was hopelessly unfashionable; he was, they said, a "billy goat."[28] His posture was bad: he loped along like a monkey.[29] He simply had no style; such a contrast to the elegant Constantius (whom the Antiochenes loved, especially now that he was dead and gone) could scarcely be imagined. With a little effort, Julian could have been a most attractive young man; the people's criticisms, however, seemed to have produced the opposite effect. He became more set in his ways than ever, more determined to cling to his own peculiar habits of fashion.

Julian's asceticism was, if anything, even more incomprehensible to the Antiochenes than his unkempt appearance.[30] His daily routine was completely lacking in the pleasures they valued so highly. He had no sex life. He disliked the theater; especially the broad farces and comedies that Antioch found so diverting. He disliked the "games" and horseraces at the circus; when protocol demanded his attendance, he brought along something to read so as not to waste his valuable time. His imperial table offered only the plainest fare; philosophical conversation was valued more than food, so much so that even his philosopher friend Libanius did not look forward to eating at Julian's table.[31] Whatever did the Emperor do for pleasure? the Antiochenes wondered. He made speeches. He conducted lavish ceremonies in honor of the various gods. He wrote; he philosophized. And for all his warmheartedness and longing to be understood, the Emperor Julian remained a stranger to most of the people of Antioch: a grotesque figure whom they could only laugh at; one whom they would never comprehend.

However low his popularity fell with most of his subjects in Antioch, the Emperor was not totally isolated there. For one thing, he was on the best of terms with his maternal uncle Julian, whom he appointed Count of the East and who came with his wife to Antioch to take up his duties there. "Uncle Julian of the East," while apparently devoted to his nephew's best interests, was not one to help his sinking popularity. A one-time Christian, he had promptly "converted" to paganism, though his wife, it seems, remained Christian. Uncle Julian's severity as an administrator was a further mark against him and a strange contrast to the more humane Emperor who nonetheless seems to have trusted him completely. When Uncle Julian died in late 362, there was widespread rejoicing in the city, particularly among the Christians, who gleefully described the distressing symptoms of his last illness as sure signs of divine punishment.[32] For the Emperor, his uncle's death meant the loss of his last close relative. His longing for kinsmen would cause him to promote the fortunes of a rather distant cousin, Procopius, who would in turn fail him badly in the upcoming Persian invasion.

Antioch also provided Julian with one who was to be among the most enthusiastic of his friends and admirers, Libanius. Libanius of Antioch was a colorful character, uncommonly so for one who followed the dignified profession of rhetor. His own voluminous writings provide the best source of information about him and unwittingly reveal his knack for getting into trouble, even when his intentions were of the best. Hostile, jealous gossips whispered about unsavory (and perhaps unfounded) scandals of his younger days;[33] by his late forties, however, he had risen to a position of eminence in his native city. If he still had a tendency to be a storm-center, so much the better for attracting students. Libanius' classes were unquestionably popular; with him, the potentially boring subject of rhetoric was never dull. And though he was outspokenly and fervently pagan, the young men who studied under his direction included many Christians, among them the future patriarch and saint, John Chrysostom.

Whatever may have been the amorous escapades of Libanius' youth he was, by the time of Julian's visit to Antioch happily settled with one mistress, an arrangement that to the Antiochenes seemed the essence of respectability.[34] It was clever, too, since by his refusal to legalize his relationship with the woman, he was sparing their little son Kimon from the future threat of curial duty. Kimon could not have avoided this obligation had he been of legitimate birth, for Libanius was wealthy by inheritance and only because he was a teacher was he exempt from curial service himself.

It was Libanius' passionate devotion to the old religion and to Hellenic learning that attracted him to Julian: these, plus the rumor that told him how Julian as a student in Nicomedia some years earlier had admired his style and surreptitiously bought copies of his lecture notes.[35] Libanius was most susceptible to flattery: Julian the Emperor was in a very real sense his former student, even if he had never attended his classes in person. Consequently, Libanius was eager to meet Julian and was among the delegation who greeted him at the village of Phlegrae, three miles north of Antioch, on the day of his arrival. Apparently Julian at first did not recognize the famous rhetor of Antioch, but once apprised of his identity, he conversed with him pleasantly and (if one can trust the rose-colored memories of the first encounter in Libanius' *Autobiography*) also told him he was looking forward to hearing him deliver an oration very soon.[36]

In the days that followed, Libanius eagerly waited for Julian to summon him to the imperial court, while the Emperor waited for him to come uninvited. There was considerable misunderstanding on this matter, smoothed over only when Julian sent him an official invitation.[37] Once the difficulties of the first visit were over, Libanius was an almost daily visitor. Apparently he did not relish Julian's daily sacrifices to the gods in the imperial garden and avoided attendance there. The rhetor's peculiar eating habits and dislike of certain foods, as well as his perennial complaints of ill health, caused him to refuse many invitations to dine with the Emperor.[38] In spite of all of this, they became close confidants, or so at least Libanius would have us believe. Julian continued to admire his speeches. On one occasion (New Year's Day of 363 when Julian and Salustius of Gaul were installed as consuls for the year), Libanius presented an oration that moved the Emperor to rise from his seat, wave his arms and flap his cloak enthusiastically in the breeze. These gestures of approval were typical of students and somewhat lacking in imperial dignity, but Libanius, needless to add, was delighted.[39]

Among the other "orations" Libanius composed for Julian is a plea for the reinstatement in office of a certain Aristophanes of Corinth who had been banished from his home city by Constans and then had lost his government post in Egypt in the reign of Constantius.[40] Aristophanes, it seems, was the victim of slanderers, including the notorious informer Paul the Chain, and Libanius promised to intervene on his behalf with the new Emperor Julian.

Obviously Julian was aware that Libanius was at work on

this appeal for Aristophanes. In an amusing letter, Julian declared he was growing old waiting for Libanius to complete the discourse and send it to him: after all he had waited for it three days.[41] With this admonition, Libanius decided to hurry. The appeal "To Julian on Behalf of Aristophanes" was promptly dispatched to the Emperor, who found it so interesting that he read most of it before breakfast. "Your speeches are not only prized by genuine Hellenes today but will still be prized in future times, unless I am mistaken in my verdict,"[42] he wrote to Libanius, a compliment that undoubtedly made the rhetor feel his efforts were worthwhile. As for Aristophanes, he was in due time pardoned and restored to a government office. In later years, deeply grateful to Julian's memory, he seems to have played an important part in collecting and preserving many of the Emperor's letters and other writings.[43]

On one point, however, Julian and Libanius remained irreconcilably at odds. Libanius loved Antioch: his native city, with all its flaws, was to him the garden city of the earth, and he was always ready to speak on Antioch's behalf to the Emperor whose dislike for the place was growing deeper with each passing day. Eventually (probably in February of 363) Julian committed to writing his bitter disillusionment with Antioch. The result was "The Misopogon" (or "Beard Hater"), a strangely undignified satirical pamphlet in which Julian gives full vent to his wounded pride and uncomprehending anger. The little treatise is like nothing else ever to come from the pen of a Roman Emperor. With biting irony, he even satirizes himself at points, and though the work contains, too, some passages of deep beauty, the overall effect is unworthy of the better side of Julian's nature. Libanius, though he would find much to praise in the literary style, cannot have been pleased by this literary memorial of Julian's running feud with the Antiochenes. Nonetheless, in spite of their differences of opinion on the city which was so dear to Libanius' heart, the Emperor and the professor remained on the best of terms, each genuinely admiring the other's abilities and respectfully tolerating his peculiarities.

When Julian left Antioch in the early spring of 363, he promised to write Libanius faithfully the details of his Persian adventure, and the Emperor's last letter is, in fact, one addressed to his friend.[44] Within a few more weeks Julian was dead, and there was none to mourn him so deeply as Libanius of Antioch. For the rest of Libanius' life (and he lived to be a very old man) it was his greatest pride that the Emperor Julian had been his friend. Forever loyal to his memory, he tended to remember only the best, the happiest, the most praiseworthy of details. His later writings on the subject of Julian are a monument to the old teacher's devotion to the young man whom he loved as if he were his own son, the young man who was also his sovereign, and who, with all the power of the Roman state in his hands, had seemed about to restore the world of Libanius' fondest dreams. It is a wonder that the Christian Byzantine copyists of the Middle Ages preserved Libanius' "Julianic Orations": how could such praises be heaped upon the dreadful "Apostate"? On the other hand, could Julian himself have read Libanius' memorials, no doubt he would have been convinced that great good came out of Antioch after all.

CHAPTER 17

Julian and the Galileans

WHENEVER Julian spoke of the Christians, he always called them "Galileans," to emphasize, he said, that they drew their origin from an obscure and rustic province.[1] The use of this term, which he considered reproachful and degrading, was but one of Julian's ways of showing his vigorous contempt for the Church to which he had belonged in his early youth.

There is, however, a vast difference between imperial scorn and persecution. Julian, who was both naturally inclined to mercy and wise enough to realize that persecution seldom achieves its desired ends, proclaimed often throughout his reign that he respected the rights of all to freedom of worship. "I affirm by the gods that I do not wish the Galileans to be either put to death or unjustly beaten, or to suffer any other injury," he declared, "nevertheless I do assert absolutely that the god-fearing [Hellenes] must be preferred to them. For through the folly of the Galileans almost everything has been overturned, whereas by the grace of the gods we are all preserved."[2]

These few sentences reveal a great deal about Julian's attitude toward Christianity. The adherents of the Galilean faith with their fanatical and intolerant ways, he believed, in their half-century of power had undermined the positive values of the classical world. They were, he frequently remarked, like people diseased, to be pitied rather than blamed. They were "insane," and needed help, not punishment.[3] Those who eagerly sought martyrdom must be possessed by evil *daimones*, so irrational was their desire "to court death in the belief that they will fly up to heaven."[4] These would-be martyrs, Julian discovered, were numerous, and he had no desire to gratify their wishes. He declared frequently his intention that no Christian

131

under his rule need face death for his faith, and indeed among the early church historians who report the activities of the "Apostate," there is the frequent complaint that Julian denied many Christians the privilege of martyrdom.[5]

Nor were the Christians particularly pleased by Julian's emphasis on religious liberty. Soon after his arrival in Constantinople, he summoned a delegation of Christian bishops to his palace.[6] Arians, previously favored by Constantius, and Orthodox, recalled from exile, were both represented as well as other smaller Christian sects, each convinced that all the others were heretics and each hoping for some sign of imperial favor. Julian made it amply clear that to him they were all the same. As Ammianus commented, he "politely advised them to lay aside their differences and each fearlessly and without opposition to observe his own beliefs."[7] Julian knew from experience, Ammianus adds, "that no wild beasts are such enemies to mankind as are most Christians in their deadly hatred of one another."[8] Left to their own devices, the Emperor was confident they would not "lay aside their differences," but might instead, by their bitter animosities, undermine the Church from within.

It was also early in his reign, when he was still in Constantinople, that Julian had a particularly unpleasant encounter with Bishop Maris of Chalcedon, a happening that the church historians relate with zest, and one that (if authentic) suggests a great deal about the character of the Galilean opposition. Maris, old and blind, was conducted into the Emperor's presence and fearlessly began to reproach Julian for his apostasy. To this attack, Julian replied with uncharacteristic rudeness, "This Galilean God of yours will never cure you." "I thank God for bereaving me of my sight," Maris retorted, "that I might not behold the face of one who has fallen into such awful impiety." Julian, the story continues, said nothing more.[9] Such stubborn Galileans as Maris, it is plain, were not to be convinced by argument.

On the other hand, at the outset of his reign, Julian clearly hoped to remain on good terms with Christian dignitaries whenever possible. One whom he may have hoped would take a lead in promoting such peaceful coexistence was Basil of Caesarea, the Emperor's onetime fellow student in Athens, now a Christian bishop. Julian wrote to Basil, urging him to visit the court, and recalling that although they had their differences of opinion, as friends they might still "refute and criticize one another with appropriate frankness whenever it is necessary."[10] Basil did not accept this invitation, nor did Bishop Aetius (Gallus' former friend) who received a similar summons.[11]

Meanwhile, Christians throughout the Empire were beginning to feel the effects of the withdrawal of imperial favors from the organized church. Gone were the immunities from curial service that Christian clerics had enjoyed;[12] gone the free transportation in the state post wagons; gone, too, the hope of generous contributions from the imperial treasury. Instead, Julian was pronouncing such strange orders as his demand to the Arian Christians of Cyzicus that they rebuild at their own expense a Novatian Christian church building they had destroyed in Constantius' day.[13] All this imperial impartiality in regard to the rival sects was proving indeed a bitter pill for many Galileans, especially those who enjoyed being on the winning side.

It was no surprise that Julian soon found he was winning a substantial number of converts to Hellenism. Because his own religious longings seem to have been genuinely satisfied by the return to the old gods, and because he naively expected that many, if sufficiently enlightened, would share his point of view, the Emperor at first seemed pleased with his missionary efforts. Confident that the Galileans who were converting to Hellenic faith were being won by reasoned argument and persuasion, he may have failed to realize at the outset how many of his new pagans were mere timeservers, with no deep religious instincts of any sort. There was, for instance, Julian's old teacher, Hecebolius, once a Christian, now seemingly an ardent pagan (but after Julian's death eager to become a Christian again.)[14] There was the Emperor's own uncle, Count Julian of the East, whose wife (a firmer Christian than he) refused to make the switch to Hellenism. There were men who accepted pagan priesthoods, but whose wives and children remained Christian.[15] Gradually the reality of the situation became very clear to Julian: like many other sovereigns of history, in fact very like his own predecessors Constantine and Constantius, he was attracting converts mainly from among those individuals who would do whatever they thought necessary to stay in their Emperor's good graces. "The Hellenic religion does not yet prosper as I desire, and it is the fault of those who profess it," he wrote, probably sometime during his trip from Constantinople to Antioch in the early summer of 362.[16]

Julian was distinctly unsatisfied; his missionary instincts frustrated. Idealistic to the point of unreality, he wanted to win converts, especially Galileans, back to the "old religion" because he genuinely believed it to be the better way. As for those who were determined to remain Christian, he had promised if they would simply mind their own business all would be well. He would say this repeatedly throughout his reign, and for the most part he would hold firmly to his stated principle. It is also true, however, that as the months passed and Julian's attempts at universal tolerance were met by intolerant rebuffs from the Galileans, he would grow somewhat more severe. As his friend Eutherius had warned him several years earlier, one of Julian's worst shortcomings was the fact that he was not always consistent in his actions.[17] So it would be with his religious policy. In his eagerness to assure the triumph of Hellenism, he was not above resorting to occasional promises of rewards to towns displaying enthusiasm for the gods, and threats to those who failed to do so. "I am ready to assist Pessinus if her people succeed in winning the favor of the Mother of the Gods," he wrote to Arsacius, the high priest of Galatia, apparently soon after his visit to Cybele's shrine. "But if they neglect her, they are not only not free from blame, but . . . let them beware of reaping my enmity also. . . . Therefore persuade them if they claim my patronage that the whole community must become suppliants of the Mother of the Gods."[18]

Similarly, Julian offered bonuses to his soldiers if they burned incense and made libations to the gods and many were glad to accept the offer.[19] "Persuasion" was giving way to bribery, and Julian himself, in his better moments, knew there must be a better, more effective way.

In the early summer of 362, Julian decided upon a repressive measure which he hoped would curtail the spread of Christianity through one of its major channels. No longer, the Emperor decreed, would Galileans be permitted to teach in any of the schools of the Empire. It was a harsh policy, one that even Ammianus Marcellinus (with all his admiration for Julian and his not especially warm feelings for Christians) condemned as unfair.[20] Throughout the Roman world numerous teachers faced the choice of losing their jobs or renouncing their faith. Reaction was divided: it would be interesting to know which category was the larger, but there seems to be no contemporary information on this point. Many Christian teachers (with the Emperor's approval) merely gave up their careers in the fields of rhetoric, literature, and philosophy and switched to private teaching of Christian theology. "Let them betake themselves to the churches of the Galileans to expound Matthew and Luke," Julian stated.[21] What the Emperor wanted to stop (and did stop to a certain extent in the one year of life remaining to him) was the teaching of the classical heritage by men who refused to accept the old Hellenic values or way of life, including reverence for the gods.

Probably realizing that there would be storms of protest over his discrimination against Christian teachers, Julian embodied his pronouncement against them in a lengthy rescript in which he attempts to justify his point of view on the entire matter. The document reveals Julian at his most logical: "When a man thinks one thing and teaches his pupils another, in my opinion he fails to educate exactly in proportion as he fails to be an honest man," he argues.[22] How can the Galileans, who openly despise the old gods, rightly teach any of the literature and philosophy of ancient Greece? "It seems to me absurd that men should teach what they do not believe to be sound," he comments.[23] The rescript then continues with his expression of hope that Galilean teachers' ears and tongues will be "born anew" to the old Hellenic faith, as no doubt many were who valued their jobs more than their faith.

Closely related to the ban on Christian teachers was the problem of whether Christian students might attend Hellenic schools. The inaccuracy of several of the early church historians is clearly seen in their allegation that Julian barred all Christians from seeking classical education.[24] On the contrary, the Emperor stated in his rescript: "Any youth who wishes to attend the schools is not to be excluded." What better way to win

some individuals away from the Galilean "disease," Julian
thought, than to fill their minds with Hellenism when they were
very young? This was, after all, the way through which he was
led to make his own lifelong commitment to the old gods.

What might have been the results of Julian's school law had
it remained in effect for any length of time are conjectural at
best. Apart from the strictly religious side of the matter, he
seems to have envisioned a well-organized, carefully regulated
system of government-funded education on a larger scale than
anything previously attempted in the Roman world.[25] In fact,
if we can believe Gregory Nazianzen, it was the Emperor's plan
to establish schools in every town.[26] As it turned out, Julian
would have no time to realize these dreams.

In the few months of life still remaining to him, however,
he would have ample opportunity to face the fact that his hopes
for peaceful co-existence with the more ardent Christians had
little real possibility for success. More and more disturbing
reports were reaching him: pagans and Christians fighting each
other in various towns of the Empire, with dreadful atrocities
being committed by both sides. Obviously Julian could do little
to curtail such incidents in remote corners of the Empire. Local
officials would have to assume these responsibilities and, as time
would prove, it was a task they handled very badly.

On the other hand, a somewhat more encouraging pattern
seemed to be present in the army. Many (perhaps the majority)
of Julian's forces were nominal Christians, yet there was apparently no widespread disaffection among them. While worship
of the gods was encouraged by the Emperor, the later Christian
historians who indicate that he forced all his troops to abjure
Christianity[27] have clearly lost sight of the fact that among them
were three future emperors, Jovian, Valentinian and Valens,
all Christians who made no attempt to conceal their adherence
to the Galilean faith. If among the soldiery Christians and Hellenes could cooperate for the common cause of the Empire, why
not in civilian society as well?

Why not? Because from Julian's point of view, many Galileans were fanatics, intent not only upon clinging to their own
opinions, but forcing them on everyone else. These were the
people who must be made to see the logical weakesses of their

dogmas. After he left Constantinople for Antioch, this thought occupied his attention increasingly: he would reach his opposition through his writing; he would convince them by logic. With this goal in mind he began preparing his treatise, "Against the Galileans," which he completed in Antioch in the winter of 362/363.[28]

Only fragments of this treatise have survived, largely in the form of lengthy quotations in a work by the fifth-century Bishop Cyril of Alexandria, who wrote with the goal of refuting Julian's statements. There was probably much more that Cyril thought too dangerous or too impious to quote. What remains, however, is still a revealing presentation of some of Julian's major objections to Galilean teachings. He attacks particularly the inconsistencies in both the Old and New Testaments, the extreme literal-mindedness with which Christians seemed determined to interpret these scriptures, and their lack of logic in explaining away contradictions.

The Galilean faith, says Julian is "a fiction of man," a "monstrous tale" if taken literally.[29] Unfortunately, in the extant text there is very little on the subject of the life of Christ. From what remains, Julian seems to have accepted as authentic the gospel accounts of Christ's acts of healing, but he did not consider them particularly remarkable: the Roman world was full of wonder-workers. Clearly, Julian was little impressed with the ethical content of Christ's teaching. He states briefly that it is not at all certain whether Jesus taught "purity of life," but he does not elaborate the point.[30] The reputed command of Christ to his disciples, "Sell what you have and give it to the poor" aroused Julian to stinging satire. "Can anyone quote a more statesmanlike ordinance than this?" he asks in obvious disgust, adding that if everyone followed it, there would be only sellers, no buyers, and "no city, no nation, not a single family will hold together."[31]

It is clear, however, that in the portions of the treatise still extant, Julian's animosity is not really directed toward the historical person, Jesus of Nazareth, so much as toward the claims the Galileans make about him. Only John among the New Testament writers actually says that Jesus Christ was God, Julian points out, a doctrine that directly contradicts the strict monothe-

ism of the Old Testament, but that Christians have accepted
enthusiastically.[32] While Julian himself had no objection to the
idea of more than one God, Christians who, he said, worshipped
"two or three" gods were betraying the regulations of Moses
and all the Hebrew prophets which they claimed as part of their
scriptures. Besides, how could a man born only a little more
than three hundred years ago be the Creator God? Julian
asks. Jesus was, moreover, born a Roman subject, not a citizen,
but an inhabitant of a defeated province, which Julian seems to
consider distinctly ungodlike. In his life on earth, Jesus could
not convert many of his own friends and kinsmen in Galilee;
this too, seemed unlikely if he were indeed God.[33]

As for the Christian claim that the Old Testament was full
of predictions of Christ's coming, Julian was not impressed.
Some of these passages, he pointed out, were actually references
to King David or some other figure, or Israel as a whole people.[34]
Since he knew the Old Testament only through Greek translation, Julian was willing to concede that Isaiah had predicted
the birth of "Immanuel" from a virgin, but, he argued, nowhere
does Isaiah say that Immanuel is God or God's Son.[35] And if
the Galileans are so intent on the doctrine that Christ was born
of a virgin, then why did Matthew and Luke go to such great
lengths to trace the ancestry of Mary's husband Joseph back to
King David? Moreover, Julian noticed that the genealogies in
these two gospels are completely different, so obviously at least
one is false.[36]

Because most of the major events of the gospels, especially
the crucifixion and resurrection, are mentioned in the extant
portions of "Against the Galileans," we must depend on small
clues to determine Julian's attitude toward them. At the outset,
when he states that the Galilean faith is "a fiction of man" and
a "monstrous tale," it is fairly clear that he intends these descriptions to apply to the dogmas most central to Christianity. The
Emperor obviously did not accept the Christian view of the
resurrection; the Jesus whom the Galileans worshipped was
"the corpse of a Jew."[37] Jesus himself had said that tombs were
"full of uncleanness," but his inconsistent followers turned them
into holy shrines, while the veneration of Christian martyrs was
in Julian's opinion, merely the adding of many additional

"corpses" to the original one. The martyrs, Julian felt, were "wretched men" undeserving of the "worship" accorded them.[38] No doubt his own unusually strong aversion to funeral rites made the veneration of saints' bones a particularly distasteful cult to him. Nor did Julian understand the Galilean tendency to "adore the wood of the cross." This relic, only recently brought to light, was the object of much superstitious attachment. The symbol of the cross also appeared on the doors of many Christian homes; and it was the sign regularly used by Christians to ward off demons. All such practices Julian considered complete nonsense.[39]

In several passages of "Against the Galileans," the apostle Paul appears as the special target of Julian's ire. Paul "surpassed all the magicians and charlatans of every place and every time." He was inconsistent; he "keeps changing his views about God." The converts Paul made were admittedly sinners of the worst sort, Julian argues, yet the apostle praises them highly in spite of their sins.[40] Paul (and many other Galileans) taught that Christian baptism cleansed individuals from sin; the result of this doctrine was the attracting of numerous converts who were simply looking for license to commit the most outrageous acts and then have them painlessly wiped away.[41]

The idea that most Christians fell far short of the virtues they professed to emulate, and that they were in fact morally lax, is one that Julian returns to in some of his other writings. In his little satire "The Caesars," an otherwise lighthearted (and, for Julian, surprisingly frivolous) spoof on his imperial predecessors, he stresses the idea that his uncle Constantine became a Christian in order to win easy forgiveness for his many moral lapses.[42] Julian is most unfair to Constantine (whom he never really knew): most early sources indicate that Constantine was a strict moralist, and aside from the series of tragedies that led him to order the death of his Empress Fausta, there is scarcely a breath of scandal in his private life.

From Julian's point of view, however, Christianity remained a religion for the most degenerate, and unregenerated, sinners—an easy way out. "Everyone who possessed even a small fraction of innate virtue has speedily abandoned your impiety," he remarks in "Against the Galileans," one of his most sweepingly unguarded statements.[43]

Then there is the matter of persecution. Although neither Jesus nor Paul recommended such things, the Galileans, once they gained the upper hand in the Roman Empire under Constantine, began persecuting pagans. Moreover, as Julian had ample occasion to observe, they frequently persecuted each other.[44] In Constantius' reign, he recalls elsewhere, "many whole communities of those who are called 'heretics' were actually butchered . . . villages were sacked and completely devastated."[45] In light of such atrocities (and probably also with the inescapable memory of the tragedies of his own childhood), he asks: "How did the Word of God take away sin, when it caused many to commit the sin of killing their fathers, and many their children?"[46] Julian, however, was wise enough to see that it would be beneath his dignity to base his critique of Christianity on the shortcomings of Constantius. "Against the Galileans" was designed as a universal work, and there is no place in it for personal invectives against his Christian predecessor.

In several sections of "Against the Galileans," Julian reveals that one of his strongest objections to Christianity was one he shared with many educated Hellenes: the extremely literal manner in which the Galileans interpreted the Bible. Since the stories he examines in detail belong to the Old Testament, they are perhaps better considered in connection with Julian's views of Judaism. It is important to note, however, that Julian's alienation from Christianity was very closely related to his inability to take certain Biblical stories in both Testaments as factual accounts. Too often, scholars in analyzing Julian's distaste for the Church have failed to see the significance of this factor. Without denying that the tragedies of his childhood would make him naturally hostile to the religion of those who were to blame for these dreadful events, it is also important to realize that Julian felt the need for a personal commitment that was intellectually satisfying. Greek mythology, he admitted, included many "incredible and monstrous stories,"[47] but they were not to be taken literally, and this point for him made a vast difference. He was an intensely religious man, but his religion was clothed in Neoplatonic logic; he could not make the leap of faith that Christians demanded. To a modern critic, Neoplatonism and the practices of theurgy that went with it seem far from logical, and Julian's strongly superstitious nature is no more "enlightened" than that of the most literal-minded Galilean. But from Julian's point of view, he had aligned himself on the side of reason; the incomprehensible, the objectionable, whatever did not seem to belong to the beautiful scheme of things that he envisioned could be classified as "allegory." It is intriguing to speculate how in another century, among Christians of a less "fundamentalist" outlook, Julian might have found the Galilean faith far less repellent than he did.

CHAPTER 18

Julian and the Jews

INTERESTING as a by-product of "Against the Galileans"
is the rich insight it provides into the Emperor Julian's
opinions of Judaism. For all his detailed knowledge of the Old
Testament, his views of the Hebrew religion are a curious mix-
ture, based partially on genuine admiration and partially, too,
on his assumption that all non-Christians were potential allies
in the cause of Hellenism.

The faithful adherence with which most Jews of his time
practiced their ancient dietary restrictions elicited Julian's enthusiastic praise. Those Jews who were "so ardent in their
belief that they would choose to die for it" rather than trangress
the Torah, he considered a striking contrast to many apa-
thetic Hellenes of his time.[1] Respect for "the customs of the
forefathers" was very much a part of the spirit of dedication
to duty that Julian longed to cultivate throughout his Empire,
and the Jews, he felt, possessed this virtue in abundance. Much
to be praised also was the spirit of charity with which the
Jews looked after their own people; the ill and the aged were
never left homeless among them; there were no Jewish beggars.[2]
Here too were ideals the Hellenes would do well to imitate.

Turning from day-to-day practices to questions of theology,
Julian thought Judaism considerably more puzzling, and though
he found much that he admired, there was also much he could
not accept. The idea that the Jews were the Chosen People he
considered particularly incomprehensible. It simply could not
be, he reasoned, that God would leave the rest of the human
race in ignorance and darkness for thousands of years and "save
only that one little tribe which less than two thousand years
before had settled in one part of Palestine."[3] The only satisfactory solution that he could find for this dilemma was one that

was, of course, completely unacceptable to the Jews of his time: that their God was a national god, one among many.

As further argument against the "Chosen People" theory, Julian pointed out how, from the standpoint of a Graeco-Roman like himself, Jewish accomplishments in world history seemed small indeed. Babylonians, Egyptians and Phoenicians had made important mathematical and scientific discoveries which they had passed on to the Greeks, but the Jews had contributed nothing in these areas. Militarily, they had been conquered often; in his own time they were subjects of Rome. Never in their history, he argued, could one find a great military man: "Point out to me among the Hebrews a single general like Alexander or Caesar!" he challenged.[4] (One can only wonder what might have been his reaction had someone reminded him of the Maccabees.) In the realm of philosophical thought, he went on, the Jews could offer nothing to compare with the great writings of Plato and many other notable Greeks. It made no impression on Julian to bring up the Hebrew prophets for comparison at this point. The prophets, he felt, were vague and since he knew them only through Greek translation, he considered them lacking in literary style. They were, moreover, often mistaken in their predictions, and in some of their utterances sounded like "silly old women."[5]

Turning to the creation story in Genesis, Julian also found much here that he considered highly unsatisfactory. If all mankind were descended from Adam and Eve, how can we account for so many racial and national differences?[6] Though he strongly believed in a sense of universal kinship among mankind, he also accepted Plato's theory that there were many sets of "first parents," not just one pair in the Garden of Eden. The Adam and Eve story he felt must be taken as "a myth that involves some secret interpretations;" otherwise it was absolutely blasphemous, implying as it did that God was both ignorant of the sin Eve and Adam were about to commit, and envious of their attempt to gain knowledge.[7] Besides, Julian adds with a touch of humor, what language are we to suppose the serpent spoke? Among other sections of the early chapters of Genesis that aroused his suspicions was the story of the Tower of Babel and the confusion of tongues, an account which he deems obviously impossible.[8]

In one section of "Against the Galileans" (where on most points, despite many criticisms, the Jews still compare favorably to the Christians), Julian reflects in detail on the Ten Commandments. Eight of them, he says, are really universal: Moses' distinct contributions have to do with keeping the Sabbath day and worshipping no other gods.[9] While he remains noncommittal on the subject of Sabbath keeping (and probably, given his love of ritual observance, admired it), Julian waxes indignant over the prohibition of the worship of other gods. Moses, he says, explained that the Jewish God was "a jealous God" and this, according to Julian was "a terrible libel upon God."[10] Jealousy was not a praiseworthy concept in human beings; so how could it be a divine quality? Neither could Julian accept the Old Testament descriptions of God as angry or resentful, or inclined to change His mind.

Yet much as he questioned many facets of Old Testament theology, Julian strongly believed that the Jewish God could be correctly described as "most powerful and most good." "He governs this world of sense and is worshipped by us also under other names."[11] These Hellenizing tendencies of the Emperor would have never found acceptance among the Jewish leadership, and what might have been the final outcome of his wishful but ill-founded assumptions had he lived longer is impossible to guess. As it turned out, during his short reign his only demand of the Jewish community was that they pray for him.[12] There was no objection, and the Emperor's relations with the Jews as a whole and particularly with the aged spiritual leader, Patriarch Hillel II, remained excellent. "I revere always the God of Abraham, Isaac, and Jacob," Julian could write in "Against the Galileans," "for they revered a God who was ever gracious to me."[13] In Abraham's practices of divination and augury and in the Jewish custom of offering animal sacrifices, Julian saw a close relation to Hellenic practices and common ground for bringing these widely divergent religions closer together.[14]

Julian was aware, however, that burnt offerings were no longer offered by the Jews of his own time. Several of the Christian historians of the following century indicate that he asked that such sacrifices be resumed.[15] This could not be done, the Jews informed him, since their Temple had been destroyed, an accomplishment of one of Julian's predecessors, Titus, in A.D. 70 and incidentally a fulfillment of many prophecies, including one ascribed to Jesus Christ. Very well, Julian responded, let the Temple be rebuilt.[16]

As it turned out however, the effort to rebuild the Temple was sorely frustrated by a whole series of eerie happenings. Julian does not mention these himself. Since not only his Christian enemies, but also the tolerant pagan Ammianus Marcellinus, saw fit to include them in their historical narratives, they must have some basis in fact, even though details differ widely in various accounts.

Funds for the rebuilding, it seems, were furnished partly by the imperial treasury, partly by the Jews themselves. Supervision of the project was entrusted to Julian's friend Alypius of Antioch (a Gentile and Hellene), while the labor force was to be made up of Jewish volunteers.[17] One account tells of the enthusiasm with which the project began, as even women joined in clearing rubble from the site, carrying away loads of it in their long skirts.[18]

But the project so happily begun was soon to be interrupted. According to most accounts there was an earthquake; Ammianus does not mention this and it may have been so slight that in itself it would have proved no deterrent. Gregory Nazianzen and somewhat later writers such as Socrates, Sozomen and Theodoret have magnified the story by adding various details, including the Jewish builders' running for cover to a nearby Christian church and a mass conversion as mysterious crosses appeared from nowhere, imprinted all over their garments.[19] More credibility attaches to Ammianus' report, though it is almost equally baffling to explain. "Terrifying balls of flame kept bursting forth near the foundations of the temple," he says. Some workmen who ventured too near were burned to death; and finally "the enterprise halted."[20] Ammianus, living in a world where logical explanations were all too rarely sought for unusual happenings, offered none himself. To the superstitious Julian, the news must have seemed a sign from the gods, though how he interpreted it is a matter for conjecture. Later historians have offered a variety of explanations for the balls of fire. Could they have been produced by gas trapped below the ground and now seeping upward through cracks opened by the recent earthquake? Or were they perhaps the work of Christian arsonists determined to protect their cherished belief that the Temple would never be rebuilt? In any case, work was not resumed in the few remaining months of Julian's lifetime, nor would any future Emperor be willing to undertake such a project.

What might have happened had Julian come back from his Persian War? If his "Letter to the Community of the Jews" (a document somewhat suspect as to authenticity) is indeed genuine, we have in it some fascinating hints of Julian's long-range plans for Jerusalem.[21] According to this letter (which well may reflect Julian's ideas even if not in his exact words), the Emperor hoped when he returned from Persia not only to rebuild the Temple but also to undertake a large-scale effort to resettle Jews of the Diaspora in Jerusalem and probably in the surrounding area as well. The *apostolè* tax, levied on Jews everywhere to support their leadership in Palestine was to be abolished, a measure that would certainly be popular with the individuals who had to pay it (even if it might not meet the enthusiastic approval of Patriarch Hillel).

There are good reasons why Julian may well have envisioned this program of fourth-century "Zionism," in addition to the explanation of the early ecclesiastical historians, who saw all of the "Apostate's" favors to the Jews as designed solely to antagonize the Christians. By sponsoring a movement for return to the homeland, he may well have hoped to win support from many of the Jews in the Persian Empire, aid that would be most valuable in his forthcoming campaign.[22] He certainly believed, too, that the resumption of the Jewish cult sacrifices would be a valuable addition to his religious revival.

But as it turned out, Julian never returned from his Persian War, and the Christian emperors who followed him had no sympathy at all for "Zionist" hopes. Thus, even though he lacked understanding of the true spirit of Judaism, Jews of later ages had good cause to look back to the tolerant and generous Emperor Julian as a last beacon light before the coming of many centuries of intolerance, hardship, and persecution in the lands that once comprised his Empire.[23]

CHAPTER 19

Galilean Resistance

JULIAN clearly opposed the entire idea of physical persecution. Both in his repeated statements granting freedom of worship to the Christians and in his generous treatment of the Jews, he is seen as a fair-minded man, true to the best principles of his Roman heritage. The Jews, few in number and victims of many an earlier emperor's discrimination, had cause to remember him gratefully. The Christians, however, at least those fortunate enough not to be considered "heretics" by the ruling clique, had enjoyed the special favor of the emperors for half a century. They were a strong and influential body in the state, convinced that they alone possessed the spiritual truths that really mattered. Trouble was inevitable, trouble too serious to be dealt with by pamphlets alone. (In fact, it seems most doubtful that Julian's treatise "Against the Galileans" swayed a single Christion who was really firm in the faith.)

It is to the question of Julian's relations with the most militant of the Christians that we must now turn. If the Emperor's conduct in this area leaves something to be desired, it is also essential to recall that in the eyes of Julian and his officials, the Galilean militants were disturbers of the public order, dangerous rabble-rousers whose unpatriotic and subversive activities must be curtailed. Their number was small, even with the enlargements of later legend; and while it is sad to find any such incidents in the record of the high-minded and usually just Emperor, it is well to remember that under many another anti-Christian ruler, their number would have been greater.[1]

The earliest writer to present detailed reports of Julian's anti-Christian activities is Gregory Nazianzen, and though he obviously hated him, his nearness in time to Julian's reign suggests that Gregory could not have fabricated his narrative completely.

147

In view of the fact that later historians and legend makers tended more and more to picture Julian as a violent persecutor, Gregory's remark that "he begrudged the honor of martyrdom to our combatants"[2] is particularly significant. Julian, he adds, was "ashamed to use force like a tyrant. . . . He forced with gentleness."[3] Among the crafty acts of the Emperor in his attempt to win converts was a habit of displayig his portrait or statue surrounded by images of the gods, so that whoever "did reverence" to the Emperor's portrait of necessity honored the gods as well.

Libanius corroborates Gregory's report that Julian had an altar for burning incense to the gods set up near his throne when he was distributing bonuses to his soldiers.[4] But while the pagan orator praises this as a splendid tactic for winning the aid of the gods and indicates that it was in any case optional, Bishop Gregory presents the matter in a vastly different light. According to him, the soldiers were required to come forward individually, kiss the Emperor's hand and then, after receiving their gold, burn incense upon the altar, although, he adds, the aspect of idolatry was so well concealed that many Christians did not realize what they were doing and sacrificed inadvertently. If Julian were really intent on winning his troops to the worship of the old gods, it seems extremely odd that it was not made clearer to them what they were doing. Julian possibly looked upon the incense ceremony in this instance as little more than a pledge of allegiance to the Empire. Apparently many Christians did it without a qualm, without realizing, as Gregory says, that they were "losing their souls."[5] Then came trouble. At supper on the evening after one such public donative, some intensely Christian soldiers (who had apparently avoided the ceremony themselves) informed their messmates that those who had burned the incense had betrayed Christ. Some of these men went to Julian straightway and returned his gold, shouting that they were Christians and would rather die than take his tainted money.

Julian, says Gregory, was "exasperated" and banished the offenders.[6] The anecdote is retold in almost identical terms in the *Ecclesiastical History* of Sozomen,[7] but by the time it reached the pen of Bishop Theodoret, additional colorful details had been added. Julian, says Theodoret, threatened to put the men to death, then relented at the last moment, and the soldiers went into exile, sad not to have been martyred.[8]

Another incident in which Julian's opposition comes from the army is found in the *Ecclesiastical History* of Theodoret who derived his information from a sermon by John Chrysostom.[9] The trouble in this case sprang from the fact that Julian had ordered all food sold in the markets of Antioch to be sprinkled with pagan holy water. Christians should not have been bothered by this measure, since the apostle Paul had plainly stated (I Corinthians 10:25) that the believer in Christ might eat such food without penalty. Two soldiers, however, protested loudly: these men, Juventius and Maximus (or Maximinus), were heard to say publicly that the Emperor Julian was "more wicked than all the nations of the earth" for having sprinkled the food. When arrested and brought before him, they continued in their outspoken defiance and were sentenced to death. This event probably occurred in January, 363, and within a few years Antioch was venerating them as martyrs. One may wonder why Julian was so much more severe than usual; the answer probably is that the actions of Juventius and Maximus were regarded as military insubordination of a very serious sort. It has even been suggested that they were actually planning to assassinate the Emperor.[10]

Although there are a few more scattered references to opposition from Christians within Julian's army, these seem less well based on fact. One is the story of two standard-bearers, Bonosus and Maximilian, who refused Julian's order to remove the Christian *labarum* or Chi-Rho symbol from their battle standards.[11] Brought before Julian, they refused to sacrifice to the gods, were tried and beheaded. While Julian's insistence on the removal of the Chi-Rho is well attested historically, Bonosus and Maximilian may simply be characters of legend invented to fit with this particular anti-Christian policy.[12] Likewise tenuous is the reference to two tribunes, Romanus and Vincentius, who were exiled for "designs beyond their power."[13] There is no indication that they were even Christians.

While later Byzantine historians insisted that Julian sought to oust all Christians from his army, they were faced with the unquestioned fact that the next three emperors, Jovian, Valentinian and Valens, had all been officers under Julian, yet all three were Christians. To explain this seeming contradiction, Socrates Scholasticus reports that Jovian offered to resign, but that Julian needed him and exempted him from his general policy.[14]

Of Valentinian a more curious story is told. This future emperor was compelled by Julian to attend a Hellenic worship service. There the priest accidentally splashed one drop of pagan holy water on Valentinian's cloak, whereupon the young Christian officer protested so loudly that Julian banished him.[15] Actually, it seems that Valentinian was at one time banished temporarily by Julian for a military blunder in Gaul that had nothing to do with religion, but he was back in the Emperor's good graces well before the Persian campaign.[16]

The Orthodox historians do not seem to have bothered making elaborate excuses for the future Emperor Valens, probably because he was an Arian, and consequently ranked in their eyes as a horrible heretic, almost as bad as "the Apostate" himself.

From the strange bits and pieces of fact and legend regarding Julian's attempt to Hellenize his troops, several inferences can clearly be drawn. First of all, there remained many Christians in Julian's army throughout his reign: would a predominantly pagan force have chosen the Orthodox Christian Jovian as Julian's successor? Secondly, the vast majority of these Christian troops must have tolerated Julian and been tolerated by him. When there were unpleasant incidents, they were almost invariably caused by hotheaded radicals and except in the most extreme cases, Julian's standard penalty was a sentence of exile.

When dealing with the civilian population, Julian tended to display similar mildness. As Socrates Scholasticus reluctantly admits, Julian abstained "from the excessive cruelties that had formerly been practiced."[17] "He considered that Paganism would be advanced by the exhibition of greater lenity and mildness toward Christians than in ordinary circumstances could be expected," adds Hermias Sozomen.[18]

Long before Socrates and Sozomen undertook their compilations of Julian's various troubles with the Christians, Gregory Nazianzen provides the original source for one of the surprisingly mild actions reported of the Emperor. A certain young man (whom Gregory does not name) was apprehended for destroying an altar of Cybele, the Great Mother goddess, and was brought before Julian. There the intense young Christian launched into an insulting tirade against the Emperor, especially mocking his speeches. Julian did nothing—could it be he judged the offender a harmless lunatic? Whatever he thought, the young man came from the Emperor's presence "with greater confidence than one returning from a feast or splendid entertainment."[19]

If Julian was mild and unperturbed at times, Gregory would have his readers believe there were also occasions when the Emperor displayed a terrible temper, kicking and hitting suppliants who came to him for justice.[20] He was, Gregory says, "like a volcano."[21] It is difficult to harmonize such details with anything that we hear of Julian from sources closer to him, and they may be no more than a reflection of Gregory's spitefulness. The overall impression of Julian in Gregory's orations is that of an Emperor who was too crafty to allow his Christian enemies a martyr's crown. The individuals who were actually killed or tortured for their Christian faith usually suffered their penalties at the hands of an infuriated pagan mob, or by order of one of Julian's subordinates, rather than at the direct command of the Emperor.

Bishop Marcus of Arethusa (in Phoenicia) is one of the most famous of these victims, an old man who reputedly had saved the child Julian from Constantius' fury in the massacres of 337 and who now refused to comply with the Emperor's order to supply funds for rebuilding a Hellenic shrine he had destroyed, or even to allow his fellow citizens to do so. Marcus' stubbornness on this point, plus the fact that he was a persecutor of pagans, incurred the hostility of the townspeople who seized him and subjected him to horrible tortures, but after suffering heroically for his faith, he was finally released by order of the pagan prefect Salustius.[22] Though he was not actually a martyr, Marcus would later be listed among the saints, and his feast day celebrated together with that of Saint Cyril of Heliopolis, a deacon whom the earlier writers ignore, but whom Theodoret describes as tortured and slain by the people of his city.[23]

While Socrates Scholasticus and Hermias Sozomen, Byzantine lawyers of the mid-fifth century, and their slightly later contemporary, Bishop Theodoret, all copied anecdotes from Greg-

ory Nazianzen in their *Ecclesiastical Histories*, they also cite
additional cases of Christian persecution. Socrates relates how
at Merus, in Phrygia, three Christians named Macedonius, Theo-
dulus, and Tatianus broke into a reopened temple of the gods.[24]
There they proceeded to smash the statues; they were arrested
and promptly confessed their deed. The governor Amachius
gave them a chance for reprieve if they would offer sacrifices
to the gods, but they refused and so were tortured until dead.
Socrates admits that provincial governors who acted as Amachius
did were exceeding Julian's instructions but, he adds, the
Emperor should have tried to stop them.[25]

Sozomen, who reports that same tale of Macedonius, Theo-
dulus, and Tatianus,[26] also has a similar tale of three brothers
from Gaza: Eusebius, Nestabis, and Zeno, who were tortured
to death by an enraged mob for desecrating a pagan temple.
"It was reported that the Emperor was filled with indignation"
when he learned of this incident, Sozomen adds, but his removal of the local governor did not really get to the heart of
the problem.[27]

Nor, if Sozomen is to be credited, were men the only victims
of the pagan mobs. In Heliopolis, he reports, some young Christian girls, "holy virgins," were barbarously slain.[28] Julian, however, when faced personally by an outspoken Christian woman
in the one recorded incident of this sort, behaved with considerable restraint.[29] Publia was a wealthy widow of Antioch, according to Bishop Theodoret; it is only in later legend that she be-
comes the mother of Saint John Chrysostom. In her home,
Publia housed a group of young virgins who served Christ by
singing psalms. One day, as the Emperor was passing by their
house, Publia and her young ladies sang especially loudly a
psalm denouncing the worship of idols. Julian soon afterwards
ordered Publia brought before him and demanded that she and
her household desist from singing, but she replied that they
would do as they pleased. Julian ordered a guard standing by
to slap the woman's face; however, he then released her, and
she returned home to sing as loudly as ever. For this defiance, she
is honored as Saint Publia.

Charges of another sort are levied by Socrates Scholasticus,
who is more adverse to Julian than are Gregory Nazianzen and

Sozomen. According to Socrates, during Julian's reign pagans in Alexandria, Athens, and elsewhere indulged in the grossest sort of rites, including human sacrifice of infants and cannibalism.[30] It is highly unlikely that such charges are true, any more than similar allegations advanced by pagans against the early Christians. If, however, they do have basis in fact, it is even more unlikely that Julian was aware of their occurrence, nor does Socrates ever say that the Emperor personally participated in or approved such rites. It is left to Theodoret, almost a century after Julian's lifetime, to record horror stories in which the Emperor is an active participant.[31] Theodoret's tales of cellars full of corpses in Julian's palace; of human sacrifices and subsequent examination of the victims' entrails have been well described as "ugly old yarns" and nothing more.[32] With the passing of a hundred years, the Apostate legend had developed to the point where the last pagan Emperor was a monster of inhumanity. It was an image that would persist throughout the Middle Ages and disappear only when Julian's own works and those of Ammianus Marcellinus and Libanius became widely known to scholars.

Since these sources are vastly to be preferred to the writings of the ecclesiastical historians, it is interesting to see what (if anything) is to be found here on the subject of the Christian "martyrs" and similar incidents. Although, as might be expected, relatively little in these writings sheds light on the problem, a few important items can be noted. One of the great public scandals of Julian's reign, the tearing to pieces of Bishop George of Alexandria by an infuriated mob, is described in detail by Ammianus Marcellinus.[33] George, an Arian, was apparently notoriously cruel and extremely unpopular with pagans and Orthodox Christians alike in the city of Alexandria. Formerly bishop of Caesarea in Cappadocia (where he had known the child Julian), George eventually rose to great power under Constantius. "Forgetful of his calling which counselled only justice and mildness, he descended to the informer's deadly pactices," Ammianus reports,[34] a sure cause for the vast hatred the populace manifested toward him. He was particularly harsh toward worshipers of the old gods, and publicly threatened to destroy the Temple of the Genius of the City, an old and historic building.

Soon after Julian took office, the new Emperor deposed and sentenced to death Artemius, the miliary commander in Egypt who was one of Constantius' notorious henchmen.[35] When this "good news" reached Alexandria in December, 361, the citizenry took it upon themselves to dispose of Bishop George. Seized by the mob, he was dragged through the city streets until dead; with him perished two of his underlings, Dracontius and Diodorus. While it was pagans who perpetrated this massacre and who subsequently burned the corpses of the victims and scattered their ashes in the sea, Ammianus reports that the Christians of the city did nothing to stop them. George and the others "might have been protected by the aid of the Christians," had they not hated the Bishop as much as the pagans did.[36] (No doubt, although Ammianus does not mention it, this was partly because George was Arian while most Alexandrian Christians were Orthodox).

Julian, Ammianus continues, was most upset on learning of the Alexandrian rioting. At first he planned to inflict a severe penalty upon the city, but decided against such harsh action and instead wrote a letter expressing "his horror at the outrage that had been committed."[37] Julian's letter "To the People of Alexandria" is extant.[38] The Emperor was not sorry that George was dead: "I might even admit that he deserved worse and more cruel treatment," he comments, but the Alexandrians had done wrong to take the law into their own hands. "You have laws which ought by all means to be honored and cherished by you all, individually." After several paragraphs of reflection along these lines, the Emperor concludes that although the perpetrators of the massacre deserve much harsher treatment, "I administer to you the very mildest remedy, namely admonitions and arguments." In spite of the fact that George was an Arian, the Byzantine church historians do not neglect his "martyrdom" and are virtually unanimous in believing that Julian was too mild in his treatment of the Alexandrian rioters.[39]

An additional sidelight on the Bishop George incident is furnished by the Emperor himself in a later letter "To Ecdicius, Prefect of Egypt."[40] Julian had remembered the bishop's splendid library. As a boy at Macellum he had borrowed books from George; where were those books now? Julian ordered that a search be made and that all of George's works on philosophy and rhetoric be sent to him, while those that contained "teachings of the impious Galileans" should be "utterly annihilated." George's former slave-secretary was assigned the task of assembling the collection with the promise of receiving his freedom when the job was done. Presumably in time Julian received the books, though there seems to be no final word on the matter.

Julian would have his difficulties, too, with another Alexandrian bishop, the fiery tempered, outspoken Athanasius. As the Orthodox rival of George, he had been banished by Constantius. At the beginning of Julian's reign, he took advantage of the upheaval in the city and returned to reclaim his see. Although Julian had clearly declared that banished Orthodox Christians were free to return to their homes, he did not grant Athanasius permission to resume his episcopal role. When he learned that the bishop had done so anyway, the Emperor dispatched a threatening edict to the city: "We publicly warn him [Athanasius] to depart from the city forthwith, on the very day that he shall receive this letter of our clemency. But if he remain within the city, we publicly warn him that he will receive much greater and more severe punishment."[41] Athanasius eventually left Alexandria, loudly remarking that Julian's hostility was "a little cloud" that would soon pass.[42] But he did not leave Egypt, and when Julian learned this several months later, and that he was still busy converting "Greek women of rank" to Orthodoxy, he ordered the prefect Ecdicius to see to it that Athanasius left the province.[43] Athanasius went into hiding and the Orthodox Christians of Alexandria petitioned Julian to allow their bishop to return. In a lengthy letter, deploring the fact that any Alexandrians at all could possibly be Christian, Julian denied their request.[44] Athanasius remained in exile in the Sudan until Julian's death a few months later, then returned triumphantly, no doubt vastly pleased by the accuracy of his "little cloud" prediction.

But if the troubles in Alexandria might indeed be described as a "little cloud," Julian's problems with stubborn Galileans in Antioch excited a storm of considerable proportions while he was there. Antioch, as we have noted, was largely a Christian city, at least nominally, and Julian's efforts to restore

the worship of the old gods there led to considerable scoffing
and sometimes to public shows of defiance from individuals like
Publia, the singing widow. By far the most serious of Julian's
encounters with Christian opposition, however, stems from the
incidents connected with Saint Babylas.

Babylas was an Antiochene martyr, who died along with
several younger men during the persecutions of the Emperor
Decius and who, a century later, lay buried with his companions in the beautiful suburb of Daphne, where their shrine
attracted many pious visitors. Julian found this cult particularly distasteful since he possessed a superstitious fear of dead
bodies and heartily disliked the Christian habit of reverence
for saints' relics. Moreover, at the Castalian spring in Daphne
in earlier centuries an oracle of Apollo had existed. Julian was
intent on restoring this oracle and ordered the removal of
stones blocking the spring. When the god seemingly still refused to speak, Julian concluded that the presence of the
corpse of Babylas and the other martyrs in the vicinity was
the obstacle. The Galileans would simply have to move their
martyrs to another resting place, the Emperor ordered.[45]

While Julian and Ammianus both mention the removal of the
bodies of Saint Babylas and his companions, it is left to the
ecclesiastical historians to supply the details of how the Christians conducted the ceremony.[46] Their seeming humiliation
was turned into a triumphal procession. As they carried away
the relics of their saints, they sang loud psalms reviling idolatry
and, by implication, insulting the Emperor. Julian, angry at this
unseemly display, ordered Salustius to arrest and imprison
several of the ringleaders. One, a young man named Theodore,
was severely beaten, but released the next day along with the
others. Theodore later reported, to the delight of his fellow
Christians, that he had not really suffered at all: while he was
being beaten, an angel appeared to him and consoled him so
that he felt "rapture rather than suffering."[47]

If Julian and his Galilean opponents hoped that the Babylas
incident was closed they were soon to be disappointed. On
October 22, 362, shortly after the removal of the martyrs, a
fire of undetermined origin destroyed the ancient and beautiful temple of Apollo in Daphne and a statue of the Olympian

Zeus inside it. While the Christians gleefully declared that the blaze was caused by a bolt from Heaven, Julian was convinced that it was the work of Christian arsonists. In retaliation he ordered the largest Arian Christian church in Antioch closed down and its treasures confiscated.[48] Because there was no convincing proof of Christian guilt in this matter, Ammianus did not approve of Julian's act; it was very possible, he reports, that the fire started accidentally, caused by sparks from a candle lit by a pious pagan.[49]

Julian's closing of the great church in Antioch was an indication of a hardening attitude toward the Galileans. With the coming of winter, however, the Emperor grew increasingly involved with preparations for the Persian campaign and with literary endeavors, and we do not find the situation of the Christians in Antioch during those months as severe as perhaps they feared it might be. By early March, 363, Julian had left for the east; by June of the same year he was dead.

Had he lived to return from Persia, would his attitude toward his Christian opponents have grown progressively harsher? Gregory Nazianzen and the later ecclesiastical historians were sure of it. Gregory, for instance, had a great deal to say about the dire restrictions Julian was planning to impose had he lived longer: he was going to debar Christians from "all meetings, markets, and public assemblies" unless they would burn the required incense.[50] Socrates and Sozomen, as we have noted elsewhere, add the patently false charge that he planned to forbid Christian children to attend school,[51] while Theodoret reports that he hoped eventually to oust all Christians from his army.[52]

As it turned out, these dire fears would not materialize, for in his decision to attack Persia, Julian's fate was sealed, and the future struggles he might have faced with the Galilean opposition remain only a matter for historical speculation.

CHAPTER 20

Julian's Persian War

THE best source by far for the ill-fated Roman invasion of
Persia in the spring of 363 is Ammianus Marcellinus.
Since Ammianus did not compose his *Histories* until some years
later, however, there is considerable scholarly controversy over
what sources (now lost) he might have utilized.[1] It is certain
that such reports did exist and highly likely that Ammianus
consulted some of them. But since he took part in the Persian
campaign in person, his chief source must have been his own
recollections and, very probably, written notes that he made
at the time.

Libanius' "Oration 18" also contains a summary of the Persian
campaign based on oral testimony of eyewitnesses, but at many
points he is extremely vague because of his unfortunate habit
of avoiding proper names. A source of a rather different sort
is the *New History* of the fifth-century pagan Byzantine historian Count Zosimus, who describes Julian's Persian campaign in detail and who at times differs considerably from
Ammianus. Unquestionably, Zosimus had access to sources
now lost, including Eunapius' *Life of Julian*, which in turn
was based on memoirs compiled by the physician Oribasius
who took part in the campaign.[2] Thus Zosimus' narrative is of
considerable importance, though Ammianus is still to be preferred at most points where data conflict. The Byzantine ecclesiastical historians also touch on the Persian expedition, but
provide few additional insights.

In retrospect, Julian's decision to attack Persia appears an
incredibly foolish move by so experienced a soldier as he. His
motives consequently have been subjected to intense scrutiny.
Did he imagine that he might in fact conquer Persia? Or did
he anticipate that the campaign would be somewhat similar to

158

his raids across the Rhine, designed to strike terror in the hearts of the enemy but not to result in permanent occupation of territory? There is much that might be argued in favor of either theory, but the latter seems a more realistic appraisal. As an avid student of history, Julian knew of the centuries-long hostility between Persia and the Roman state and of the many times Rome had met defeat on Persian soil. On the other hand, it is possible that he had convinced himself that having been uncommonly fortunate in war heretofore, he would succeed where many of his predecessors had failed, and would unite the Hellenic and Persian worlds under one ruler as Alexander of Macedon had done nearly seven centuries before.

It is in connection with Alexander that Socrates Scholasticus advances what is perhaps the most bizarre of all attempts to explain Julian's determination to invade Persia.[3] Maximus the theurgist, says Socrates, convinced the Emperor that he, Julian, was Alexander reincarnated, that Alexander's soul inhabited his body. The greatest flaw in this theory is the fact that whatever peculiar mystical ideas he may have entertained, Julian nowhere seems to have expressed belief in reincarnation.[4] Moreover, although he certainly admired Alexander's generalship, he has very little else to say in praise of the famous Macedonian conqueror; rather when he mentions him at all, it is usually to deplore Alexander's many moral failings.[5]

Julian claimed to have inherited the present hostility with Persia from Constantius, who for years off and on had battled with King Sapor along the frontier. Sapor may well have anticipated that Julian would be a more formidable foe than Constantius, for the Persian monarch appeared eager to initiate peace talks. Persian envoys came to Antioch while Julian was there, but the Roman Emperor refused to have anything to do with negotiations.[6] The Persians, he professed to believe, could not be trusted. Perhaps he was right; on the other hand, perhaps he was looking forward to this Persian war, which he could have avoided, as a chance to rebuild his rapidly sinking popularity. Should he succeed in Persia, was it not likely that all his enterprises at home would flourish the more readily? Was not the aggressive attack on Sapor's domain clearly the mandate of the gods to their chosen one?

This he must accomplish, and in doing so, win the glory and support for the old religion that he was failing to gain by other means.

As a prop for his expansionist designs, Julian took with him on his Persian expedition King Sapor's half-brother, Prince Ormisdas, an old man who had spent most of his life at the Roman court, a perennial pretender to Sapor's throne.[7] Should the Romans have conquered Persia, Ormisdas presumably would have been installed as a puppet king. During Julian's campaign he would serve as a top-level interpreter and negotiator and also as commander of the cavalry forces.

On March 5, 363, Julian left Antioch, loudly proclaiming that he would never return to the city that had treated him so badly.[8] Libanius, emotional as ever, wept openly to see him go;[9] Julian promised to write him faithfully, and in fact his last extant letter is one written March 10 and addressed to Libanius. From it come ample details on the first five days of the eastward march.[10]

Upon leaving Antioch the Emperor and his forces journeyed along the rough swampy road to the village of Litarbae and then on to Beroea. There the army halted for a day while Julian offered sacrifices, checked omens, and spoke to the local Senate on the worship of the old gods. The omens, he says, were good. (Ammianus, however, says they were distinctly bad during the whole march, but that Julian had closed his mind to negative warnings from the gods.)[11] As for the city fathers of Beroea, "they all applauded my arguments," Julian reports, but "very few were converted by them, and these few were men who even before I spoke seemed to me to hold sound views."[12] It is the Emperor's final word on his missionary efforts, and in it one senses plainly the futility he was beginning to feel.

From Beroea, the army proceeded to Batnae, an outpost in a heavily forested area that Julian describes as almost as beautiful as Daphne. Here, he informs Libanius, he stayed in an unpretentious house of "clay and logs," that made up for its lack of elegance by the magnificent gardens and orchards which surrounded it. There is unconscious irony in the glimpse that Julian gives us of himself at this point, wandering amidst the cypress trees of Batnae, fully alert to the beauty of the world around him and seeking to learn the will of his gods, yet at the same time wholeheartedly determined upon a needless war.[13]

The next stop after Batnae was Hierapolis, the rendezvous point where additional Roman forces had convened and where, on the nearby Euphrates River, a fleet of supply boats was assembled. Julian stayed at the home of a Hellenic scholar, Sopater, and tended to numerous important details which he barely mentions in his letter to Libanius. It would take "too long" to tell everything, he says, but he does mention that he sent an embassy to the Saracens of Arabia, inviting volunteers to join the campaign.[14] Sometime earlier, Ammianus reports, he had also summoned King Arsaces of Armenia, an ally of Rome, to provide auxiliary forces.[15]

From Hierapolis, it was Julian's plan to send the river fleet of some eleven hundred boats southeastward down the Euphrates. The entire army crossed the river by a pontoon bridge; but next we find Julian and the main body of his forces headed northeastward, away from the river, toward another town called Batnae (this one "Batnae of Osdroëne") and then on farther east toward the city of Carrae.[16] This apparent change of plans was probably an effort to confuse the enemy. At Carrae, Julian lingered to offer sacrifices. The omens continued to be very bad; at Batnae some fifty men were accidentally crushed to death when a huge heap of fodder fell upon them. Julian was himself continually troubled by bad dreams. Fully aware that he might not survive the Persian invasion, he met with his distant cousin Procopius at Carrae and gave him one of his purple cloaks as a sign that he was his designated successor—at least, so Procopius would claim later on. Julian also entrusted Procopius with command of a large force of auxiliaries (some thirty thousand troops according to Ammianus; Libanius says twenty thousand).[17] They were to patrol the area east of Carrae where at least one surprise incursion by the enemy had just been reported. Then when King Arsaces and his Armenians appeared, they would proceed southward to serve as reinforcements for Julian who by then would be inside Persia. Such was the plan; but as it turned out, when Julian needed him, Procopius failed to appear.

In late March, on the morning when Julian was about to leave Carrae, an ominous incident took place that must have caused the Emperor some alarm, though he managed to interpret it as a favorable sign. Julian's favorite horse was named "Babylonius" for one of Persia's great cities. That morning just as the Emperor was preparing to mount, one of the Roman archers shot Babylonius and the horse fell to the ground in terrible pain, shaking off its gold and jewelled ornaments. "Babylon has fallen, stripped of all its adornments," Julian cried out; it was a sure sign of victory over the Persians.[18]

From Carrae the army marched due south and on March 27th reached the town of Callinicum on the Euphrates, where they were to rendezvous with the river fleet which apparently arrived the next day. A band of Saracen volunteers also arrived with a golden crown to present to Julian as a token of their loyalty to his service. Though they were welcomed enthusiastically, later it seems that many of these Saracen volunteers deserted to the Persians.[19]

From Callinicum to the frontier fortress of Cercusium, a journey of several days, the army stayed close to its supply fleet on the Euphrates. About one thousand of these vessels, Ammianus informs us, were simply cargo boats, stocked with food, weapons, and siege equipment. There were also fifty large warships and fifty more designed to support pontoon bridges.[20]

The rations carried by the fleet were far from elaborate, the usual dry bread and sour wine, while drinking water was obtained from the river itself. At one point along the way, the army was approached by a camel caravan laden with fine wines and other delicacies. The enterprising merchants who hoped to unload these wares on the Roman army were disappointed, however, for Julian promptly sent word that no such luxuries would be permitted until such time as they might all drink the "wine of victory." Nor could the merchants persuade the Emperor to purchase some of their wares for his own use; he was (as Libanius says) "one of the soldiers, and it was proper that his rations should be the same as the rest."[21]

The army reached Cercusium at the border between the two

empires around the first of April. Here more troops joined the expedition including the historically-minded young officer, Ammianus Marcellinus, who describes in detail the walled fortress city of Cercusium, nestled in an angle between the Euphrates and the Abora (or Chaboras) Rivers. To enter enemy territory, the Romans had to cross the Abora by pontoons, an operation that extended for several days. Bad omens of various sorts, Ammianus adds, continued to appear.[22] Julian received a very discouraging letter from his friend the prefect Salustius, back in Gaul, urging him not to fight the Persians at all. The other Salustius, one of Julian's highest ranking officers and ordinarily an unusually merciful man, ordered the execution of a quartermaster who had failed to supply provisions on schedule as promised. Then, after the man was killed, it was discovered that he was innocent of any misdoing; the supplies he had promised arrived late, delayed by accident. In spite of these misfortunes, nothing would dissuade Julian from his planned attack on Persia. The Abora was duly crossed and the Romans disembarked on enemy soil.

Soon after they had crossed the border, the Romans came to the monumental tomb of the teen-aged Emperor Gordian III, slain by one of his own men while on campaign in Persia in A.D. 244. While Julian paused here to pay his respects to the memory of his predecessor, some of his men went hunting and slew a lion which they brought back to the Emperor. The death of this king of beasts signified to the omen-conscious Romans the death of a human king, and Julian cheerfully declared it meant Sapor.[23]

In the best tradition of ancient historiography, Ammianus includes in his narrative of Julian's Persian war a long speech which the Emperor is supposed to have made to his troops soon after the visit to Gordian's tomb.[24] Presuming that its basic content is fairly authentic, Julian seemed particularly anxious to convince his forces that the Romans had won victories in Persia before; omitting the many disasters the Empire had suffered at the hands of the Persian foe, he concentrated on the few notable (if temporary) successes won by previous emperors. On the other hand, he added, "if fickle fortune should overthrow me in any battle, I shall be content with

having sacrificed myself for the Roman world." The Emperor
also promised to undergo whatever hardships awaited them on
equal terms with his soldiers, a standard to which he had
adhered faithfully throughout his career and which was surely
the secret of much of his popularity. The troops who heard
him speak (presumably including many Christians) cheered
him enthusiastically and waved their shields about in token of
their loyalty to him and their eagerness to follow him on to
victory. Zosimus adds at this point that Julian also distributed
a bonus of 130 silver coins to each of his soldiers.[25]

It was about a month since the Emperor had left Antioch,
a month in which the army had traveled through several hundred miles of frontier territory and effected a successful
crossing of the border. Throughout the rest of April and on
into May, the Romans moved from one victory to another, and
it seemed that Julian's highest aspirations were to be fulfilled.

Two days after crossing the Abora, the Romans arrived at
Dura, the first major stronghold on the Persian side of the
frontier. The city was deserted and the soldiers occupied themselves by hunting deer in the nearby area and feasting on their
prey. It was another four days' march to Anatha, an island fortress
in the Euphrates, where their first major victory took place.
Ammianus presents a vivid narrative of how the Roman warships surrounded the island in the dark of the night. When
morning came, there was a great outcry when the inhabitants
of the town discovered their predicament. Defenders hastily
manned the walls, but Julian, suspecting that the townspeople
might prefer surrender to a long-drawn-out siege, sent Prince
Ormisdas to negotiate. It was decided that the inhabitants should
be allowed to take their possessions and evacuate to Roman
territory (Chalcis in Syria). After the army had helped itself to
a vast stock of provisions, the fortress of Anatha was burned
to the ground.[26]

Among the evacuees, Ammianus reports, was an aged man
almost a hundred years old, who had served in the Roman army
as a teen-aged boy about eighty years earlier. He had been
taken as a prisoner of war by the Persians and eventually became
integrated into Persian society, marrying several local women
and raising a large family. He had, however, always prophesied

(or so he alleged when Anatha surrendered) that he would
live to return to the Roman Empire and be buried on Roman
soil.[27] This strange incident no doubt seemed an encouraging
omen to Julian and his forces.

The next day a fierce windstorm arose, destroying some of the
soldiers' tents. The Euphrates overflowed its banks and some
of the supply boats were sunk. Despite these setbacks, Ammianus reports, the army was in good spirits because of the
capture of Anatha and eager to press on to the next stronghold.
On the way, they lived off the land, helping themselves to Persian crops and then burning everything they could not use.[28]

Still following the course of the Euphrates, the Romans came
to another island fortress, Thilutha, which refused Julian's offer
to come to terms. Because the place was extremely well fortified and because the local officials promised to submit to Rome
if the Romans were victorious further on, it was decided to
bypass the fortress. The same thing was done at Achaiachala.
Another unnamed fortress a little further down the river was
abandoned when the Romans reached it, so they destroyed it
by fire. Two additional towns, Diacira and Ozogardana, received
the same treatment; the Romans helped themselves to supplies
and, following the standard practice of the time, killed the few
civilians they found lingering in these deserted cities.[29]

Soon after, Prince Ormisdas, leading a reconnaissance force,
narrowly escaped death in an ambush planned by Saracen allies
of the Persians.[30] Still the main body of the Persian army had
not appeared, though by now the Romans were deep inside the
province of Assyria. On the day after Ormisdas' narrow escape
the first major encounter between Julian's forces and the Persians
took place. "At daybreak," Ammianus recalls, "the enemy were
already in sight, and we saw them for the first time in their
gleaming helmemts and bristling with stiff coats of mail; but our
soldiers rushed to battle at quick step and fell upon them most
valiantly."[31] In this encounter the Romans beat off the Persians
and in the days that followed continued their progress down
river till they reached the Naarmalacha Canal which branched
off eastward toward the Tigris. The Romans' crossing of the
Naarmalacha was somewhat hindered by Persian archers. Moreover, some of the Roman calvarymen and their horses were

drowned while attempting to ford the stream. In spite of these obstacles the crossing was made and the Romans moved on toward the large fortress city of Pirisabora.[32]

There are lengthy details in both Ammianus and Zosimus on the siege of Pirisabora, which turned out to be one of the major battles of Julian's Persian war.[33] Zosimus calls the city Bersabora (the particle *sabor* was a variant of the name of King Sapor). Although many citizens had fled before the Romans arrived, the defenders were confident of the strength of their excellent walls and rejected Julian's preliminary invitation to surrender. When Prince Ormisdas attempted to negotiate with them, they reviled him as a traitor to his native Persia.

It was on the second day of the siege that one of the Roman battering rams effected a breach in the city wall. When the Romans pressed into the city, the Persian defenders congregated in their fortified citadel; the struggle went on, with the Persians in their tower showering down a constant barrage of arrows, stones, and other "missiles" upon the Romans.

Casualties were heavy on both sides. On the third day of the siege, Julian, as usual involved in the thick of the fighting, with a group of picked men attempted to break through the gate of the citadel. The maneuver failed; some of the men were injured by stones hurled down upon them, and they were forced to withdraw to a safer spot. Julian was not hurt, but if Ammianus can be believed, he was embarrassed that he had not been and "blushed with shame."[34]

The same day Julian ordered the Romans to assemble a *helepolis* and bring it into position beside the Persian citadel. This powerful structure, one of the most dreaded weapons of ancient war, was a tall, mobile tower full of soldiers (archers and slingers), who as soon as the *helepolis* was in place, might rain down death upon the heads of the enemy below. The Persians in the citadel of Pirisabora needed only to look at the *helepolis* to begin thinking about surrender. According to Ammianus, Ormisdas conducted negotiations; the defenders, who numbered about twenty-five hundred, were taken prisoners but their lives were spared.[35] Zosimus indicates that five thousand townspeople were allowed to leave the city freely, taking clothing and money with them, a detail which Ammianus does not mention.[36] Both writers agree that again the Romans took for themselves a great amount of plunder, not only food but weapons. There were in fact more than they could carry off. Some weapons were sunk in the Euphrates and some left to the flames as the city itself was burned to the ground.

After the victory at Pirisabora, Julian made a speech praising his troops, and presented them a bonus of one hundred silver coins each.[37] When he announced the amount, there was open muttering among the soldiers that it was too small, and Julian was full of "deep indignation" as he spoke on the subject of their ingratitude and his own lack of unlimited wealth his men seemed to think he possessed. As usual, it is reported, his words had a calming effect on his restless troops, particularly since there was hope of further victories soon.

It was near the end of April when the Romans, pressing further southeastward, began to encounter serious difficulties. A Roman reconnaissance force was surprised by Persians, who inflicted heavy casualties and captured one of their dragon banners.[38] Julian's troops in a counterattack retook the lost standard, but in the next few days they were faced with a new enemy: a flooded countryside. The Persians deliberately broke many of the dikes along their elaborate system of canals in the Euphrates-Tigris valley. Everywhere the ground was covered with "gluey mud," too shallow for the fleet to be of any use, too deep for crossing on foot except with the greatest of difficulty. Zosimus has a vivid description of Julian in this difficult terrain, wading up to his knees in mud, followed by a special task force of loyal men who "felt ashamed not to do what they observed their Emperor doing."[39] That night Julian's task force began cutting down trees to make light bridges across the swamp lands and thus get the main body of troops through more easily.

The next major action probably took place early in May. In Ammianus' report the Romans besieged the city of Maioza-malcha; Zosimus calls this fortress Besuchis, but there is little doubt they refer to the same place.[40] Both report that on a preliminary scouting expedition, Julian narrowly escaped death at the hands of a small band of Persians who had sallied forth from their fortress. In fierce hand-to-hand combat, Julian slew one of his attackers; his men killed another and the rest fled.

There was more skirmishing outside Maiozamalcha as the Romans were setting up their siege equipment. Then for two days, while the main force of the besiegers employed the standard devices of ancient warfare, pounding away at the heavy walls with their battering rams, a select troop under the leadership of the Gallic barbarians, Nevitta and Daiglaif, undertook mining operations. A tunnel was dug under the city wall and the Romans entered Maiozamalcha, spreading terror before the defenders on the wall realized what had happened. At about the same time, several breaches were made in the town wall and thousands of Romans poured into the city. There are several reports of the killing of civilians, a standard practice in warfare of that time, though Libanius adds that Julian had forbidden it here and that the soldiers were disobeying his specific orders. Many Persians were taken as prisoners, while some, who preferred death to captivity, committed suicide before they could fall into Roman hands.[41] Following their usual procedure, Julian's forces destroyed Maiozamalcha by fire.

The Romans were now only a few days distant from Ctesiphon on the Tigris, one of the capitals of Persia and the apparent goal of the expedition. As Julian's forces pressed eastward, there were several small flare-ups of fighting with the Persians,[42] in which the Romans usually got the better of their foes. A more difficult problem was getting the fleet through the network of canals back toward the great Naarmalacha, in order to reach the Tigris. Ammianus lingers on many details of the march toward Ctesiphon. Particularly memorable was the occupation of King Sapor's personal hunting preserve, where the soldiers spent several days hunting lions, bears, wild boars and other beasts. Julian housed himself in Sapor's magnificent hunting lodge and declared the building was far too beautiful to be destroyed, since it was built in Roman style.[43]

When the nearby city of Seleucia-Coche was found to be deserted, Julian ordered most of his army to encamp there for a few days' rest while he went ahead with a reconnaisance force to explore the surrounding countryside. A large troop of Persians caught the Roman scouting party completely by surprise, inflicted heavy casualties, and took a number of prisoners. Julian, says Ammianus, was "in a rage" and so eager for reprisal that he went straightway to reconnoiter the nearest Persian fortress. The defenders on the wall recognized him and sent down a volley of "various missiles."[44] Had he not been hastily covered by his armor-bearer's shield, he almost certainly would have been killed or seriously wounded; it is tempting to wonder if the Emperor's daredevil action at this point was inspired by something more than hot headedness. The historians do not stress Julian's growing despair throughout the Persian venture, but there are hints of it. Could it be that he actually longed to die gloriously in battle and thus find release from the difficulties of living?

Within a few days the Romans succeeded in taking the fortress where Julian had so narrowly escaped death. Ammianus does not name this place, reporting only that it was very near Ctesiphon. He makes it clear, however, that the Roman war effort was meeting increased opposition, since the Persians sallied forth from their stronghold at night to attack the Roman camp.[45]

To reach Ctesiphon the Romans faced another crossing of a branch of the Naarmalacha Canal. (Earlier, heading southward, they had crossed where it joined the Euphrates; now they had doubled back, moving north toward Ctesiphon on the Tigris.) Now they discovered that the Persians had drained and dammed the canal to halt their enemies. The Romans immediately set to work to dismantle the huge stone dam the Persians had built so that water again flowed in the canal and the fleet was able to enter the waters of the Tigris.[46] Since Ctesiphon stood on the east bank of the Tigris, they still had to cross the river, a maneuver complicated by the steep height of the east bank where the Persian forces were massed, waiting for them.

After several days of rest and recreation, including horse races and prizes, Julian determined on the night of May 26–27 for the crossing of the Tigris. Several of the largest ships under the infantry commander, Count Victor, were ordered across the river first.[47] As feared, there was immediate and fierce opposition from the Persians on the east bank, who attacked with firebrands and set the Roman ships ablaze. Julian, watching from the west bank and fully aware of what was happening, craftily announced to his men that the fires they saw in the distance were a pre-arranged Roman victory signal. He now ordered the entire army and fleet across the river. By their superior numbers and sudden arrival, the Romans were able after heavy fighting to effect a landing on the riverbank just outside Ctesiphon and rescue the burning ships and most of the troops who had taken part in the first crossing.[48] All day long on May 27th, battle raged outside Ctesiphon. Julian was in the thick of the fighting throughout the day; in the words of Ammianus, the Emperor "was busily engaged in giving support to those who gave way and in spurring on the laggards, playing the part both of the valiant fellow-soldier and a commander."[49]

   Towards late afternoon the Persians began retreating to Ctesiphon. The Romans followed in hot pursuit, but when the city gates opened to receive the Persians, the Roman Count Victor forbade his men to follow. Victor was himself wounded; his men were exhausted by long hours of combat and eager to pick up spoils. Should they enter Ctesiphon, he reasoned, they would most likely find themselves trapped in the city and slaughtered by Persian reserves who had not spent the entire day fighting.[50]

   There is considerable logic in Count Victor's decision, but as it turned out, from the Roman point of view it was an unfortunate one, for thus the opportunity to take Ctesiphon was irretrievably lost.

CHAPTER 21

Julian's Death

THE Romans had failed to enter the Persian capital, but the battle outside Ctesiphon was still a great victory for Julian's forces, so great that if Libanius' account is reliable, King Sapor sent an envoy to Prince Ormisdas asking for peace talks. Ormisdas was eager to accept the offer, but Julian refused.[1] Since neither Ammianus nor Zosimus mention the Persians' abortive peace feeler, and since it is hard to understand why Julian would have made such an incredibly foolish decision, the account is somewhat suspect.

The military historians, however, do indicate something of the sense of elation that possessed the Romans immediately after the battle at Ctesiphon. Reportedly, only about seventy-five Romans were slain compared to about twenty-five hundred Persians.[2] The day following the battle, May 28th, was set aside for celebration. Julian presented wreaths to many of the soldiers who had performed noteworthy deeds. This presentation was to be followed by the sacrifice of ten bulls to Mars the Avenger. Then, ominously, when the animals were led forth for the sacrifice, nine of them "sank in sadness to the ground" before they could be slaughtered, while the tenth ran away and was recaptured only with great difficulty. Julian may have suspected that the nine bulls who showed such distressing symptoms had been drugged; but to the ordinary soldiers and perhaps to the superstitious Emperor as well, the happening nonetheless must have seemed a sign from the gods. When the runaway bull was retaken and duly sacrificed, the omens observed in its entrails were distinctly bad. Julian, Ammianus reports, "cried out in deep indignation" that he would sacrifice to Mars no more.[3]

In the days that followed, the Emperor's despair and obvious weariness were more discouraging than any number of omens. Had Julian begun to realize that in spite of his victories, the Roman army under his direction had maneuvered itself into a most uncomfortable position, far from home, without a regular source of supplies other than what they might take as spoils? The fortress of Ctesiphon glared at them from one side; to the north, the way of retreat was marked by the Tigris River, and while the Mesopotamian rivers were easily navigable southward, the journey back again without a favorable current would be difficult in the extreme. The large number of men who would have to row or haul the fleet upstream simply could not be detailed to this task without great risk to the land army. The fleet had suddenly become more of a hindrance than an asset. If abandoned, however, the Persians would seize it.[4]

For several days the Romans remained outside Ctesiphon at a place called Abuzatha while Julian conferred with his officers on the problem of the ships, but also on the prospects of besieging Ctesiphon, which he personally still hoped to do. He was dissuaded from this idea by the opinion of the majority of his staff. Ctesiphon, they told him, was impregnable; moreover, King Sapor (who had not yet taken part in any of the action) was rumored to be en route to his capital with a large army of reinforcements. The summer weather was already almost unbearably hot. Better to leave Ctesiphon and begin a strategic diversion toward the north.[5]

Julian unhappily agreed. He also decided, apparently on his own initiative, to burn the fleet. A few boats (Ammianus says twelve) would be saved to make pontoon bridges and transported on wagons overland until such time as they were needed.[6] (The Romans were leaving the banks of the Tigris; Julian planned to move northeast through an area reportedly more fruitful, where they could live off the land.) When the boats were put to the torch, however, soldiers of all ranks protested so loudly that Julian eventually relented and gave orders to stop the blaze if possible. It was too late; the ships were already damaged beyond repair.[7]

As the army began its northward diversion (the ancient writers, loyal to Julian's memory, are reluctant to call it a "retreat"), new troubles arose. The area through which they marched was indeed a rich farming district, but Persian forces began to ravage the countryside, burning their own people's crops so that nothing might be left for the Roman enemies.[8] Almost daily, small bands of Persian cavalry appeared to harass Roman stragglers, while thick swarms of flies and gnats added to the army's misery. If only Procopius and King Arsaces would arrive with their promised reinforcements! Daily, Julian expressed hope for the help that never came, while the army gradually shifted back toward the east bank of the Tigris, deciding, after all, to follow the river back to Roman territory.

The northward retreat proved to be a ghastly experience. Without reliable guides, deep in enemy territory, the Romans now faced vast stretches of semi-desert country and "scorched earth" as the summer grew increasingly hotter and food supplies dwindled. The Persians still avoided a major battle, but swift riders appeared frequently, seemingly from nowhere, and then disappeared as suddenly as they had come. On several encounters in mid-June there was sharp fighting, with the Romans almost always victorious,[9] yet for all their slaying of individual Persians, there was still the inescapable reality that the Romans had lost their war. Many were dead; many who lived were grievously wounded and now these survivors were going back where they came from with little to show for the vast invasion their Emperor had undertaken.

Julian, ever a good soldier, bore the hardships of the retreat with exemplary courage. He was still very much in command; and while there were continued rumblings of discontent among his men, they apparently were not widespread or seriously threatening. The men knew that their Emperor was suffering as much as they were: he ate nothing but porridge and distributed to his troops all extra rations that he might have claimed.[10] Somehow, in spite of all their difficulties, Julian was managing the retreat efficiently. He had fought well and would no doubt fight again in a more auspicious season. Most of the troops who had served with him in better days were still with him in adversity.

The historical sources hint strongly, however, that Julian, despite his outward show of bravery, was deeply depressed. Ill omens continued to appear, a trend sure to cause unrest in one so superstitious as he.[11] On a deeper level he must have feared the long-range consequences of his Persian adventure: how would this failure affect his chances of retaining his position when the news spread throughout the Empire? Many of his predecessors, whose history he knew well, had lost their thrones—and their lives—against a similar background of military disaster. The way was clear for an ambitious rival to claim the crown. It could be practically any one of the top army officers: no one but Julian himself was left of the imperial house of Constantine. As for Procopius, Julian's mother's cousin, his failure to appear with reinforcements negated his chances of recognition as heir.

It was probably on the night of June 25th as Julian lay on the pallet in his tent, exhausted and more nearly asleep than he realized, that he seemed to see a frightening vision. As he reported it the next morning, the Genius Publicus, the guardian spirit of Rome, had appeared before him; a veil covered the spirit's head and the cornucopia he carried. The dream, for such it must have been, was startlingly real: the guardian spirit was in mourning, turning his favor away from the Emperor. Julian arose, fully awake now, and went outdoors to pray and to search the heavens for a sign. As fate would have it, he saw a falling star, a bad omen, he believed, from the god Mars, who had been distinctly unfriendly ever since the incident of the ten bulls. The next morning, Julian consulted the Etruscan soothsayers who accompanied the expedition; they counselled remaining in camp for the whole day.[12]

For all his fear of omens, Julian disregarded them whenever he was so minded. His common sense was stronger than his superstitious qualms: why waste a whole day in the Persian desert when there were still so many miles to travel? Camp was broken and the Romans resumed their march.

It was mid-afternoon on June 26th when a large mounted troop of Persians swooped down on the Roman forces. Julian was himself in the thick of the fighting, attempting to organize the Roman defense amid dense clouds of dust which swirled across the desert battlefield. Suddenly a lance hurled by an unknown hand pierced Julian's side. The Emperor was not wearing armor; it was a very hot day, and the Persian attack had come without warning. His first impulse was to extract the weapon, but as he attempted to do so, he only succeeded in cutting his right hand badly. The wound in his side was obviously deeper than he had realized. In great pain, he fell from his horse, bleeding profusely. In moments he was surrounded by loyal soldiers who carried him out of the combat on his shield.[13] Back in his own tent, his wounds were tended immediately by his friend, the physician Oribasius.[14] For several hours, the young Emperor hovered between life and death, fully conscious all the while.

The events of the long summer evening when Julian lay dying in his tent have been subject to intense historical scrutiny. Ammianus' account is the lengthiest and in most respects the best. While he was not likely an eyewitness, he was among Julian's troops and undoubtedly learned the details very soon afterward from those who were present.[15] Libanius, too, obtained information directly from eyewitnesses.[16] Several of his orations contain reflections on Julian's death; while he is a careful reporter, he is also deeply emotional, for he was both devoted to Julian in life and full of apprehension as to what the world would be like without him. In substance, Ammianus and Libanius agree, as does Zosimus, whose report is very brief and contributes no additional information. Most of the other narratives of Julian's death, especially those of the Christian historians, are full of later legends and must be used with extreme caution.[17]

At first Julian seemed unaware that his injury would be fatal and longed to rejoin the battle. The attendants who dressed the wound in his side realized, however, that the weapon had penetrated deep into his body and probably pierced his liver. Only with great difficulty did they succeed temporarily in stanching the flow of blood. Julian, too weak to rise from the "soft bed" where he lay, at length realized that he was dying.[18]

There is no positive evidence whether, in those crucial hours, anyone raised the question of the identity of Julian's assailant. Ammianus at least seems to accept the idea that it was one of the enemy.[19] On the other hand, there is the dreadful possibility that, amid the thick dust, Julian was wounded—deliberately or accidentally—by one of his own men. In later years, Julian's admirers, particularly Libanius, professed to believe that the fatal lance was hurled by a Christian who had taken it upon himself to rid the world of the "Apostate" Emperor.[20] No one will ever know now; and if Julian knew, or even suspected, he thought it best to say nothing.

Not far away the battle still raged; many of Julian's men were fighting more recklessly and boldly than ever to avenge their fallen leader. At length the Persians were routed, though not without heavy losses on both sides.[21]

Night came, and inside the imperial tent the Emperor Julian struggled with his last great adversary: death. Never was his great courage displayed more clearly than in these final hours. He was a young man, still in his early thirties, yet he expressed no word of regret for his fate. Surrounded by weeping friends, he shed no tears himself.[22] While the long speech that Ammianus puts in his mouth cannot be taken verbatim, it probably reflects some of the content of his dying words.[23] He had striven to live uprightly and to rule justly, he said, and he had no regrets for the past. To die by "the sword" was a noble death; he was grateful that the gods had found him worthy of it. Long before, it had been prophesied that he would die in this manner; he was not surprised. To some of his close friends who were standing by, he distributed certain personal effects. There was much weeping, and Julian, still calmer than any of those who surrounded him, remarked, "It is unworthy to mourn for a prince who is called to union with heaven and the stars." As the long hours dragged by, the philosophers Maximus and Priscus (themselves so unlike, but both so greatly respected by Julian) remained at the bedside of their Emperor, talking with him about the nobility of the human soul. Around midnight, the wound in his side began to bleed again; gasping for breath, he called for a cup of water, drank some, and died.[24]

Julian's personal religion had never placed much emphasis on the life beyond this world, but clearly he believed in it, and when the time came, he went to his death firm in the conviction that he was returning to his gods. Neither in Ammianus' narrative nor Libanius' orations is there any hint of the disillusioned Julian of later legend, crying in anguish, "Helios, thou hast ruined me!"[25] Nor does he speak the famous words first ascribed to him by Bishop Theodoret almost a century later: "Galilean, thou hast conquered!"[26] Though these tales gained widespread currency and have even had their modern defenders, everything we know of Julian's character warns against accepting them as fact. Is it credible that he who had served the gods so long and so faithfully would deny them with his last breath? Perhaps he realized that in fact the Galileans had conquered, since he refused to name a successor, leaving the choice to the army who would almost certainly select a Christian. But constancy in matters of faith was ever one of Julian's strong points, and one can feel confident that he died as he had lived, committed to the gods he had chosen to follow in his early youth.

As the next Emperor, the army chose a compromise candidate: Jovian, a likable, easygoing young officer—and a Christian.[27] He was a very tall man; when they dressed him in one of Julian's purple cloaks, it was so much too short that it seemed almost comical. From the start there were various estimations of Jovian's chances for effective rulership. Everyone agreed that he was good-natured, but would this be a help or a hindrance? To Ammianus, he seemed too much a playboy, overly fond of wine and women, and lacking in dignity. In time, as he became accustomed to the responsibility of rulership, he might improve. . . .[28]

Jovian most of all wanted peace, a worthy ambition, but scarcely enough to justify the extreme concessions he was willing to make to the Persians. Yielding a large amount of territory (including several important border fortresses) to the enemy, he hastened his troops back to Roman soil.[29]

His popularity was rapidly sinking, but it mattered little. Within a few more months Jovian, too, was dead, reportedly asphyxiated by the fumes of a charcoal stove beside his bed.[30] The Roman world passed into the hands of another army officer, Valentinian, and his brother Valens, Christians both of them, and noticeably lacking in Jovian's good humor. Pagans throughout the Empire realized that a time of great change was beginning. For those who clung to the old ways, it was a fearful time, a time to reach out in desperation to the memory of the young man who had wanted to change the world by restoring the best of the past.

True to Julian's statement that when he came back from Persia he planned to winter in Tarsus, Jovian had arranged for his predecessor's burial in that city.[31] It is not clear who selected his epitaph, perhaps some Hellenic-minded scholar in the employ of Valens. With a clear echo of the language of the *Odyssey*, the plaque on the Emperor's tomb read simply: "Here lies Julian who fell by the swift-flowing Tigris. He was both a good king and a mighty warrior."[32]

It is interesting to contemplate how Julian, who was unenthusiastic about ruler-worship, would have reacted to Hellenism's final pronouncement upon his memory. Within a few months after his death, loyal pagans declared him a god, *Divus Julianus*. Pilgrims journeyed to Tarsus to pray to him at the spot where his mortal remains rested, or simply to touch the marble of his sarcophagus.[33]

At least one artifact of the Julian cult survives: a charming ivory plaque, depicting his ascension into the heavens.[34] This piece, probably made in 431 to commemorate the centennial of his birth, was originally a part of a diptych; the other half, which is lost, may have been a representation of his birth scene. The surviving plaque is crowded with Mithraic symbols, with elephants symbolizing Julian's eastern victories, and other elaborate details. Julian himself, borne skyward in the arms of two figures representing the winds, is dressed as he often was in life, not in imperial robes, but in the simple garb of a philosopher. If 431 is the correct date for this object, it indicates that worship of the last pagan Emperor went on for some decades after his death, though it would be frowned upon and eventually wiped out by Christian authorities.

Yet, shocking as the "Julian cult" must have been to Christian sensibilities at the time, it was in its way no more surprising than the Galileans' own veneration of martyrs.[35] Perhaps Libanius explained it best (in his Oration 18, and again in the later Oration 24, addressed to Valens' successor, the Christian Emperor Theodosius). Julian, he indicates, would definitely answer prayers, for surely was it not logical that he who had loved and fought for the Roman state while he lived, would continue to do so in the world beyond the grave?[36]

The reaction of the intensely Orthodox Theodosius to this argument is not recorded. It is to be noted, however, that it was Theodosius (probably acting upon a suggestion from the Empress Constantia of the West) who decided to have Julian's body brought to Constantinople for burial in the Church of the Holy Apostles.[37] There he would lie through the long centuries of medieval Byzantium, in this great burial hall of the Byzantine emperors, but in a place apart from the others, in a sarcophagus unadorned by the symbols of the faith he rejected.[38]

And on the other side of the Roman world, in Spain, the Christian poet Prudentius wrote what might well have been Julian's epitaph. Prudentius deplored the Emperor's "apostasy," but remembered, as Christians and pagans alike agreed:

"Faithful he was to the Roman State."

CHAPTER 22

A Note on Sources

JULIAN'S surviving literary works fall into several categories. Although most of these are discussed in the foregoing chapters, the reader may find a brief summary convenient at this point. From the standpoint of autobiographical detail, one of the most important of Julian's writings is his "Letter to the Senate and People of Athens," written in late 361 to justify his assumption of the title of Augustus. While he naturally tries to present himself in the best possible light, this work is nonetheless a frank and revealing disclosure of the tumult in the young Emperor's mind and heart as he faced the seemingly inevitable showdown with his rival Constantius.

Very different in character is "The Misopogon" ("Beard-Hater"), the satirical pamphlet Julian wrote early in 363, expressing his disgust with the city of Antioch after living there several months. Precisely because it is a satire and because Julian is satirizing himself, "The Misopogon" is open to much misinterpretation. At times he is straightforward enough; but at other times he deliberately makes himself seem unattractive, even repulsive, which he certainly was not in real life. All in all, it is a puzzling document, a cry of anguish from a deeply disappointed and misunderstood soul, and as such it must be used with caution.

Julian's letters, almost all of them from the brief twenty months of his reign, are also invaluable for their autobiographical glimpses. Compositions of a very different sort are the three "Panegyrics" written by Julian while Caesar of Gaul. The first "Panegyric in Honor of Constantius" and "The Heroic Deeds of Constantius" are so full of flattery of the Emperor whom Julian distrusted and perhaps despised that some have viewed them as practically worthless, though on closer inspection they are interesting repositories of Julian's thought on the ideals of rulership. His "Panegyric in Honor of the Empress Eusebia," which contains autobiographical material, is an apparently sincere act of gratitude to the Empress whose friendship may well have saved his life.

Also written in Gaul is Julian's "Consolation on the Departure of the Excellent Salustius." Though somewhat effusive in tone, it is a revealing insight into Julian's thought (and, after all, the effusiveness itself is very much a part of his character).

The rest of Julian's important works date from after his accession to Constantius' throne. In the realm of pure theology, he has left two prose hymns, "To King Helios" and "To the Mother of the Gods." Both were written very rapidly and are not as clear as one might wish, but nonetheless are crucial to understanding Julian's own particular interpretation of Neoplatonism and (especially in the piece on Helios) of the Mithraic religion. In two treatises against the Cynics, Julian attacks the only "school" of Greek philosophy that seemed to him almost as uncooperative and misguided as the Christians.

"The Caesars," a light-hearted satire on his own predecessors, comes as a surprise from the usually serious Julian, yet beneath the obvious frivolity this piece too has its message and its condemnation of the pro-Christian policies of the Constantinian emperors.

While it survives only in fragments, Julian's treatise "Against the Galileans" is extremely interesting for its insights into some of his objections to Christianity. The extant portions of this work center around Christianity's inconsistencies and its departure from its Jewish roots.

On the more positive side, in a long fragment entitled "Letter to a Priest," Julian outlines his plans for the new-old Hellenism he hopes to organize into a "church" that will offer an appeal surpassing that of the Galileans.

Between the fourth century and the introduction of printing more than a thousand years later, Julian's literary works, while forgotten in Western Europe, were preserved and recopied by Byzantine scholars. In some ways, it is curious to think of the Orthodox Christian Byzantines making an effort to save the writings of the "Apostate" emperor; but while they detested his

religious ideas, they admired his "style." Perhaps, too, something
of the same spirit that prompted them to bury him in the Orthodox Church of the Holy Apostles impelled them to keep copies
of his writings: after all, he was one of their emperors, a great
soldier, a learned man, and in spite of his "apostasy," a Byzantine
himself, the third *basileus* in the succession from the Great Constantine. Not that they preserved everything. Julian's commentaries on his Gallic wars have disappeared, as have many of
his letters. A large part of his treatise "Against the Galileans"
which the Orthodox must have found too shocking to copy is
also irretrievably lost.

With the coming of the Renaissance, the original Greek text
of Julian's works began to appear in printed editions in Western
Europe. Translations into Latin and later into other languages
followed.[1] The most authoritative modern edition is that planned
by Joseph Bidez and completed after his death by other
scholars, with Greek text and French translation.[2]

Although it is somewhat older and lacking in the detailed
notes of the Bidez edition, the English reader can use with
confidence the three volume set of *The Works of the Emperor
Julian,* edited and translated by Wilmer Cave Wright ("Loeb
Classical Library," Cambridge, Mass., 1913–23). For the con-
venience of the general reader who will find this edition most
readily accessible, all references to Julian's works in our text
include page citations from Mrs. Wright's volumes.

Also available in the Loeb Classical Library series are *The
Histories* of Ammianus Marcellinus, translated by J. C. Rolfe
(three volumes, 1935–40). Ammianus, a native of Antioch and
a professional soldier, was stationed in Gaul during part of
Julian's caesarship and later served in the ill-fated Persian campaign. While apparently he was never a close friend of Julian,
he admired him deeply. Nevertheless, Ammianus does not hesitate to criticize his hero's faults; he is determinedly objective,
a careful and usually accurate reporter. Strangely enough, although Greek was his native language, he chose to write in
Latin. Though his work is frequently ignored by students of
ancient history (since the fourth century is too "recent" to be
truly "ancient"), many Latin scholars consider him the greatest
Roman historian after Tacitus. His chapters on Julian are very

full and more than any other source are valuable for developing the chronology of Julian's career.

Material of an altogether different sort is provided by Libanius, who was in his day the most famous, successful, and controversial teacher in Antioch. An excellent edition of his *Selected Works* with translation by A. F. Norman has recently (1969) appeared in the Loeb Classical Library series. The volume is devoted to Libanius' specifically "Julianic" orations and includes almost all of his most important writings that have to do with Julian in any way. Particularly important is his lengthy "Oration 18," a funeral oration (never actually delivered) in which he gives a detailed summary of the Emperor's life.

Libanius knew Julian very well. For the seven months that the Emperor lived in Antioch, he saw him almost every day, and they spent many hours together in the philosophical discussions both of them so much enjoyed. In reading Libanius' work one must be alert to the fact that his deep and sincere devotion to Julian at times warped his objectivity. He actually contemplated suicide when he learned of Julian's death, but persuaded himself to keep on living for the purpose of celebrating Julian's memory for all eternity.[3] Needless to say, "Oration 18" and the other pieces he composed with this end in view present a somewhat idealized hero, but the very fact that one who knew him so well could admire him so much reveals a great deal about Julian's character.

Also of importance is Libanius' *Autobiography* ("Oration 1"), published as a separate volume with Greek text and English translation by A. F. Norman (London: Oxford University Press, 1965). Here will be found some interesting recollections of Libanius' contacts with Julian during the Emperor's stay in Antioch.

From the highly favorable works of Libanius, we turn next to the derogatory orations of Saint Gregory Nazianzen, composed a few years after Julian's death. The two "Invectives Against Julian" are available in English translation by C. W. King in *Julian the Emperor* ("Bohn's Classical Library," London, 1888), and are usually cited respectively as Orations 4 and 5. Saint Gregory knew Julian in Athens; that he hated him with passionate intensity is evident on every page of his work. Yet because of his nearness to Julian's own time, Gregory cannot be dismissed simply as a hate-monger; mixed with the rumors and gossip are valid criticisms of the Emperor, at least from the Christian viewpoint. And if much of the later "black legend of the Apostate" derives ultimately from Saint Gregory, he is also most revealing in the allegations he does *not* lay at Julian's doorstep: even Gregory has nothing disparaging to say of the Emperor's personal morality.

Within the next generation, in the early fifth century, appeared the work of Eunapius, who utilized many sources, oral and written, among them recollections furnished him by Julian's friend, the physician Oribasius. Eunapius' *Lives of the Sophists* (translated by Mrs. W. C. Wright, "Loeb Classical Library," 1921) contains a wealth of data on Julian's student years and his philosopher friends. Even more important, however, would have been another work, now almost completely lost—Eunapius' *Histories*, including a "Life of Julian." The few fragments that remain (as well as *The Lives of the Sophists*) reveal the Eunapius, himself a pagan, esteemed Julian highly. There is no English translation of the fragments of the "Life," but the Greek text is available in C. Müller's edition, *Fragmenta Historicorum Graecorum*, Vol. V (Paris, 1885).

Somewhat later than Eunapius, we come to Count Zosimus, also a pagan and a devoted admirer of Julian. (His dates are uncertain, but he most likely belongs to the late fifth century.)[4] Utilizing sources no longer extant for his *Historia Nova* ("New History"), Zosimus concentrates on Julian as a military man. An English translation of the Greek original has been published as *Historia Nova: The Decline of Rome*, translated by James J. Buchanan and Harold T. Davis (San Antonio: Trinity University Press, 1967).

Turning again to the Christian side, we find in the fifth century the works of the three ecclesiastical historians: Socrates Scholasticus (born c. 380), Hermias Sozomen (born c. 400), and Theodoret of Cyrrhus, whose very unfavorable image of Julian was widely disseminated throughout the Middle Ages both in their original Greek and in Latin translation. Socrates Scholasticus and Hermias Salamenes Sozomen were contemporaries; and though Socrates was somewhat the elder, they composed their books at almost exactly the same time in the 440's. Both were lawyers in Constantinople, and as such almost certainly knew each other. Both were intensely Christian, and consequently had little good to say of Julian, though Sozomen on the whole is much the fairer and tries to present both sides.

Far more malicious than either Sozomen or Socrates is the slightly later Theodoret, Bishop of Cyrrhus, whose *Ecclesiastical History* was often published together with theirs. In his narrative on Julian, Theodoret copied all the worst that his historical predecessors had reported and added a good deal of his own that apparently has little if any basis in fact.

Another distinctly hostile reporter is Philostorgius, an Arian Christian (born c. 364). Earlier than the Socrates-Sozomen-Theodoret trio, his work is less well known, since it survives only in an epitome prepared by the learned ninth-century Byzantine Patriarch Photios.

The Greek texts of these various ecclesiastical historians are to be found in *Patrologia Graeca*, edited by J.-P. Migne. There are several English translations although none is recent. Perhaps most easily accessible are those in the Bohn's Ecclesiastical Library series published in London: Philostorgius (1855), Socrates (1853), Sozomen (1855), and Theodoret (1854).

With such a diversity of source material to draw from it is little wonder that Julian has been interpreted in vastly differing lights through the centuries. Though medieval historians did little but repeat the charges of his early critics, the coming of the Renaissance brought with it the beginning of a reappraisal of Julian's role in history.[5] A hint of this appears already in 1489 in a play by the colorful Florentine statesman, Lorenzo de'Medici.[6] As years went by, the dissemination of Julian's own writings and those of Ammianus caused historians more and more to consider the "Apostate" in a favorable light, a view popularized by Michel de Montaigne in his essay, "Of Liberty of Conscience" (1578).[7] Julian, the famed essayist declared, was "in truth a very great and rare man," to be praised for his many virtues.

Julian received considerably more attention in the eighteenth century, when the *philosophes* of the Enlightenment imagined that they had found in him a kindred spirit. Montesquieu, Voltaire, Diderot, and others praised him extravagantly, picturing him as a genuine "enlightened despot," and by implication, the sort of king that the France of their own time needed and sadly lacked. Such praise was risky: Diderot was imprisoned for writing, among other things, that Julian was "the prince of philosophers" and definitely not an apostate.[8]

While the French *philosophes* generally tried to explain away Julian's "unenlightened" superstitiousness (if they mentioned it at all) and his very real commitment to his own variety of religion, their contemporary, the Englishman Edward Gibbon, in his famous *Decline and Fall of the Roman Empire,* takes a more balanced view. One modern commentator has pronounced Gibbon's account as still the best biographical narrative of Julian in English.[9] Gibbon, no friend of Christianity, plainly admired Julian, but although he praises him enthusiastically at many points, he also deplores his superstitious inclinations.[10]

If Julian failed to conform perfectly to the eighteenth-century ideal of the "enlightened despot," he fell just as far short of exemplifying the role in which he was cast by the early nineteenth century, that of the tragic young Romantic rebel. This view, which is not without its measure of truth, was altogether overdrawn. Just as the *philosophes* before them, the Romantics tended to lift Julian out of the context of his own time and to transfer him to their own thought milieu. An interesting example of this view is that of Alfred de Vigny who declared he would have rather been Julian than anyone who ever lived, and who composed a long philosophical dialogue carried on in his imagination between Julian and Libanius.[11]

Modern scholarly work on Julian has been extensive and diverse.[12] (For a sampling, see the Selected Bibliography.) Of the many modern studies Joseph Bidez's *La vie de l'Empereur Julien* (Paris, 1930; reprint, 1965), although now more than forty years old, still holds a place of foremost importance. Concise yet thorough, it is a treasure-trove of information for any serious student of Julian's career.

Quite apart from the many scholarly studies devoted to Julian, the intrinsic fascination of his career has also made him the subject of several important works of fiction. The great Norwegian playwright Henrik Ibsen (following the example of

Lorenzo de'Medici) made him the subject of a drama, *Emperor and Galilean*. The play, which is historically inaccurate at many points, also proved to be one of Ibsen's few failures, though he is reported personally to have had high hopes for it.[13]

From early in the twentieth century comes Dmitri Merezhkovski's widely read novel, *The Death of the Gods*. (There is an English translation of the Russian original by Herbert Trench, London, 1901, reprint 1926.) For good or ill, Merezhkovski's highly imaginative portrayal of Julian probably contributed more than any other book to shaping the average reader's impressions of the Emperor for two generations, a role that in more recent times is being fulfilled by Gore Vidal's best-seller, *Julian* (Boston, 1964). Vidal's work is very movingly written and overall is far sounder historically than was Merezhkovski's, though the reader will find many scenes that derive strictly from the author's imagination and some of these, at least, are surprisingly un-Julianic.

In conclusion, it is well to ponder what the very existence of such diverse literature suggests about Julian's historical reputation. Dating over a span of sixteen centuries and interpreting their subject in widely varied lights, countless authors and readers have found Julian a fascinating person—one who, whatever else he may have been, is never boring. Idealized by some, cordially hated by others, he has captured the imagination of the centuries. His short life has all the elements of high drama; while his death will forever carry with it the unanswerable question: what might have been had he lived longer? Julian failed; yet in a negative way, his influence in later history is very real. In the decline of the Roman Empire and the rising authority of the Christian Church, in the whole of the Middle Ages and on into modern times, the historian can recognize what happened *without* Julian to guide the state through the crises of the late fourth century.

And thus Julian has become, in a sense, something more than an interesting and well-documented historical figure. He is a symbol of unrealized but ardent hope for those who, like himself, continue to believe even amid despair that the world can yet become a better place.

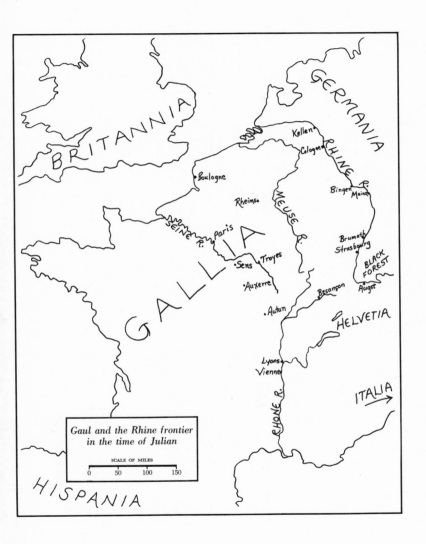

Gaul and the Rhine frontier
in the time of Julian

SCALE OF MILES

0   50   100   150

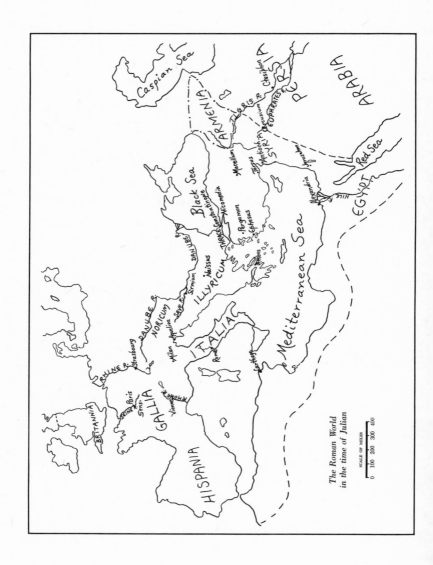

*The Roman World
in the time of Julian*

SCALE OF MILES

0   100 200 300 400

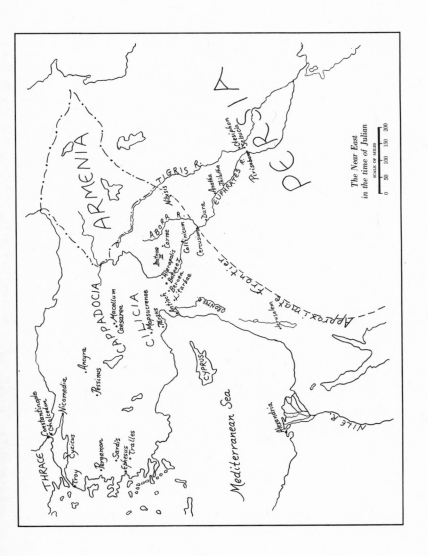

The Near East
in the time of Julian

SCALE OF MILES

0   50   100   150   200

Notes and References

Preface

1. Julian's status as the "last" pagan emperor might be challenged by those who would accord this distinction to the usurper Eugenius (392–394), but Eugenius' allegiance to the old gods is far from clear, and in any event he was not recognized empire-wide. Julian is unmistakably the last *effective* pagan emperor.

2. Throughout this work, references to classical sources will be given according to traditional book, chapter and section divisions based on the ancient manuscripts, numberings that are repeated in the best modern editions and translations. References to Julian's own writings will also be followed by a citation of volume and page numbers in the Loeb Classical Library edition prepared by Mrs. Wilmer Cave Wright. For additional information on texts and editions, see Chapter 22, "A Note on Sources."

3. Libanius, *Selected Works*, ed. and trans. A. F. Norman ("Loeb Classical Library"; Cambridge, Mass., 1969), Vol. I. Oration 18.303.

Chapter One

1. Also called Constantia.

2. Julian mentions the massacre in his "Letter to the Senate and People of Athens," 270C-D (Wright II, 249), but he is not completely clear on the identity of all the victims.

3. "Letter to the Senate and People of Athens," 271B (Wright II, 249), hereinafter cited as "Ath."

4. The name of Constantius' first wife is uncertain. Joseph Bidez, *La vie de l'Empereur Julien* (Paris, 1930; reprint 1965), p. 8, calls her Constantia, while Giuseppe Ricciotti, *Julian the Apostate* (Milwaukee, 1960), p. 6, suggests Fausta.

5. Gallus' full name was Flavius Claudius Julius Constantius Gallus.

6. Libanius 18.10.

7. Gregory Nazianzen, Oration 4.91. (Hereinafter cited as G.N.) The story is copied from Gregory by several of the fifth-century historians.

8. Gallus' mother was an Italian lady named Galla, first wife of

Julius Constantius. Ammianus Marcellinus, *Histories*, 14.11.27. (Hereinafter cited as A.M.)

9. Julian's birthday is uncertain, but November 6, the date of his coronation as Caesar, was accepted by some of the older authorities; it is certainly possible, since one's birthday was sometimes deliberately selected as one's coronation date, and he seems to have been born late in the year. On the other hand, Frank D. Gilliard in "Notes on the Coinage of Julian the Apostate," *Journal of Roman Studies*, 54 (1964), 139–41, suggests that Julian was a "Taurus," born in late May or early June of 332, and that this explains the otherwise mysterious bull figure that appears on some of his coins.

10. Bidez, *Julien*, pp. 8–9.

11. Julian, "The Misopogon," 352B (Wright II, 461).

12. The name Basilina ("Little Queen") is simply a variant of Basilia. Richard Delbrueck, *Spaetantike Kaiserportraets* (Berlin, 1933), pp. 174–75.

13. "To the Cynic Heracleios," 230 (Wright II, 139).

14. Most of Julian's recollections of Mardonius are to be found in "The Misopogon," 351–52 (Wright II, 459–63).

15. Julian never mentions Mardonius' religious affiliation, a strong "argument from silence" that he was a nominal Christian and that his former student did not want to remember it. See A. J. Festugière, "Julien à Macellum," *Journal of Roman Studies*, 47 (1957), 54. (Hereinafter referred to as *JRS*.)

16. "Misop.," 351 (Wright II, 457).

17. "Misop.," 351C-D (Wright II, 459).

18. Libanius 18.11.

19. Libanius 18.12.

20. Norman H. Baynes, "The Early Life of Julian the Apostate," *Journal of Hellenic Studies*, 45 (1925), 252. (Hereinafter referred to as *JHS*.)

21. Julian's description of his grandmother's home is found in his letter no. 25, "To Evagrius" (Wright III, 77–81). After he became Emperor, Julian gave this property to his friend Evagrius, a rhetor.

22. Julian, "Hymn to King Helios," 130C-D (Wright I, 353).

Chapter Two

1. Regarding the date, see Baynes, "Early Life of Julian, *JHS*, 45 (1925), 252. Anne Hadjinicolaou, "Macellum, lieu d'exil de l'Empereur Julien," *Byzantion*, 21 (1951), 16, prefers 341. The later date of 345, once accepted by many scholars, has now been universally abandoned.

2. "Ath.," 271B (Wright II, 251).

3. "Ath.," 271D (Wright II, 251).

4. Julian's letter no. 23 "To Ecdicius, Prefect of Egypt" (Wright III, 73–75).

5. Julian's ability to quote passages of the Bible from memory years later is evidenced in his treatise "Against the Galileans."

6. For example see Julian's letter no. 41 "To the Citizens of Bostra" (Wright III, 129).

7. On this matter see the detailed analysis of Festugière, "Julien à Macellum," *JRS*, 47 (1957), 56–58.

8. G.N. 4.52.

9. Festugière, "Julien à Macellum," *JRS*, 47 (1957), 54.

10. "King Helios," 130C (Wright I, 353).

11. "To Heracleios," 229C ff. (Wright II, 137 ff.).

12. G.N. 4.23. See also Hermias Salamenes Sozomen, *Ecclesiastical History*, 5.2; Theodoret of Cyrrhus, *Ecclesiastical History*, 3.2.

13. G.N. 4.30.

14. G.N. 4.25 is the first to report this story though he does not designate St. Mamas by name. See also Sozomen, 5.2; Theodoret, 3.2. On the exact location of the shrine to St. Mamas, see Hadjinicolaou, "Macellum," *Byzantion*, 21 (1951), 20–21.

15. "Ath.," 271C (Wright II, 251).

16. Baynes, "Early Life of Julian," *JHS*, 45 (1925), 254.

Chapter Three

1. We learn of Julian's beard in "Ath.," 274C (Wright II, 259), where he tells of his regret when Constantius later required him to have it shaved off.

2. A.M. 14.11.28.

3. The much later Byzantine historian Cedrenus says, however, that Julian's hair was black. Delbrueck, *Spaetantike Kaiserportraets*, p. 25.

4. A.M. 25.4.22 has a number of interesting details. On Julian's appearance see also Andrew Alföldi, "Some Portraits of Julianus Apostata," *American Journal of Archaeology*, 66 (1962), 403–405.

5. Julian's most vivid description of himself is to be found in "Misop.," 238B–239C (Wright II, 423–27). Because this work is satire, however, one must beware of taking Julian literally at every point; rather, he seems determined to exaggerate his unattractiveness.

6. Eunapius, *Lives of the Sophists*, is most readily available in the Loeb Classical Library edition (Cambridge, Mass., 1921). Ed. & trans. Mrs. W. C. Wright.

7. Libanius 18.13.

8. Eunapius, *Sophists*, section 474 (Wright, p. 429).

9. Ibid.

10. Julian's epigram 2, "On the Organ" (Wright III, 305).

11. Libanius 18.13.

12. Libanius 18.13–14.

13. Libanius 18.15.

14. Sozomen, 5.2; Socrates, 3.1.

15. Julian, "Letter to Themistius," 259C-D (Wright II, 217–19).

16. Eunapius, *Sophists*, sec. 474 (Wright, p. 431).

17. Eunapius, *Sophists*, sec. 474 (Wright, p. 429).

18. Eunapius, *Sophists*, sec. 475 (Wright, p. 435).

19. Ibid. Contrariwise, Socrates Scholasticus, 3.1, says that Maximus came to Nicomedia to meet Julian. Eunapius' account is preferrable.

20. Eunapius, *Sophists*, sec. 473 (Wright, p. 427).

21. Julian's letter no. 47 "To the Alexandrians" (Wright III, 149).

22. The classic study of Mithraism is Franz Cumont, *The Mysteries of Mithra*, trans. Thomas J. McCormack (1903; reprint New York, 1956). See also Francis Legge, *Forerunners and Rivals of Christianity* (New York, 1915; reprint 1964), II, 227–73.

23. Legge, *Forerunners and Rivals*, II, 240.

24. Cumont, *Mysteries*, p. 156.

25. R. Jonas, "A Newly Discovered Portrait of the Emperor Julian," *American Journal of Archaeology*, 50 (1946), 281.

26. G.N. 4.70.

27. G.N. 4.55.

28. Gabriel Rochefort, "Les lectures latines de l'Empereur Julien," *Revue des études grecques*, 75 (1962), xxiii; see also Christian Lacombrade, "L'Empereur Julien et la tradition romaine," *Pallas*, 9 (1960), 160–61.

29. The extent of Julian's ability in Latin has been the subject of considerable scholarly discussion. In addition to the foregoing references, see E. A. Thompson, "The Emperor Julian's Knowledge of Latin," *Classical Review*, 58 (1944), 49-51, representative of the older view that Julian's Latin was far from outstanding, and that he read practically none of the Roman classics.

30. Libanius 18.20.

31. "To Heracleios," 232 (Wright II, 143–45).

Chapter Four

1. "Ath.," 271 (Wright II, 249).

2. A full page color reproduction of this portrait may be found in André Grabar, *Early Christian Art* (New York, 1968), p. 189.

3. A.M. 14.1.2.

4. This more favorable view of Gallus stems from the fragmentary *Ecclesiastical History* of Philostorgius, an Arian Christian who admired Gallus' allegiance to Arianism and his patronage of missionary efforts. For a modern defense of Gallus, see E. A. Thompson, *The Historical Work of Ammianus Marcellinus* (Cambridge, England, 1947), pp. 56 ff.; also W. Den Boer, "Two Letters from the *Corpus Iulianeum*," *Vigiliae Christianae*, 16 (1962), 179–81. (Hereinafter referred to as *VC*.)

5. Much of A.M.'s Book 14 is devoted to the reign of Gallus. See especially sections 1, 7, 9, and 11.

6. "Ath.," 271D–272C (Wright II, 251-53).

7. "Ath.," 273 (Wright II, 255).

8. Philostorgius, 3.27, mentions Gallus' concern about Julian's religious activities and says Aetius visited Julian several times. There is also a "Letter from Gallus Caesar to his Brother Julian" (letter no. 82 in Wright III, 289–91), in which Gallus expresses his relief on hearing from Aetius that Julian was a practicing Christian. It is not certain if this is an authentic composition of Gallus, but Den Boer, "Two Letters," *VC*, 16 (1962), 182 ff. defends it.

9. "Letter from Gallus Caesar" (Wright III, 289).

10. A.M. 15.2.7–8.

11. A.M. 14.11.6.

12. A.M. 14.11.12.

13. A.M. 14.11.19–23. See also Libanius 18.24.

14. A.M. 15.1.2.

15. "Ath.," 271D–272 (Wright II, 251–53).

16. Libanius 18.26.

17. "Ath.," 273 (Wright II, 255).

Chapter Five

1. Julian's letter no. 19 "To a Priest" (Wright III, 49–55), is the sole source for his visit to Troy. It is interesting to note that Julian's descriptions of the Homeric shrines as they appeared in his time have proved of considerable value to modern archaeological study of the Trojan ruins.

2. On the Christian custom of hissing at pagan relics see Charles A. Bolton, "Emperor Julian Against Hissing Christians," *Harvard Theological Review*, 61 (1968), 496–97.

3. "To a Priest" (Wright III, 49).

4. "Ath.," 273 (Wright II, 255).

5. Libanius 18.25.

6. A.M. 15.2.7.

7. Bidez, *Julien*, p. 106 (inferred from A.M. 18.4.3).

8. A.M. 15.2.7–8.

9. A.M. 15.3.4–6.

10. "Ath.," 273B (Wright II, 255).

11. Julian, "Panegyric in Honour of the Empress Eusebia," 118B-C (Wright I, 315); see also Libanius 18.27.

12. Libanius 13.19; 18.29.

13. "Eusebia," 118D (Wright I, 317).

14. Bidez, *Julien*, p. 113.

15. Eunapius, *Sophists*, section 476 (Wright, p. 437). This prediction, incidentally, turned out to be true.

16. Eunapius, *Sophists*, section 476 (Wright, pp. 437–39), who provides the sole source for Julian's acquaintance with the hierophant at this time, plainly does not say that Julian was initiated, though many modern historians have assumed that he was.

17. Libanius 18.29–30.

18. Eunapius, *Sophists*, section 481 (Wright, pp. 461–63).

19. G.N. 5.23.

20. Libanius 18.31.

21. "Ath.," 275 (Wright II, 259); see also Libanius 12.38.

Chapter Six

1. "Letter to the Athenians," 275B (Wright II, 261).

2. "Ath.," 275C (Wright II, 261).

3. "Ath.," 275C-D (Wright II, 261).

4. "Ath.," 274C-D (Wright II, 259).

5. Ibid.

6. "Ath.," 275 (Wright II, 259).

7. A.M. 15.8.4–17.

8. A.M. 15.8.18, quoting *The Iliad*, 5.83.

9. "Eusebia," 123 (Wright I, 327).

10. "Ath.," 277 (Wright II, 265).

11. Bidez, *Julien*, p. 130.

12. "Ath.," 277C (Wright II, 265).

13. "Eusebia," 123 (Wright I, 327).

14. Her mother Fausta was executed in 326. While Helena was the youngest of Fausta's children, the exact year of her birth is not recorded.

15. "Eusebia," 123D (Wright I, 329); "Ath.," 284C (Wright II, 283); see also following note.

16. Julian's letter no. 29 "To His Uncle Julian" (Wright III, 103).

17. "Eusebia," 123D (Wright I, 329).
18. "Eusebia," 124 (Wright I, 329).
19. A.M. 16.5.3.

Chapter Seven

1. Julian, "The Shorter Fragments," no. 5 (Wright III, 299); see also Zosimus, *Historia Nova*, 3.3.
2. "Ath.," 277D (Wright II, 267).
3. A.M. 15.8.22.
4. Libanius 18.41.
5. Libanius 12.24.
6. A.M. 16.2.1.
7. A.M. 16.5.10.
8. A.M. 16.5.4–8.
9. Libanius 12.25.
10. A.M. 15.5.22. For additional biographical background on A.M. see Thompson, *Historical Work of Ammianus Marcellinus*, pp. 1–12.
11. Libanius 18.36–110.
12. A.M. 16.1.1.
13. Zosimus 3.3.
14. "Ath.," 278 (Wright II, 267).
15. André Piganoil, "La couronne de Julien César," *Byzantion*, 13 (1938), 246–47.
16. "Ath.," 278 (Wright II, 267).
17. A.M. 16.2.1.
18. A.M. 16.2.1–3; Libanius 18.43–44.
19. A.M. 16.2.3–7.
20. A.M. 16.2.9.
21. A.M. 16.2.10–11; Libanius 18.45.
22. A.M. 16.2.12–3.2; Libanius 18.46.
23. "Ath.," 278 (Wright II, 267).
24. A.M. 16.4.2.
25. A.M. 16.7.1; Libanius 18.48.
26. A.M. 16.11.1–2.
27. A.M. 16.7.3–8.
28. A.M. 16.7.3.
29. Ricciotti, *Julian*, p. 89.
30. First "Pan. on Constantius," 48 (Wright I, 123).
31. First "Pan. on Constantius," 45D (Wright I, 117).
32. On this matter see especially Francis Dvornik, "The Emperor Julian's 'Reactionary' Ideas on Kingship." In *Late Classical and*

Mediaeval Studies in Honor of Albert Mathias Friend Jr., ed. Kurt Weitzmann (Princeton, 1955), pp. 71–81.

33. First "Pan. on Const.," 46D–47 (Wright I, 121).
34. First "Pan. on Const.," 41B (Wright I, 107).
35. First "Pan. on Const.," 16C (Wright I, 43).
36. A.M. 16.10.19.
37. A.M. 16.10.18.
38. Alice Gardner, *Julian, Philosopher and Emperor* (New York, 1895), pp. 92–93.
39. Julian does not mention Helena but he does refer to the Roman triumphal ceremonies of Constantius which Helena attended in 357 in "Eusebia," 129B (Wright I, 343).

Chapter Eight

1. A.M. 15.11.2. Libanius 18.49 says thirty thousand.
2. A.M. 16.11.3–6.
3. A.M. 16.11.8, 12.
4. A.M. 16.11.9–11.
5. A.M. 16.11.11.; Libanius 18.52.
6. A.M. 16.11.12.
7. A.M. 16.11.14–15; Libanius 18.50–51.
8. A.M. 18.3.1–4.
9. A.M. 16.12.1–3; Libanius 18.52.
10. A.M. 16.12.8.
11. A.M. 16.12.13. See also Libanius 18.53.
12. A.M. 16.12.36.
13. A.M. 16.12.22.
14. Libanius 18.59.
15. A.M. 16.12.43.
16. A.M. 16.12.53–57.
17. A.M. 16.12.63. Libanius 18.60 says eight thousand Germans fell. Zosimus 3.3 is certainly wrong when he numbers the enemy dead at sixty thousand.
18. Zosimus 3.3.
19. A.M. 16.12.65–66; Libanius 18.61–62; "Ath.," 279C-D (Wright II, 271).
20. Libanius 18.63–64.
21. "Ath.," 279D (Wright II, 271).
22. A.M. 17.1.1.
23. A.M. 17.1.2.
24. Libanius 18.65.
25. A.M. 17.2.4–13; Libanius 18.68–69.
26. A.M. 17.2.1–4; Libanius 18.70.

Chapter Nine

1. "Misop.," 340D–342 (Wright II, 429–33).
2. "Misop.," 341B–342 (Wright II, 431–33).
3. Julian's letter no. 5 "To Priscus" (Wright III, 15). Mrs. Wright is almost certainly mistaken in her guess that he refers to his semi-asphyxiation, since Julian says ("Misop.," 342) that he had fully recovered from that experience by the next day.
4. Julian, "The Heroic Deeds of the Emperor Constantius," 87C (Wright I, 233).
5. A.M. 16.5.4.
6. A.M. 18.1.4.
7. A.M. 16.5.12.
8. A.M. 17.3.2.
9. A.M. 17.3.5.
10. Julian's letter no. 4 "To Oribasius" (Wright III, 11–13).
11. A.M. 17.3.5.
12. A.M. 16.5.14.
13. In Mrs. Wright's edition (II, 167–97) "A Consolation to Himself upon the Departure of the Excellent Sallust." Hereinafter cited as "Salustius." (The classical form of his name is to be preferred to the Anglicized "Sallust.")
14. "Salustius," 245B (Wright II, 179).
15. "Salustius," 248D (Wright II, 187).
16. "Salustius," 251D (Wright II, 195).
17. "Salustius," 252C-D (Wright II, 197). Incidentally, the references to a singular God are not so surprising as they might seem from a devout pagan, since the philosophical Hellenists tended to believe that all gods were manifestations of The One.
18. A.M. 21.8.1.
19. See especially "Heroic Deeds," 85D–93D (Wright I, 229–49).
20. "Heroic Deeds," 89 (Wright I, 237).
21. Dvornik, "Julian's Ideas on Kingship," *Late Classical and Mediaeval Studies*, p. 74.
22. Julian's letter no. 3 "To Eumenius and Pharianus" (Wright III, 7).
23. Ibid.
24. Julian's letter no. 2 "To Priscus" (Wright III, 5).
25. Libanius 12.55–56.
26. Libanius 12.55; see also 18.74.
27. Eunapius, *Sophists*, section 476 (Wright, p. 439).
28. A.M. 16.5.1–3.

29. Julian's epigram no. 1 "On Wine Made from Barley" (Wright III, 305).

Chapter Ten

1. "Ath.," 279D–280 (Wright II, 271); Libanius 18.83.
2. "Ath.," 280B (Wright II, 271-73).
3. Libanius 18.87 ff.; Zosimus 3.4.
4. "Ath.," 280C-D (Wright II, 273).
5. A.M. 17.9.3.
6. A.M. 17.10.1.
7. A.M. 17.10.5–9.
8. Zosimus 3.4. On prisoner return, see also Libanius 18.78–79.
9. A.M. 18.2.4–6.
10. A.M. 18.2.2–3.
11. A.M. 18.2.7ff.
12. "Ath.," 280C-D (Wright II, 273).
13. Ibid.
14. A.M. 16.12.69–70.
15. A.M. 16.12.67.
16. Piganoil, "La couronne de Julien César," *Byzantion*, 13 (1938), 248.
17. A.M. 17.11.1.
18. A.M. 16.10.9–11; 21.16.1–7.

Chapter Eleven

1. For details, see Walter Emil Kaegi, Jr., "Research on Julian the Apostate, 1945–1964," *The Classical World*, 58 (1965), 231–32.
2. A most important study of this problem is Ilse Müller-Seidel, "Die Usurpation Julians des Abtrünnigen im Lichte siener Germanenpolitik," *Historische Zeitschrift*, 180 (1955), 225–44. (Hereinafter referred to as *HZ*.) See also Ricciotti, *Julian*, pp. 143–44.
3. Eunapius, *Sophists*, section 498 (Wright, p. 533). Eunapius also wrote a *Life of Julian*, part of his *Histories*, of which only a few small fragments have been preserved. In "fragment 14" there are similar indications of "planning ahead" by Julian and his friends.
4. Julian's letter no. 4 "To Oribasius" (Wright III, 9–15).
5. Ibid.
6. Ibid. (Wright III, 9–11).
7. Eunapius, *Sophists*, section 476 (Wright, pp. 439–41).
8. Philostorgius 4.7. The exact date of Eusebia's death is not clear. Müller-Seidel, "Die Usurpation," *HZ*, 180 (1955), 242, believes she died shortly before spring, 360.

9. Eunapius, *Sophists*, section 476 (Wright, p. 441).
10. A.M. 20.4.1–2; Libanius 18.90–93; Zosimus 3.8.
11. A.M. 20.1.2–3.
12. Müller-Seidel, "Die Usurpation," *HZ*, 180 (1955), 228, 232 ff.
13. A.M. 20.4.4.
14. A.M. 20.4.6–8; "Ath.," 283 (Wright II, 279).
15. Libanius 18.95; 12.58.
16. "Ath.," 283B (Wright II, 279).
17. A.M. 20.4.10. See also Zosimus 3.9.
18. A.M. 20.4.11.
19. A.M. 20.4.12.
20. "Ath.," 284C (Wright II, 283).
21. A.M. 20.5.10.
22. Libanius 13.24; 12.60.
23. "Ath.," 284D (Wright II, 283).
24. A.M. 20.4.7.
25. A.M. 20.4.17–18; "Ath.," 284D (Wright II, 283); Libanius 18.99.
26. "Ath.," 285 (Wright II, 283-85).
27. Libanius 18.100.

Chapter Twelve

1. A.M. 20.4.19–22; "Ath.," 285D (Wright II, 285); Libanius 18.102.
2. A.M. 20.5.5–17.
3. A.M. 20.8.18.
4. A.M. 20.9.2. See also Zosimus 3.9.
5. "Ath.," 285 (Wright II, 287).
6. A.M. 20.9.4–5.
7. A.M. 20.9.6–8.
8. Müller-Seidel, "Die Usurpation," *HZ*, 180 (1955), 232 ff.
9. A.M. 20.9.9.
10. A.M. 20.9.5. About a year later, suspected by Julian of disloyalty, Gomoarius was relieved of his command and replaced by Nevitta.
11. A.M. 20.10.2.
12. Julian's letter no. 8 "To Maximus" (Wright III, 23).
13. A.M. 21.1.5.
14. Libanius 18.179.
15. A.M. 21.6.4.
16. A.M. 21.2.1–2.
17 A.M. 21.1.8–14.

18. A.M. 21.2.2; Zosimus 3.9 identifies the deity as Helios (Mithra). See also Libanius 18.105.

19. Julian's letter no. 8 "To Maximus" (Wright III, 23–25).

20. A.M. 21.1.4.

21. Zosimus 3.9.

22. A.M. 21.2.4–5.

23. "Ath.," 286B (Wright II, 287).

24. A.M. 21.3.1–3. See also "Ath.," 286B (Wright II, 287); Libanius 18.107.

25. A.M. 21.3.4–4.6.

Chapter Thirteen

1. A.M. 21.5.10.

2. Libanius 18.110; A.M. 21.5.11–12.

3. A.M. 21.5.12.

4. Libanius 18.109.

5. "Ath.," 287B-C (Wright II, 289–91).

6. "Ath.," 286C (Wright II, 287).

7. Ibid.

8. A.M. 21.8.3.

9. A.M. 21.9.2. Zosimus 3.10 says that Julian had the boats built.

10. Libanius 13.38.

11. A.M. 21.9.4; Zosimus 3.10.

12. A.M. 21.9.5–6.

13. A.M. 21.9.7–8.

14. A.M. 21.10.1.

15. Libanius 18.114.

16. See Glanville Downey, "Julian the Apostate at Antioch," *Church History*, 8 (1939), 313.

17. There is also a small fragment of Julian's "Letter to the Corinthians" in which he mentions the fact that his father once lived in Corinth. Julian's fragment no. 3 (Wright III, 297). See also Libanius 14.29–30; 12.64.

18. Julian's letter no. 8 "To Maximus" (Wright III, 25).

19. A.M., 21.12.22.

20. A.M. 21.11.2–3.

21. A.M. 21.7.6–7; 13.1–8.

22. A.M. 21.14.2.

23. Socrates Scholasticus 2.47.

24. A.M. 21.15.2.

25. G.N. 4.48. Gregory also hints that Julian poisoned Constantius, a charge completely without evidence.

26. A.M. 21.15.6.

Chapter Fourteen

1. Julian's letter no. 9 "To his Uncle Julian" (Wright III, 27–29).
2. Libanius 18.119.
3. A.M. 22.2.2.
4. Julian's letter no. 13 "To Hermogenes, formerly Prefect of Egypt" (Wright III, 33).
5. Julian's letter no. 48 "To the Alexandrians" (Wright III, 153).
6. The Church of Sancta (or Hagia) Sophia of Julian's time was completely destroyed in the Nika Riots of 532, early in the reign of the Emperor Justinian I. Justinian's magnificent "new" Hagia Sophia, built on the same spot and still standing in Istanbul, probably bears little resemblance to its predecessor.
7. A.M. 22.2.4; see also Zosimus 3.11.
8. As is evident from his coins and statues. See Pierre Lévêque, "Observations sur l'iconographie de Julien dit l'Apostat d'après une tête inédite de Thasos," *Momuments Piot*, 51 (1960), 118.
9. Libanius 18.191.
10. Libanius 18.190.
11. A.M. 21.16.20–21.
12. Libanius 18.120. See also G.N. 5.17; Philostorgius 6.6.
13. Zosimus 3.11.
14. Libanius 18.130; A.M. 22.4.1 ff.
15. A.M. 22.4.9.
16. "Misop.," 352B (Wright II, 461); see also A.M. 22.4.1–6.
17. Socrates Sch. 3.1.
18. Libanius 18.131 ff.
19. Libanius 18.134.
20. See, for instance, Libanius 12.85.
21. Libanius 18.146–48; see also A.M. 22.9.12.
22. See, for instance, Glanville Downey, *The Late Roman Empire* (New York, 1969), pp. 32–33.
23. Julian's letter no. 31 "A Decree concerning Physicians" (Wright III, 107–109).
24. A.M. (22.9.12 and 25.4.21) is not at all enthusiastic about the curial reforms and indicates that Julian was not immune to an occasional bribe. A.M.'s failure to appreciate benefits of this reform is most likely due to the fact that he had avoided curial duty himself only by making the military service his lifelong career.
25. Libanius 13.42; 18.143–45; G.N. 4.75.
26. See, for example, such free passes mentioned in Julian's letters: no. 8 "To Maximus" (Wright III, 27); no. 15 "To Bishop Aetius" (Wright III, 37); no. 26 "To Basil" (Wright III, 83).

27. Eunapius, *Sophists*, section 476–77 (Wright, pp. 441–43).

28. Libanius 18.154.

29. A.M. 22.7.3; Libanius 18.155–56.

30. Eunapius, *Sophists*, section 477 (Wright, p. 445).

31. Eunapius, *Sophists*, section 476–77 (Wright, pp. 441–47).

32. A.M. 22.3.1–2. See also Julian's letter no. 13 "To Hermogenes" (Wright III, 33). Salustius Secundus (or, perhaps more correctly, Salutius) is not to be confused with Julian's friend Salustius of Gaul.

33. See especially Thompson, *Ammianus Marcellinus*, pp. 73-78.

34. A.M. 21.8.1 and 22.7.1.

35. Thompson, *Ammianus Marcellinus*, p. 74.

36. A.M. 22.3.10.

37. Libanius 18.152; see also A.M. 22.3.8.

38. A.M. 22.7.5.

39. A.M. 22.7.1.

40. Mamertinus is the author of a panegyric on Julian, *Gratiarum Actio*, delivered on this occasion.

41. Kaegi, "Research on Julian," *CW*, 58 (1965), 238.

42. A.M. 22.10.8.

43. A.M. 22.7.1.

44. A.M. 22.7.2.

45. Julian's letter no. 29 "To his Uncle Julian" (Wright III, 97–99).

46. Libanius 18.189.

Chapter Fifteen

1. "To the Cynic Heracleios," 216B–217D (Wright II, 103–105). See also Julian, "Hymn to King Helios," 137C (Wright I, 373); "Hymn to the Mother of the Gods," 170C (Wright I, 475–77); Bidez, *Julien*, p. 252.

2. "To Heracleios," 217C (Wright I, 105).

3. "Mother of the Gods," 167D–168 (Wright I, 469). Practically the entire treatise (Wright I, 443-503) is instructive along these lines. See also Bidez, *Julien*, pp. 256–57.

4. "King Helios," 132C-D (Wright I, 359); "Against the Galileans" (Wright III, 337). See also Charles Norris Cochrane, *Christianity and Classical Culture* (New York, 1940; reprint 1957), pp. 274 ff.

5. "Fragment of a Letter to a Priest," 289C–290 (Wright II, 299–301).

6. "Letter to a Priest," 299 (Wright II, 321). See also Julian's letter no. 20 "To the High-Priest Theodorus" (Wright III, 57).

7. "Against the Galileans" (Wright III, 387–89).

8. "Against the Galileans" (Wright III, 389).

9. "Against the Galileans" (Wright III, 375).

10. "King Helios," 153B (Wright I, 419) and 144B (I, 393).

11. Julian's letter no. 20 "To the High-Priest Theodorus" (Wright III, 61); "Against the Galileans" (Wright III, 345).

12. "King Helios," 136 and passim (Wright I, 369 ff.). See also Cochrane, *Christianity and Classical Culture*, p. 274.

13. "Mother of the Gods," 166 (Wright I, 463) and 179 (I, 499).

14. "King Helios," 157C-D (Wright I, 433).

15. "Letter to a Priest," 298C (Wright II, 321).

16. A.M. 22.12.6 criticizes Julian for holding entirely too many sacrifices. Libanius, on the other hand, praises this practice highly (see especially 12.79–82).

17. "Letter to a Priest," 293C–294B (Wright II, 309–11).

18. A.M. 22.12.6; Libanius 18.126.

19. On this matter, see especially Julian's letters to two priestesses, nos. 32, 33, and 34 "To Theodora" (Wright III, 109–15), and no. 42 "To Callixeine" (Wright III, 135–37).

20. Julian's letter no. 22 "To Arsacius, High Priest of Galatia" (Wright III, 69).

21. Ibid. See also "Letter to a Priest," 296D–297D (Wright II, 317–19).

22. "Letter to a Priest," 292D–293 (Wright II, 309).

23. Libanius 18.179; A.M. 25.4.2–3.

24. "Misop.," 345D (Wright II, 443).

25. Libanius 18.128.

26. "Misop.," 357D (Wright II, 477). See also "Letter to a Priest," 300D (Wright II, 325) and especially 304B-C (Wright II, 335).

27. "Letter to a Priest," 300D–301D (Wright II, 325–27).

28. "Letter to a Priest," 300C (Wright II, 325).

29. "Misop.," 340C (Wright II, 429).

30. On Julian's eating and drinking habits see especially Libanius 18.171, 174; A.M. 25.4.4.

31. "Misop.," 340B (Wright II, 429).

32. "Mother of the Gods," 175B–177D (Wright I, 489–97).

33. Julian's letter no. 29 "To His Uncle Julian" (Wright III, 99).

34. A.M. 22.9.10–11. It might be noted that red shoes, the status symbol *par excellence* of the Byzantine emperors, derived their prestige from the fact that red and purple hues were the rarest and most expensive dyes in the Roman world. Centuries earlier, Roman Senators had originated the custom of wearing red shoes as a sign of rank.

35. "Letter to a Priest," 303B (Wright II, 331–33).

36. Julian's letter no. 22 "To Arsacius, High Priest of Galatia" (Wright III, 69).

37. "Letter to a Priest," 290D (Wright II, 303).

38. "Letter to a Priest," 291B (Wright II, 303–305); "To Arsacius" (Wright III, 71).

39. "To Arsacius" (Wright III, 69).

40. "Letter to a Priest," 305C (Wright II, 337).

Chapter Sixteen

1. A.M. 22.9.1–2.

2. For background, see Glanville Downey, *A History of Antioch in Syria* (Princeton, 1961), especially pp. 380-97, and the same author's delightful little book, *Antioch in the Age of Theodosius the Great* (Norman, Okla., 1962).

3. Downey, *History of Antioch*, p. 382.

4. Glanville Downey, "Julian the Apostate at Antioch," *Church History*, 8 (1939), 304–306.

5. Libanius 18.159.

6. Libanius 18.193.

7. A.M. 22.9.4–5.

8. A.M. 22.9.5.

9. "Mother of the Gods," 178D–179 (Wright I, 499).

10. "Mother of the Gods," 159C–161B (Wright I, 445–49) and 175B–178 (I, 489–97).

11. "Mother of the Gods," 180B-C (Wright I, 503).

12. A.M. 22.9.9 and 22.10.1–6.

13. A.M. 22.14.4–5.

14. A.M. 22.9.13; Libanius 18.159.

15. A.M. 22.9.15.

16. Soc. Sch. 3.17 is the only one of the ancient historians who seems to have realized the negative effects of the heavy troop concentration. Two detailed and interesting analyses of the Antioch grain crisis appeared within a short time of each other: P. DeJonge, "Scarcity of Corn and Corn Prices in Ammianus Marcellinus," *Mnemosyne*, ser. 4, vol. I (1948), 238–45, and Glanville Downey, "The Economic Crisis at Antioch under Julian the Apostate," *Studies in Roman Economic and Social History in Honor of Allan Chester Johnson*, Paul Robinson Coleman-Norton, ed. (Princeton, 1951), pp. 312–21. Both are most helpful in harmonizing the events mentioned by Julian in his "Misopogon" with data from other ancient sources.

17. DeJonge, "Scarcity of Corn," p. 242.

18. "Misop.," 365B (Wright II, 497).

19. "Misop.," 367D–368B (Wright II, 503).

20. "Misop.," 368C-D (Wright II, 505).

21. Downey, "Economic Crisis," p. 316.

22. "Misop.,"368D–369 (Wright II, 505); Libanius 18.195. A.M. 22.14.1 ff. (whose understanding of the grain crisis is grossly inadequate) says Julian lowered prices "merely from a desire for popularity."

23. "Misop.," 369B (Wright II, 505).

24. "Misop.," 365B (Wright II, 497) and 370D (II, 509–11).

25. Libanius 1.126.

26. Libanius 18.198.

27. "Misop.," 369D–370 (Wright II, 507).

28. A.M. 22.14.3. Julian's sensitivity on the subject of his beard is also evident in many passages of "The Misopogon."

29. A.M. 22.14.3.

30. "Misop." throughout, but especially 339-40 (Wright II, 427–29) and 345–46 (II, 443). See also Libanius 18.170–71; A.M. 22.10.1; Zosimus 3.11.

31. Libanius, *Autobiography* ("Oration 1"), p. 73.

32. Sozomen 5.8; Theodoret 3.13; Philostorgius 7.10. The ecclesiastical historians also report that Uncle Julian on his deathbed returned to Christianity.

33. Eunapius, *Sophists*, section 495 (Wright, p. 521). Eunapius' very obvious dislike for Libanius renders his report suspect, especially since it is not attested elsewhere.

34. Eunapius, *Sophists*, section 495 (Wright, p. 523).

35. Libanius 18.15.

36. Libanius, *Autobiography* ("Oration 1"), p. 71. Some years ago there was a flurry of scholarly "notes" subjecting the story of Libanius' meeting with Julian to minute analysis, mainly on the question of whether the two of them were deliberately imitating a famous meeting between Emperor Marcus Aurelius and the philosopher Aelius Aristides. See: Roger Pack, "Two Sophists and Two Emperors," *Classical Philology*, 42 (1947), 17–20; A. F. Norman, "Philostratus and Libanius," *CP*, 48 (1953), 20–23; R. Pack, "Julian, Libanius, and Others: A Reply," *CP*, 48 (1953), 173–74; and A. F. Norman, "Julian and Libanius Again," *CP*, 48 (1953), 239.

37. Libanius, *Autobiography* ("Oration 1"), pp. 73–75.

38. Libanius, *Autobiography* ("Oration 1"), p. 73.

39. Libanius, *Autobiography* ("Oration 1"), pp. 75–77. The speech

itself is Libanius' "Oration 12: An Address to the Emperor Julian as Consul."

40. Libanius, Oration 14.

41. Julian's letter no. 51 "To Libanius" (Wright III, 181–83).

42. Julian's letter no. 52 "To Libanius" (Wright III, 183–85).

43. A. F. Norman, footnote "a" in Libanius, *Selected Works*, I, 144–45.

44. Julian's letter no. 58 "To Libanius" (Wright III, 201–209). See also, Libanius, *Autobiography* ("Oration 1"), p. 79.

Chapter Seventeen

1. G.N. 4.76.

2. Julian's letter no. 37 "To Atarbius" (Wright III, 123).

3. Julian's letter no. 36 "Rescript on Christian Teachers" (Wright III, 123). See also Libanius 18.122–23.

4. "Letter to a Priest," 288B (Wright II, 297).

5. G.N. 4.58; Soc. Sch. 3.12; Sozomen 5.4.

6. A.M. 22.5.3; Soc. Sch. 3.1; Theodoret 3.4.

7. A.M. 22.5.3.

8. A.M. 22.5.4.

9. Soc. Sch. 3.12; see also, Sozomen 5.4.

10. Julian's letter no. 26 "To Basil" (Wright III, 81–83).

11. Julian's letter no. 15 "To Bishop Aetius" (Wright III, 35–37).

12. Sozomen 5.4; Theodoret 3.6. See also Julian's letter no. 39 "To the Citizens of Byzacium" (Wright III, 125) on his cancellation of curial immunities of Galilean priests.

13. Soc. Sch. 3.11.

14. Soc. Sch. 3.13.

15. Julian's letter no. 22 "To Arsacius" (Wright III, 69). See also Sozomen 5.16.

16. "To Arsacius" (Wright III, 69).

17. A.M. 16.7.6.

18. "To Arsacius" (Wright III, 73).

19. Libanius 18.168.

20. A.M. 22.10.7. Julian's school policy, however, has found at least one staunch modern defender: B. Carmon Hardy, "Emperor Julian and his School Law," *Church History*, 37 (1968), 131–43. Hardy emphasizes the outspoken Christian anti-intellectualism and scorn for pagan learning, in light of which he believes Julian's law completely reasonable and constructive.

21. Julian's letter no. 36 "Rescript on Christian Teachers" (Wright III, 121).

22. Ibid., p. 117.
23. Ibid., p. 121.
24. Soc. Sch. 3.16; Sozomen 5.18; Theodoret 3.8.
25. See Glanville Downey, "The Emperor Julian and the Schools," *Classical Journal*, 53 (1957–58), 97–103.
26. G.N. 4.111.
27. Soc. Sch. 3.22 and 4.1; Sozomen 5.17, and especially Theodoret 3.8 and 3.16.
28. Libanius 18.178.
29. "Against the Galileans" (Wright III, 319). Hereinafter cited as "A.G."
30. "A.G." (Wright III, 377).
31. "A.G.," additional fragment 5 (Wright III, 431).
32. "A.G." (Wright III, 413–15).
33. "A.G." (Wright III, 377–81).
34. "A.G."(Wright III, 395); also additional fragment 7 (III, 433).
35. "A.G." (Wright III, 399).
36. "A.G." (Wright III, 397).
37. "A.G." (Wright III, 373).
38. "A.G." (Wright III, 375 and 417).
39. "A.G." (Wright III, 373).
40. "A.G." (Wright III, 341–43 and 391–93).
41. "A.G." (Wright III, 393).
42. "The Caesars," 336B (Wright II, 413).
43. "A.G." (Wright III, 385).
44. "A.G." (Wright III, 377).
45. Julian's letter no. 41 "To the Citizens of Bostra" (Wright III, 129).
46. "A.G." additional fragment 6 (Wright III, 433).
47. "A.G." (Wright III, 325).

Chapter Eighteen

1. Julian's letter no. 20 "To the High Priest Theodorus" (Wright III, 59).
2. Julian's letter no. 22 "To Arsacius, High Priest of Galatia" (Wright III, 71).
3. "A.G." (Wright III, 343–45).
4. "A.G." (Wright III, 367 and 381).
5. "Letter to a Priest," 295D (Wright II, 315).
6. "A.G." (Wright III, 325–27 and 347). See also "Letter to a Priest," 291D–292C (Wright II, 305–307) for Julian's version of Plato's theory of creation.

7. "A.G." (Wright III, 327).

8. "A.G." (Wright III, 349–51).

9. "A.G." (Wright III, 361).

10. "A.G." (Wright III, 361).

11. Julian's letter no. 20 "To the High Priest Theodorus" (Wright III, 61).

12. Julian's letter no. 51 "To the Community of the Jews" (Wright III, 179–81). See also Sozomen 5.22.

13. "A.G." (Wright III, 423).

14. "A.G." (Wright III, 423–25).

15. The major ecclesiastical historians of Julian's attempt to rebuild the Temple are G.N. 5.7; Soc. Sch. 3.20; Sozomen 5.22; Theodoret 3.20; Philostorgius 7.9.

16. Julian speaks of the rebuilding as being planned in "Letter to a Priest," 295C (Wright II, 313), and as underway in his "fragment no. 11" (Wright III, 301) . . . "I am rebuilding with all zeal the temple of the Most High God."

17. A.M. 23.1.2–3; G.N. 5.3 ff.

18. G.N. 5.4.

19. G.N. 5.7.; Soc. Sch. 3.20; Sozomen 5.22; Theodoret 3.20.

20. A.M. 23.1.3.

21. "To the Community of the Jews" (Wright III, 177–81). J. Vogt, *Kaiser Julian und das Judentum* (*Morgenland*, 30, 1939) summarized in detail the arguments against the authenticity of this letter. Vogt's opinions were generally accepted until the question was reopened by W. Den Boer, "Two Letters from the *Corpus Iulianeum*," *Vigiliae Christianae*, 16 (1962), 187–97, who argues very convincingly for Julian's authorship of the document.

22. Den Boer, "Two Letters," p. 194.

23. For an interesting examination of what it might have meant for Judaism had Julian lived longer, see Harry Sacher, "If Julian, Not Constantine: a Might-Have-Been of History," *Menorah Journal*, 36 (1948), 304–10.

Chapter Nineteen

1. A detailed and very important study of the Christians reportedly martyred during Julian's reign is B. De Gaiffier, " '*Sub Iuliano Apostata*' dans de martyrologe romain," *Analecta Bollandiana*, 74 (1956), 5–49. De Gaiffier examines not only the incidents reported by the early ecclesiastical historians, but also later stories of martyrs under Julian, many of which are obviously legendary, including those which picture Julian as personally present in Rome, a city he never visited.

2. G.N. 4.58.
3. G.N. 4.79.
4. Libanius 18.168.
5. G.N. 4.83.
6. G.N. 4.84.
7. Sozomen 5.17.
8. Theodoret 3.17.
9. Theodoret 3.15.
10. Libanius 18.199 mentions such an assassination attempt. See also Downey, *History of Antioch*, p. 393.
11. They are not mentioned by any of the earlier sources. For details see De Gaiffier, " '*Sub Iuliano*,' " *AB*, 74 (1956), 6–7; Downey, *History of Antioch*, p. 392.
12. De Gaiffier, " '*Sub Iuliano*,' " *AB*, p. 6.
13. A.M. 22.11.2.
14. Soc. Sch. 3.22.
15. Sozomen 6.6; Theodoret 3.16. A variant of this story also appears in Philostorgius 7.7.
16. A.M. 16.11.6–7.
17. Soc. Sch. 3.12.
18. Sozomen 5.4.
19. G.N. 5.40.
20. G.N. 5.21.
21. G.N. 4.85.
22. G.N. 4.88–91; Sozomen 5.10; Theodoret 3.7.
23. Theodoret 3.7.
24. Soc. Sch. 3.15.
25. Soc. Sch. 3.14.
26. Sozomen 5.11.
27. Sozomen 5.9.
28. Sozomen 5.10.
29. Theodoret 3.19.
30. Soc. Sch. 3.13.
31. Theodoret 3.26–27.
32. Stebelton H. Nulle, "Julian *Redivivus*," *The Centennial Review*, 5 (1961), 328.
33. A.M. 22.11.1–11.
34. A.M. 22.11.5.
35. A.M. 22.11.2, 8. The industriousness of the anti-Julian legend makers can be clearly seen in the fact that even this Artemius, whom the Alexandrians found guilty of "a mass of atrocious charges" and who was an Arian besides, has been transformed into an Orthodox Christian saint. See De Gaiffier, " '*Sub Iuliano*," *AB*, 74 (1956), 15–16.

36. A.M. 22.11.10.

37. A.M. 22.11.11.

38. Julian's letter no. 21 "To the People of Alexandria" (Wright III, 61–67). Also quoted in Soc. Sch. 3.3.

39. Soc. Sch. 3.2–3; Sozomen 5.7.

40. Julian's letter no. 23 "To Ecdicius, Prefect of Egypt" (Wright III, 73–75). See also the more threatening and possibly spurious letter no. 38 "To Porphyrius" (Wright III, 123–25) on the same subject.

41. Julian's letter no. 24 "To the Alexandrians, an Edict" (Wright III, 77).

42. Sozomen 5.15. See also Soc. Sch. 3.4.

43. Julian's letter no. 46 "To Ecdicius, Prefect of Egypt" (Wright III, 141–43).

44. Julian's letter no. 47 "To the Alexandrians" (Wright III, 143–51).

45. "Misop.," 361B-C (Wright II, 485); A.M. 22.12.8.

46. Soc. Sch. 3.18; Sozomen 5.19; Theodoret 3.10.

47. Soc. Sch. 3.19; see also Sozomen 5.20; Theodoret 3.11.

48. A.M. 22.13.2. See also Theodoret 3.12.

49. A.M. 22.13.3.

50. G.N. 4.96.

51. Soc. Sch. 3.16; Sozomen 5.18; Theodoret 3.8.

52. Theodoret 3.8.

Chapter Twenty

1. For details see Walter R. Chalmers, "Eunapius, Ammianus Marcellinus, and Zosimus on Julian's Persian Expedition," *Classical Quarterly*, n.s. 10 (1960), 152–60; Thompson, *Ammianus Marcellinus*, pp. 20–33.

2. Chalmers, "Eunapius, Ammianus Marcellinus, and Zosimus," pp. 155 ff. It is not known whether Zosimus utilized the work of Ammianus, and the question has been argued both ways.

3. Soc. Sch. 3.21. For more detail see Walter E. Kaegi, Jr., "The Emperor Julian's Assessment of the Significance and Function of History," *Proceedings of the American Philosophical Society*, 108 (1964), 37, who considers Socrates' report "extraordinary" but possible. See also Norman H. Baynes, "Julian the Apostate and Alexander the Great," *Byzantine Studies and Other Essays* (London, 1960), pp. 346–47. Baynes is inclined to believe Socrates' theory.

4. "King Helios," 136B (Wright I, 369) seems in fact a clear denial of any belief in reincarnation on Julian's part.

5. See for instance "Letter to Themistius," 257B, 264C-D (Wright II, 211–13, 229–31); "Salustius," 250D–251B (II, 191–93; "Pan. on Const.," 45D (I, 119); and particularly Julian's letter no. 50 "To Nilus, surnamed Dionysius" (III, 169–71).

6. Libanius 18.164–66; 17.19.

7. On Prince Ormisdas' background see Zosimus 2.27.

8. A.M. 22.2.4; Libanius, "Oration 1" (*Autobiography*), p. 77.

9. Libanius, "Oration 1" (*Autobiography*), p. 77.

10. Julian's letter no. 58 "To Libanius, Sophist and Quaestor" (Wright III, 201–209).

11. A.M. 23.1.5–7; 2.6. See also Zosimus 3.12.

12. "To Libanius" (Wright III, 203).

13. "To Libanius" (Wright III, 205–207).

14. "To Libanius" (Wright III, 207).

15. A.M. 23.2.2. See also Julian's (possibly spurious) letter no. 57 "To Arsaces, Satrap of Armenia" (Wright III, 197–201).

16. A.M. 23.2.6–3.1; Zosimus 3.12; Libanius 18.214.

17. A.M. 23.3.5; Libanius 18.214; see also Zosimus 3.12.

18. A.M. 23.3.6.

19. A.M. 23.3.8.

20. A.M. 23.3.9; see also Zosimus 3.13.

21. Libanius 18.216.

22. A.M. 23.5.4–6.

23. A.M. 23.5.8.

24. A.M. 23.5.16–23.

25. Zosimus 3.13.

26. A.M. 24.1.6–9; Zosimus 3.14. See also Libanius 18.218.

27. A.M. 24.1.10.

28. A.M. 24.1.14.

29. A.M. 24.2.1–3; Zosimus 3.15; Libanius 18.219 ff.

30. A.M. 24.2.4; Zosimus 3.15.

31. A.M. 24.2.5.

32. A.M. 24.2.7–8; Zosimus 3.16; Libanius 18.222 ff.

33. A.M. 24.2.9 ff.; Zosimus 3.17–18; Libanius 18.227 ff.

34. A.M. 24.2.15.

35. A.M. 24.2.21; Zosimus 3.18; Libanius 18.228.

36. Zosimus 3.18.

37. A.M. 24.3.3; Zosimus 3.18.

38. A.M. 24.3.1; Zosimus 3.19.

39. Zosimus 3.19; see also Libanius 18.226.

40. A.M. 24.4.1 ff. Zosimus 3.20–22; Libanius 18.235 ff.

41. A.M. 24.4.25; Zosimus 3.22; Libanius 18.240–41.

42. A.M. 24.4.31; 5.5 ff.

43. A.M. 24.5.1–2; Zosimus 3.23.

44. A.M. 24.5.6; Zosimus 3.20.

45. A.M. 24.5.8–9.

46. A.M. 24.6.1–2; Zosimus 3.24; Libanius 18.245–47.

47. A.M. 24.6.4; Zosimus 3.25; Libanius 18.250 ff.

48. A.M. 24.6.5–7; Zosimus 3.25; Libanius 18.252.

49. A.M. 24.6.11. Zosimus 3.26, however, indicates that Julian had remained on the other side of the Tigris.

50. A.M. 24.6.13.

Chapter Twenty-one

1. Libanius 18.257–60. See also Soc. Sch. 3.20, who appears to have gotten his information from Libanius.

2. A.M. 24.6.15; Zosimus 3.25.

3. A.M. 24.6.17.

4. Libanius 18.262.

5. A.M. 24.7.1 ff.; Zosimus 3.26.

6. A.M. 24.7.4. Zosimus 3.26 says twenty-two. See also G.N. 5.12.

7. A.M. 24.7.5.

8. A.M. 24.7.7; Zosimus 3.26–28.

9. A.M. 24.7.7; 25.1.1 ff.; Zosimus 3.26–28; Libanius 18.264.

10. A.M. 25.2.2.

11. A.M. 25.2.3–4.

12. A.M. 25.2.7–8.

13. A.M. 25.3.1 ff.; Libanius 18.268–69; Zosimus 3.29.

14. Philostorgius 7.15 reports the detail of Oribasius' presence which seems highly likely although not mentioned by the principal sources.

15. Thompson, *Ammianus Marcellinus*, p. 33, suggests that A.M. got his information on Julian's death from "one of his Neoplatonist friends." He also suggests (p. 20) that data used by Ammianus came from Eutherius.

16. Libanius, ep. 1220 (cited by Thompson, *Ammianus Marcellinus*, p. 40) says he collected data on this subject from "strangers" who had been in Julian's army.

17. G.N. 5.13–14; Philostorgius 7.15; Soc. Sch. 3.21; Sozomen 6.1; Theodoret 3.25.

18. A.M. 25.3.8; Libanius 18.269–70.

19. A.M. 25.3.6. However, in 25.6.6 A.M. adds that the Persians soon heard of "an unfounded rumor that Julian had been killed by a Roman weapon."

20. Libanius' "Oration 24" is devoted to this theme. See especially 24.21 ff.; also 18.274.

21. A.M. 25.3.10; Zosimus 3.29.

22. A.M. 25.3.22; Libanius 18.272.

23. A.M. 25.3.15 ff.

24. A.M. 25.3.23.

25. Philostorgius 7.15. See also Sozomen 6.2 who retails this as one of his several accounts of Julian's last moments.

26. Theodoret 3.25. For further variations on this theme see Norman H. Baynes, "The Death of Julian the Apostate in a Christian Legend," *Byzantine Studies and Other Essays* (London, 1960), 271–81.

27. A.M. 25.5.4 ff.; also 25.10.14 ff.

28. A.M. 25.10.15.

29: A.M. 25.7.5–14; Zosimus 3.31.

30. A.M. 25.10.13. A.M. also hints that Jovian's death may not have been so "accidental" as it seemed.

31. A.M. 25.10.5; Libanius 18.306.

32. Zosimus 3.34.

33. Libanius 18.307.

34. For a detailed description and picture see Archer St. Clair, "The Apotheosis Diptych," *Art Bulletin*, 46 (1964), 205–11. This article also contains an excellent summary of earlier scholars' opinions on the diptych. Ms. St. Clair believes it to have been manufactured in Alexandria where, she hypothesizes, the Julian cult was particularly strong.

35. See Arthur Darby Nock, "Deification and Julian," *JRS*, 47 (1957), 123.

36. Libanius 18.304, 306; 24.40.

37. For details see Philip Grierson, "The Tombs and Obits of the Byzantine Emperors (337–1042)," *Dumbarton Oaks Papers*, 16 (1962), 6–7, 25, 38, 40–41. It seems likely that the body of Julian's wife Helena was also moved to Constantinople and placed in the same tomb with Julian.

38. Grierson, "Tombs and Obits," pp. 40–41, describes the cylindrical sarcophagus still preserved in Istanbul that is widely believed to have been Julian's.

Chapter Twenty-two

1. For details see Stebelton H. Nulle, "Julian and the Men of Letters," *Classical Journal*, 54 (1959), 258–59.

2. Julian, *Epistulae, Leges, Fragmenta*, ed. and trans. J. Bidez and F. Cumont (Paris, 1922), and *Oeuvres complètes*, ed. and trans. J. Bidez, G. Rochefort, and C. Lacombrade, 2 vols. in 4 (Paris, 1924–64).

3. Libanius, "Oration 1" (*Autobiography*), p. 79.

4. James J. Buchanan and Harold T. Davis, "Introduction" to Zosimus, *Historia Nova* (San Antonio, 1967), pp. vii–ix.

5. An important article on the medieval and Renaissance views of Julian is Nulle, "Julian *Redivivus*," *Centennial Review*, 5 (1961), 320–38.

6. See Nulle's analysis of Lorenzo's play in "Julian *Redivivus*," pp. 324–27.

7. Michel Eyquem de Montaigne, "Of Liberty of Conscience," II, xix, in *The Essays of Michel Eyquem de Montaigne*, trans. Charles Cotton ("Great Books of the Western World," vol. 25; Chicago, 1952), pp. 324–26. Many other editions of Montaigne also contain this essay.

8. Nulle, "Julian and the Men of Letters," *CJ*, 54 (1959), 257–66, contains an excellent analysis of Julian's literary reputation through the centuries; for the *philosophes*, see especially pp. 260–63.

9. Kaegi, "Research on Julian," *CW*, 58 (1965), 231.

10. Many editions of Gibbon's *Decline and Fall* are available, but the best is that with editorial notes by J. B. Bury (London, 1923).

11. Nulle, "Julian and the Men of Letters," *CJ*, 54 (1959), 264.

12. Kaegi, "Research on Julian," *CW*, 58 (1965), 229–38, is a most helpful bibliographic article for the years it covers (1945–64). For earlier studies there is a wealth of bibliographic material in André Piganoil, *L'Empire chrétien (325–395)* (Paris, 1947), pp. 110–48.

13. Nulle, "Julian and the Men of Letters," *CJ*, 54 (1959), 264.

Selected Bibliography

Major primary sources are discussed in Chapter 22, "A Note on Sources." Secondary works on Julian and his times are extensive. The following bibliography does not claim to be definitive, but lists some of the most significant and readily available materials for those seeking additional background. For the aid of the student, chief emphasis is placed on works in English.

1. General Background

COCHRANE, CHARLES NORRIS. *Christianity and Classical Culture.* New York, 1940. Reprint, 1957.
CUMONT, FRANZ. *The Mysteries of Mithra.* Translated by Thomas J. McCormack. New York, 1903. Reprint, 1956.
DELBRUECK, RICHARD. *Spaetantike Kaiserportraets.* Berlin, 1933.
DODDS, ERIC ROBERTSON. *The Greeks and the Irrational.* Berkeley, 1968.
DOWNEY, GLANVILLE. *Ancient Antioch.* Princeton, 1962.
—————. *Antioch in the Age of Theodosius the Great.* Norman, Okla., 1962.
—————. *A History of Antioch in Syria.* Princeton, 1961.
—————. *The Late Roman Empire.* New York, 1969.
GIBBON, EDWARD. *The Decline and Fall of the Roman Empire.* Edited by J. B. Bury. London, 1923.
GLOVER, TERROT REAVELEY. *Life and Letters in the Fourth Century.* New York, 1901. Reprint, 1968.
GRABAR, ANDRÉ. *Early Christian Art.* Translated by Stuart Gilbert and James Emmons. New York, 1968.
JONES, ARNOLD HUGH MARTIN. *The Later Roman Empire.* 3 vols. Oxford, 1964.
LEGGE, FRANCIS. *Forerunners and Rivals of Christianity.* 2 vols. Hyde Park, N. Y., 1915. Reprint, 1964.
LEITZMANN, HANS. *A History of the Early Church.* Translated by Bertram Lee Woolf. Cleveland, 1950. Reprint, 1961 (Vol. 3).
MURRAY, GILBERT. *Five Stages of Greek Religion.* Garden City, N. Y., 1955.

PIGANOIL, ANDRÉ. *L'empire chrétien* (325–395). Paris, 1947.
THOMPSON, E. A. *The Historical Work of Ammianus Marcellinus.* Cambridge, England, 1947.

2. Books on Julian

BIDEZ, JOSEPH. *La vie de l'Empereur Julien.* Paris, 1930. Reprint, 1965.
GARDNER, ALICE. *Julian, Philosopher and Emperor and the Last Struggle of Paganism against Christianity.* New York, 1895.
MEREZHKOVSKI, DMITRI. *The Death of the Gods.* Translated by Herbert Trench. London, 1901. Reprint, 1926. (Fiction.)
SIMPSON, W. DOUGLAS. *Julian the Apostate.* Aberdeen, 1930.
RENDELL, G. H. *The Emperor Julian: Paganism and Christianity.* London, 1879.
RICCIOTTI, GUISEPPE. *Julian the Apostate.* Translated by M. Joseph Costelloe, S.J. Milwaukee, 1960.
VIDAL, GORE. *Julian.* Boston, 1964. (Fiction.)

3. Shorter monographs and articles on special topics

ALFÖLDI, ANDREW. "Some Portraits of Julianus Apostata," *American Journal of Archaeology*, 66 (1962), 403–405.
BAYNES, NORMAN H. "The Death of Julian the Apostate in a Christian Legend." In *Byzantine Studies and Other Essays.* London, 1960. 271–81.
—————. "The Early Life of Julian the Apostate." *Journal of Hellenic Studies*, 45 (1925), 251–54.
—————. "Julian the Apostate and Alexander the Great." In *Byzantine Studies and Other Essays.* London, 1960. 346–47.
BOLTON, CHARLES A. "Emperor Julian Against Hissing Christians." *Harvard Theological Review*, 61 (1968), 496–97.
CHALMERS, WALTER R. "Eunapius, Ammianus Marcellinus, and Zosimus on Julian's Persian Expedition." *Classical Quarterly*, n.s. 10 (1960), 152–60.
DE GAIFFIER, B. " 'Sub Iuliano Apostata' dans le martyrologe romain." *Analecta Bollandiana*, 74 (1956), 5–49.
DE JONGE, P. "Scarcity of Corn and Corn Prices in Ammianus Marcellinus." *Mnemosyne*, ser. 4, 1 (1948), 238–45.
DEN BOER, W. "Two Letters from the *Corpus Iulianeum.*" *Vigiliae Christianae*, 16 (1962), 179–97.
DOWNEY, GLANVILLE. "The Economic Crisis at Antioch under Julian the Apostate." In *Studies in Roman Economic and Social History*

in Honor of Allan Chester Johnson, edited by Paul Robinson Coleman-Norton. Princeton, 1951. 312–21.

————. "The Emperor Julian and the Schools." *Classical Journal,* 53 (1957–58), 97–103.

————. "Julian and Justinian and the Unity of Faith and Culture." *Church History,* 28 (1959), 339–49.

————. "Julian the Apostate at Antioch." *Church History,* 8 (1939), 303–15.

DVORNIK, FRANCIS. "The Emperor Julian's 'Reactionary' Ideas on Kingship." In *Late Classical and Mediaeval Studies in Honor of Albert Mathias Friend Jr.,* edited by Kurt Weitzmann. Princeton, 1955. 71–81.

FESTUGIÈRE, A. J. "Julien à Macellum." *Journal of Roman Studies,* 47 (1957), 53–58.

GILLIARD, FRANK D. "Notes on the Coinage of Julian the Apostate." *Journal of Roman Studies,* 54 (1964), 135–41.

GRIERSON, PHILIP. "The Tombs and Obits of the Byzantine Emperors (337–1042)." *Dumbarton Oaks Papers,* 16 (1962), 3–63.

HADJINICOLAOU, ANNE. "Macellum, lieu d'exil de l'Empereur Julien." *Byzantion,* 21 (1951), 15–22.

HARDY, B. CARMON. "Emperor Julian and his School Law." *Church History,* 37 (1968), 131–43.

JONAS, R. "A Newly Discovered Portrait of the Emperor Julian." *American Journal of Archaeology,* 50 (1946), 277–82.

JONES, A. H. M. "The Social Background of the Struggle between Paganism and Christianity." In *The Conflict Between Paganism and Christianity in the Fourth Century,* edited by Arnaldo Momigliano. Oxford, 1963. 17–37.

KAEGI, WALTER E. JR. "The Emperor Julian's Assessment of the Significance and Function of History." *Proceedings of the American Philosophical Society,* 108 (1964), 29–38.

————. "Research on Julian the Apostate, 1945–1964." *Classical World,* 58 (1965), 229–38.

KENT, J. P. C. "An Introduction to the Coinage of Julian the Apostate." *Numismatic Chronicle,* ser. 6, 19 (1959), 109–17.

LACOMBRADE, CHRISTIAN. "L'Empereur Julien et la tradition romaine." *Pallas,* 9 (1960), 155–64.

LÉVÊQUE, PIERRE. "De nouveaux portraits de l'Empereur Julien." *Latomus,* 22 (1963), 74–84.

————. "Observations sur l'iconographie de Julien dit l'Apostate d'après une tête inédite de Thasos." *Monuments Piot,* 51 (1960), 105–28.

MONTAIGNE, MICHEL EYQUEM DE. "Of Liberty of Conscience" (Essays II, xix). In *The Essays of Michel Eyquem de Montaigne*. Translated by Charles Cotton. ("Great Books of the Western World," Vol. 25) Chicago, 1952. Many other editions also available.

MÜLLER-SEIDEL, ILSE. "Die Usurpation Julians des Abtrünnigen im Lichte siener Germanenpolitik." *Historische Zeitschrift*, 180 (1955), 225–44.

NOCK, ARTHUR DARBY. "Deification and Julian." *Journal of Roman Studies*, 47 (1957), 115–23.

NORMAN, A. F. "Julian and Libanius Again." *Classical Philology*, 48 (1953), 239.

––––––. "Philostratus and Libanius." *Classical Philology*, 48 (1953), 20–23.

NULLE, STEBELTON H. "Julian and the Men of Letters." *Classical Journal*, 54 (1959), 257–66.

––––––. "Julian *Redivivus*." *The Centennial Review*, 5 (1961), 320–38.

PACK, ROGER. "Julian, Libanius, and Others: A Reply." *Classical Philology*, 48 (1953), 173–74.

––––––. "Two Sophists and Two Emperors." *Classical Philology*, 42 (1947), 17–20.

PIGANOIL, ANDRÉ. "La couronne de Julien César." *Byzantion*, 13 (1938), 243–48.

ROCHEFORT, GABRIEL. "Les lectures latines de l'Empereur Julien." *Revue des Études Grecques*, 75 (1962), xxii–xxiii.

SACHER, HARRY. "If Julian, Not Constantine . . . A Might-Have-Been of History." *Menorah Journal*, 36 (1948), 304–12.

ST. CLAIR, ARCHER. "The Apotheosis Diptych." *Art Bulletin*, 46 (1964), 205–11.

THOMPSON, E. A. "The Emperor Julian's Knowledge of Latin." *Classical Review*, 58 (1944), 49–51.

VOGT, JOSEPH. "Pagans and Christians in the Family of Constantine the Great." In *The Conflict Between Paganism and Christianity in the Fourth Century*. Edited by Arnaldo Momigliano. Oxford, 1963. 38–55.

Index

(The works of Julian are listed under his name)